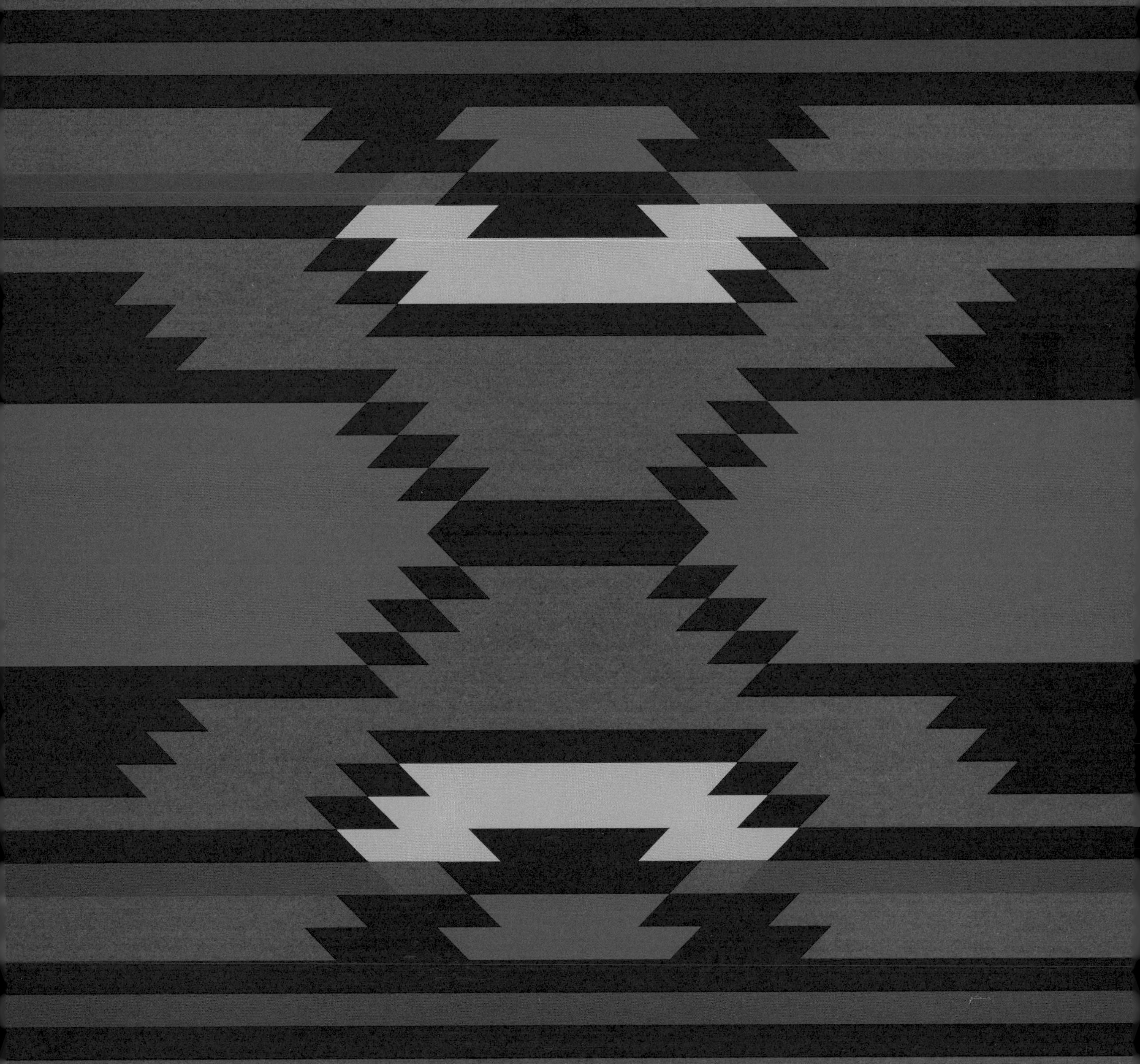

George Herriman, c. 1940. From the collection of and many thanks to Philippe Ghielmetti.

⊕. KRAZY & IGNATZ. ⚡

by George Herriman.

"A Brick Stuffed with Moom-bims."

Congregating the Complete Full-Page Comic Strips,
with Addenda.

1939-40.

Edited by Bill Blackbeard
with an Introduction by Jeet Heer.

Fantagraphics Books, SEATTLE.

Published by Fantagraphics Books.
7563 Lake City Way North East,
Seattle, Washington, 98115, United States of America.

Edited by Bill Blackbeard.
Except where noted, all research materials appear courtesy of the San Francisco Academy of Cartoon Art.
Additional research and cutlines by Jeet Heer and Kim Thompson.
Design, decoration, and occasional cutlines by Chris Ware.
Production assistance and scanning by Paul Baresh.
Promoted by Eric Reynolds.
Published by Gary Groth and Kim Thompson.

First Fantagraphics Books edition: January 2007.

ISBN13: 978-1-56097-789-6.

Printed in Korea through Print Vision.

Special thanks to Philippe Ghielmetti and Jeet Heer.

"KRAZY
KAT"

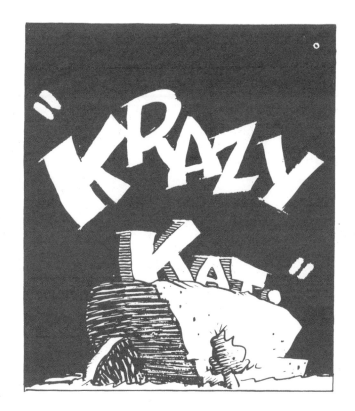

KRAZY & IGNATZ.

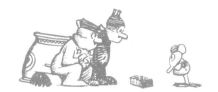

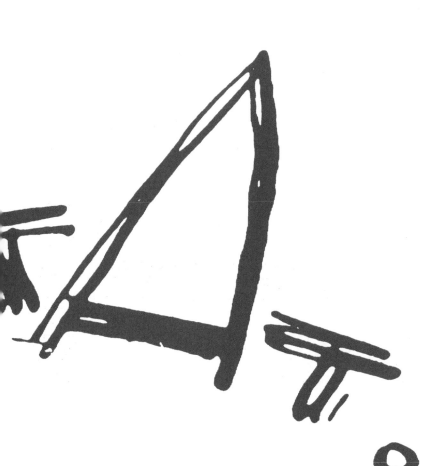

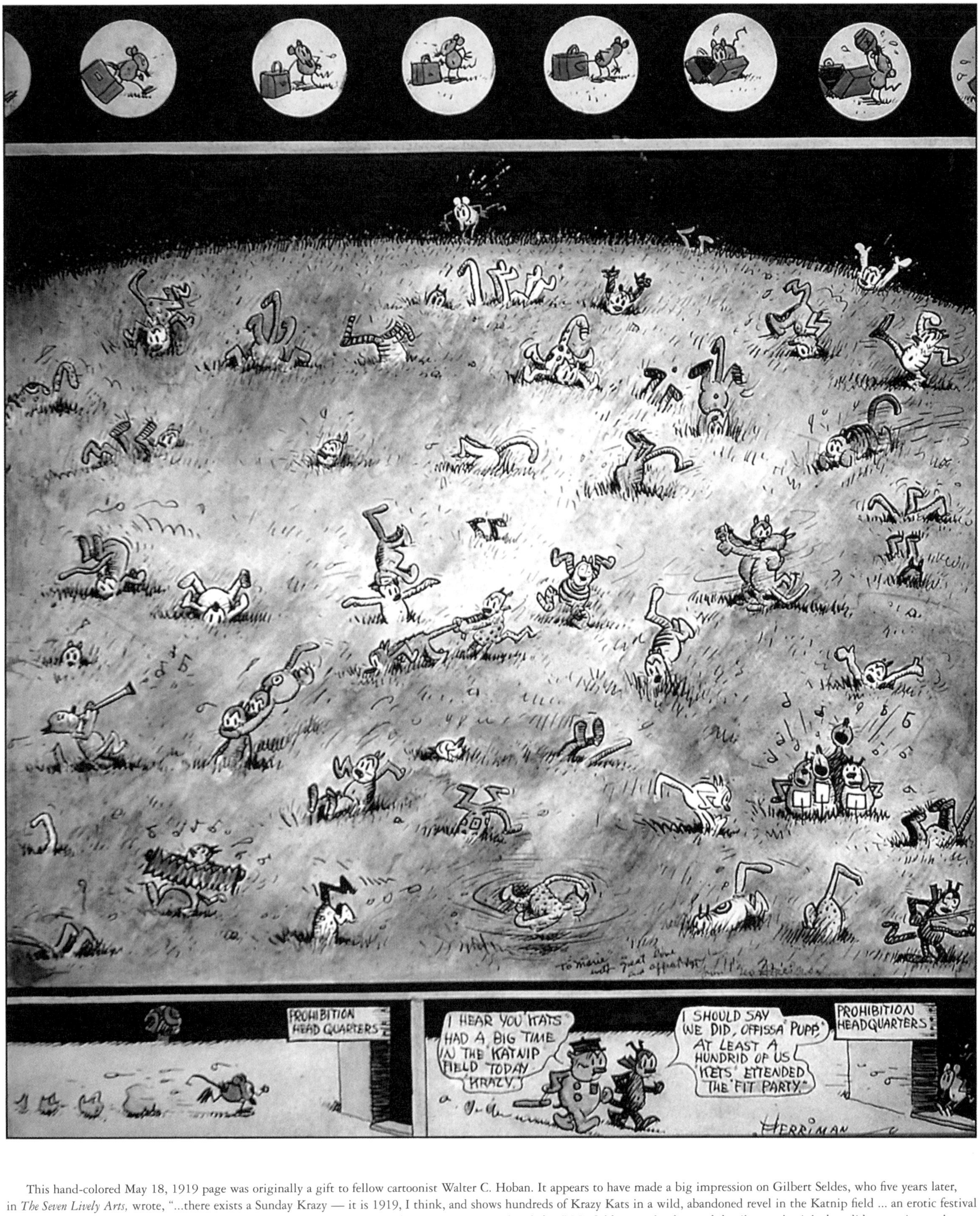
PROHIBITION HEAD QUARTERS
I HEAR YOU KATS HAD A BIG TIME IN THE KATNIP FIELD TODAY "KRAZY."
I SHOULD SAY WE DID, OFFISSA PUPP. AT LEAST A HUNDRID OF US "KETS" ETTENDED THE "FIT PARTY."
PROHIBITION HEADQUARTERS
HERRIMAN

This hand-colored May 18, 1919 page was originally a gift to fellow cartoonist Walter C. Hoban. It appears to have made a big impression on Gilbert Seldes, who five years later, in *The Seven Lively Arts,* wrote, "...there exists a Sunday Krazy — it is 1919, I think, and shows hundreds of Krazy Kats in a wild, abandoned revel in the Katnip field ... an erotic festival ... with our own Krazy playing the viola and Ignatz, who has been drinking, going to sign the pledge." Mr. Seldes got the date and details exactly right but did overestimate the number of Kats by a bit. From *The Illustration Art Auction Catalogue* for 11/20/2004. — K.T.

Kat of a Different Color.

Introduction
by Jeet Heer.

As a newspaper cartoonist, George Herriman began in color and ended in color, but he spent many years in the black and white desert between his vibrant alpha and omega.

Herriman made his comic strip debut on September 29th, 1901 with a four panel vignette for the *New York World,* a brief farce about a sly photographer who takes a trick photo in order to discredit a romantic rival. The last regular Herriman feature to appear in newspapers ran on June 25th 1944, a rather somber *Krazy Kat* Sunday page, with most of the panels framed in black, showing Offisa Pupp rescuing Krazy from drowning while an unexpectedly tearful Ignatz looks on. A final look at the mismatched love affair between Herriman's three main characters, this farewell Sunday page is divided at the top by an upside-down triangle, floating above a white-space V that cuts into the heart of the strip.

Herriman's first comic strip, garishly awash in primary colors, is a byproduct of the early twentieth world of slapstick comedy. His last page testifies to a lifetime spent honing comics into a private language, using the full design of the page and the color scheme to achieve a total effect. Between his beginning and ending, Herriman clearly spent a fair bit of time thinking about the uses of color in comics, so it is worthwhile asking how he developed his unique palette.

When Herriman was starting out, color was very much a selling point with comics: a vivid new technique that set the newspaper supplement apart from old fashioned black and white images. In 1896, William Randolph Hearst, Herriman's future employer and patron, boasted that his Sunday comics offered "eight pages of iridescent polychromous effulgence that makes the rainbow look like a lead-pipe." These florid words testify to the cocky showmanship of the early comics, where the colors were as bright and glaring as a circus poster.

Herriman's earliest strips, done mostly for Pulitzer family newspapers, partook in the rowdy spirit of the time. They were visual explosions full of movement and action. Depending on the resources of the local newspapers, strips like *Professor Otto* (1902) or *Major Ozone* (1906) could appear in four colors or in two or in black and white. Therefore, the color scheme itself couldn't be central to the story. Rather, color had to serve as an additive, often functioning like an exclamation mark, to make the joke louder. Although he was a quick success as a yuck-maker, Herriman wasn't entirely pleased by this situation. "Inspiration! Who ever heard of a comic artist being inspired?" He complained in the pages of *Bookman* in 1902. "What does he know of the inspiration to be obtained from blue, azure, turquoise skies with fleecy clouds riding on and on, whither no one knows." Instead, Herriman noted, the newspaper cartoonist has to try and please the "inartistic majority."

Yet within a few years, Herriman would see his best cartooning peers bring artistic inspiration and even subtlety to the Sunday funnies. In *Little Nemo,* Winsor McCay would unfold multi-hued butterfly wings; in *Wee Willie Winkie's World,* Lionel Feininger distilled the fading half-light of a sunset; in *Polly and Her Pals,* Cliff Sterrett draped female sexuality with a suave sleekness; in *Gasoline Alley,* Frank King marked nature's annual course from budding spring and blooming summer to russet fall and white winter. Like all these cartoonists, Herriman would develop his own personal color scheme but he must have taken inspiration from their achievements.

Whatever lessons he drew from his contemporaries, it took a long time for Herriman to bring the same level of coloring mastery to his cartooning. In 1910 he signed on with Hearst, his final employer till his death. For his first 25 years at the Hearst chain, Herriman created a wide variety of strips (most famously *Krazy Kat*) but almost always in black and white.

After beginning as an offshoot of *The Dingbat Family* in 1910, *Krazy Kat* became its own independent daily strip in 1913. By 1916, Herriman was doing a full page *Krazy Kat* strip for the weekend arts section, setting it apart from the color strips that appeared in their own supplement. There was a brief-lived *Krazy Kat* color page 1922 and a few of the strips Herriman created in the 1920s (*Stumble Inn* and *Us Husbands*) also appeared in color. It was only in 1935 that the color *Krazy Kat* returned for the duration. By and large, Herriman spent a good quarter of century largely working in black and white, at the very time when so many of the best comics appeared in color.

There are a variety of reasons to explain Herriman's long exile from the color pages. For one thing, color was seen childish and the Sunday supplement a branch of children's art. When cartoonists did adult themed work (for example, McCay's *A Pilgrim's Progress*) they usually worked in black and white on weekdays, saving the Sunday page for work that appealed more to kids (like *Little Nemo*). Since *Krazy Kat* was geared towards a sophisticated adult audience, it was deliberately segregated from the other comics.

The early *Krazy Kat* pages were hardly suited for color, in any case. Dense with narrative, often featuring a large cast of characters crammed into two dozen panels and overseen by a loquacious narrator, these strips had so much going on that color would have been a distraction. Moreover, Herriman himself might have stayed away from color out of artistic scruples. The Hearst papers were notoriously vulgar in their use of color, especially compared the *New York Herald* (for whom McCay did his best *Little Nemo* pages) and the *Chicago Tribune* (the home of Feininger and King). Whereas the engravers at the *Herald* and *Tribune* worked hard to capture finely marked graduations of color, the Hearst pressmen tended to be slapdash, dropping dollops of red, blue and yellow on every page.

To be sure, Sterrett was also a Hearst man and did fine things with color. But it's noticeable that Sterrett's colors tended to ostentatious and brassy, like the early comic strips, rather than the more subtle effects

Cliff Sterrett's *Polly and Her Pals* in an August 28th, 1927 example. For jazzy design and colorful, syncopated cartoon compositions, Sterrett was unparalleled. Collection C. Ware.

achieved by McCay or King. It was Sterrett's genius to forge a jazzy style that suited the Hearst colors perfectly. Herriman's style was less suited to the brightness of the Hearst Sunday pages. We know from the many hand-colored strips that Herriman gave away to his friends, what his own ideal color preferences were: the color on these pages is almost translucent, a delicate, watery wash.

When Herriman agreed to re-launch the full page *Krazy Kat* as a color strip in 1935, he faced an artistic challenge: how to take the blunt colors of the Hearst papers and use them for his own refined purposes? He solved this problem by re-conceptualizing the Sunday page. Gone were the complicated narratives of the early days (these were moved over to the daily strip: the lengthy saga of Tiger Tea appeared between Monday and Saturday). Instead the pages were pared down: sometimes featuring only a handful of panels, with the bottom third often blocked off as a large pedestal on which the rest of the page sat. This allowed Herriman to re-cast each page as large coherent unit, with each decorative touch part of an overall pattern.

With larger shapes to work with, Herriman made each page like a poster. Perhaps an even better metaphor is a carpet. Herriman took inspiration from the Navajo art he saw in Monument valley and kept Navajo rugs in his house. These rugs are clearly on Herriman's mind when he worked on many of these Sunday pages, with their combination of jagged lines working towards overall symmetry.

In keeping with the Navajo theme, landscape became increasingly prominent in the late Sunday pages. Of course, from the start Herriman used Monument Valley as a backdrop for his strip, but in the late Sunday pages, gains an extra dimension of depth. The distances behind the character seems larger, the environment harsher and more alien. Herriman achieved this effect largely through his bold use of un-naturalistic colors.

With Sterrett as an example, Herriman knew that he didn't have to be naturalistic in his color choices. Of course, Herriman is not completely arbitrary: the water is often blue, the ground yellow or green, and the main characters mostly stay the same color from beginning to end. But he feels no compunction in varying these basic colors in pursuit of his grand designs. The sky, in particular, can often become unexpectedly black or purple, not just to indicate night but also for greater contrast.

The many years doing black and white also left their mark. Black and white are never default choices for Herriman: he always uses them with intent. This can most clearly be seen in the famous page of November 5th, 1939 (page 56) when black ink spills down the page like in a raging torrent. This page reminds us that for the artist black is not a lack of color but rather a force in its own right.

One way of defining Herriman's genius is to say that he didn't tran-scend comics, rather he took the special language of comics and gave it a personal lilt as no artist did before. The basic brick-throwing plot of Krazy Kat is pure vaudeville: farce based on physical violence. Yet as he matured Herriman didn't abandon this abusive theme but rather high-lighted the pathos of Krazy's love for Ignatz, bricks and all. Similarly, the colors that Hearst had to offer were a blunt instrument. But rather than letting these colors drown his art, Herriman re-drafted his strip so that the colors became integral to the story. The use of color reinvigorated Herriman as an artist, giving him new challenges and opening the way for his best work.

Regular readers of this series will already know of Herriman's seemingly countless gifts of personalized hand-colored drawings to family members, friends and professional acquaintances; the translucent tones he used for such work were not as evident in his published color strips, except possibly in the earliest examples. He seems to have realized that bold flat coloration complemented his newsprint work — and *Krazy Kat* — more readily. Additionally, 1930s methods of coloring had changed from the early days of newspapering, in some cases paper plate matrices of the ink separations sent out to subscribing newspapers rather than a local production department re-interpreting a master guide.
From *The Illustration Art Auction Catálogue* for 11/2/1996. Following page: an example of Herriman's non-*Krazy Kat* color work, a *Stumble Inn* from 1923. Collection C. Ware.

COMIC SECTION SATURDAY, MARCH 24, 1923 NEW YORK EVENING JOURNAL

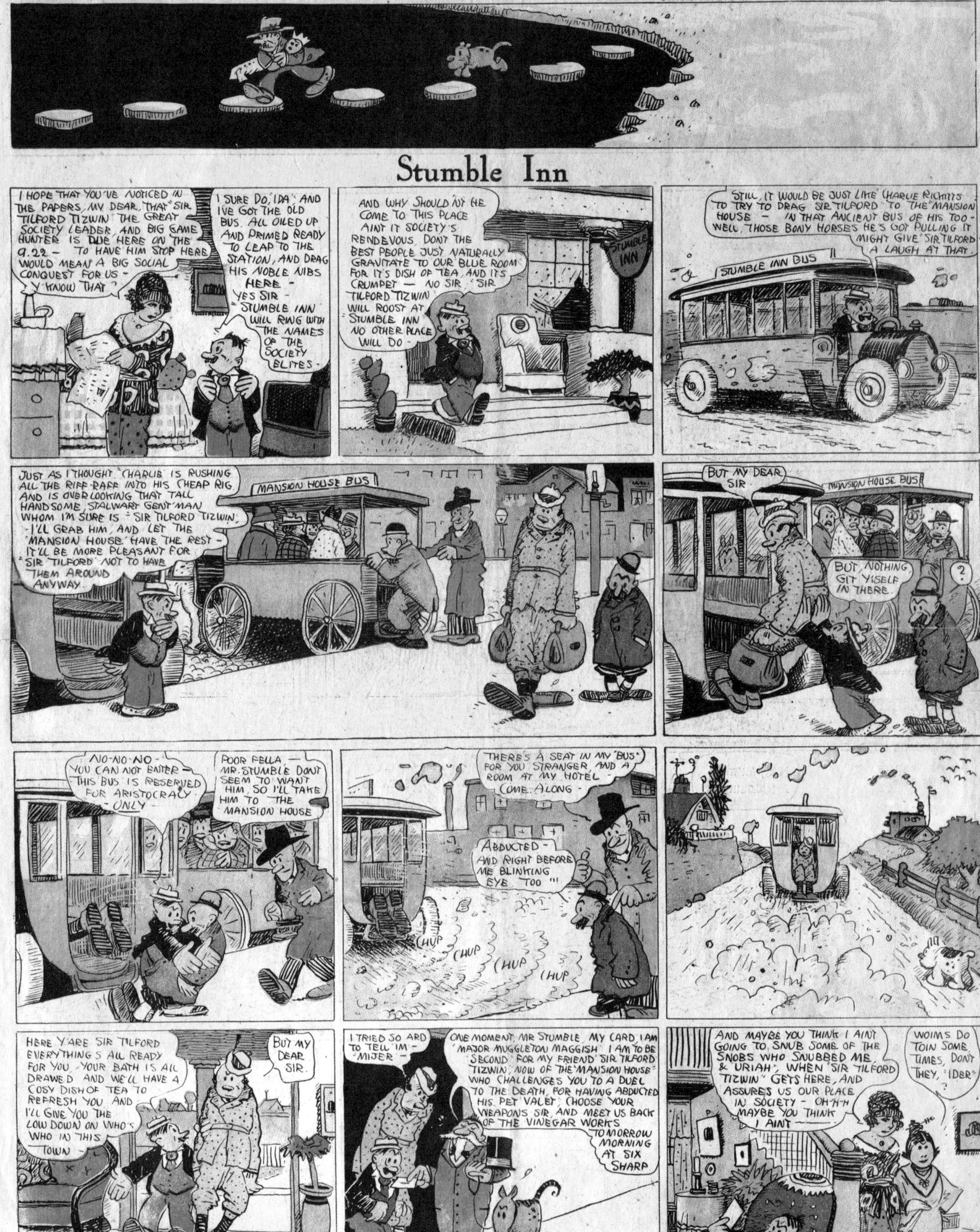
Stumble Inn
I HOPE THAT YOU'VE NOTICED IN THE PAPERS, MY DEAR, THAT "SIR TILFORD TIZWIN" THE GREAT SOCIETY LEADER, AND BIG GAME HUNTER IS DUE HERE ON THE 9.22 - TO HAVE HIM STOP HERE WOULD MEAN A BIG SOCIAL CONQUEST FOR US - Y'KNOW THAT?
I SURE DO, IDA AND I'VE GOT THE OLD BUS. ALL OILED UP AND PRIMED READY TO LEAP TO THE STATION, AND DRAG HIS NOBLE NIBS HERE -
YES SIR - STUMBLE INN WILL RING WITH THE NAMES OF THE SOCIETY ELITES -
AND WHY SHOULD'NT HE COME TO THIS PLACE AINT IT SOCIETY'S RENDEVOUS. DONT THE BEST PEOPLE JUST NATURALLY GRAVITATE TO OUR BLUE ROOM FOR IT'S DISH OF TEA, AND ITS CRUMPET - NO SIR, SIR TILFORD TIZWIN WILL ROOST AT STUMBLE INN NO OTHER PLACE WILL DO -
STUMBLE INN
STILL, IT WOULD BE JUST LIKE CHARLIE RICHITTS TO TRY TO DRAG SIR TILFORD TO THE MANSION HOUSE - IN THAT ANCIENT BUS OF HIS TOO - WELL, THOSE BONY HORSES HE'S GOT PULLING IT MIGHT GIVE SIR TILFORD A LAUGH AT THAT.
STUMBLE INN BUS
JUST AS I THOUGHT CHARLIE IS RUSHING ALL THE RIFF-RAFF INTO HIS CHEAP RIG. AND IS OVERLOOKING THAT TALL HANDSOME, STALWART GENT'MAN WHOM I'M SURE IS "SIR TILFORD TIZWIN" - I'LL GRAB HIM, AND LET THE MANSION HOUSE HAVE THE REST - IT'LL BE MORE PLEASANT FOR "SIR TILFORD" NOT TO HAVE THEM AROUND ANYWAY.
MANSION HOUSE BUS
BUT MY DEAR SIR
MANSION HOUSE BUS
BUT, NOTHING GIT YISELF IN THERE.
?
NO-NO-NO - YOU CAN NOT ENTER - THIS BUS IS RESERVED FOR ARISTOCRACY - ONLY -
POOR FELLA, - MR. STUMBLE DONT SEEM TO WANT HIM, SO I'LL TAKE HIM TO THE MANSION HOUSE
THERE'S A SEAT IN MY "BUS" FOR YOU STRANGER, AND A ROOM AT MY HOTEL - COME ALONG -
ABDUCTED - AND RIGHT BEFORE ME BLINKING EYE TOO !!!
CHUP
CHUP
CHUP
CHUP
HERE Y'ARE SIR TILFORD EVERYTHING'S ALL READY FOR YOU, YOUR BATH IS ALL DRAWED AND WE'LL HAVE A COSY DISH OF TEA TO REFRESH YOU AND I'LL GIVE YOU THE LOW DOWN ON WHO'S WHO IN THIS TOWN -
BUT MY DEAR SIR.
I TRIED SO ARD TO TELL IM - MIJER -
ONE MOMENT, MR STUMBLE, MY CARD, I AM "MAJOR MUGGLETON MAGGISH" I AM TO BE SECOND FOR MY FRIEND SIR TILFORD TIZWIN, NOW OF THE "MANSION HOUSE" WHO CHALLENGES YOU TO A DUEL TO THE DEATH, FOR HAVING ABDUCTED HIS PET VALET, CHOOSE YOUR WEAPONS SIR, AND MEET US BACK OF THE VINEGAR WORKS TOMORROW MORNING AT SIX SHARP
AND MAYBE YOU THINK I AINT GOING TO SNUB SOME OF THE SNOBS WHO SNUBBED ME, & URIAH", WHEN "SIR TILFORD TIZWIN" GETS HERE, AND ASSURES US OUR PLACE IN SOCIETY - OH-H-H MAYBE YOU THINK I AINT ——
WOIMS DO TOIN SOME TIMES, DONT THEY, "IDER"?

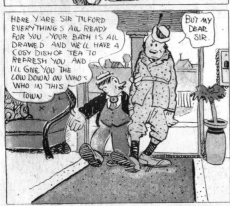

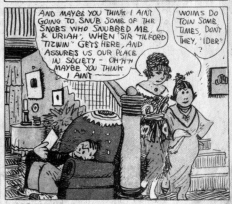

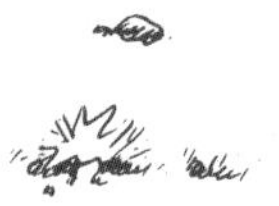

1939.

Readers, please note: an Ignatz "dingbat" placed below a strip indicates a relevant or related footnote at the volume's end for that particular selection, all to be found in the "Ignatz Debaffler" section.

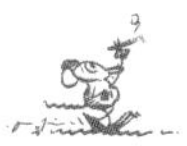

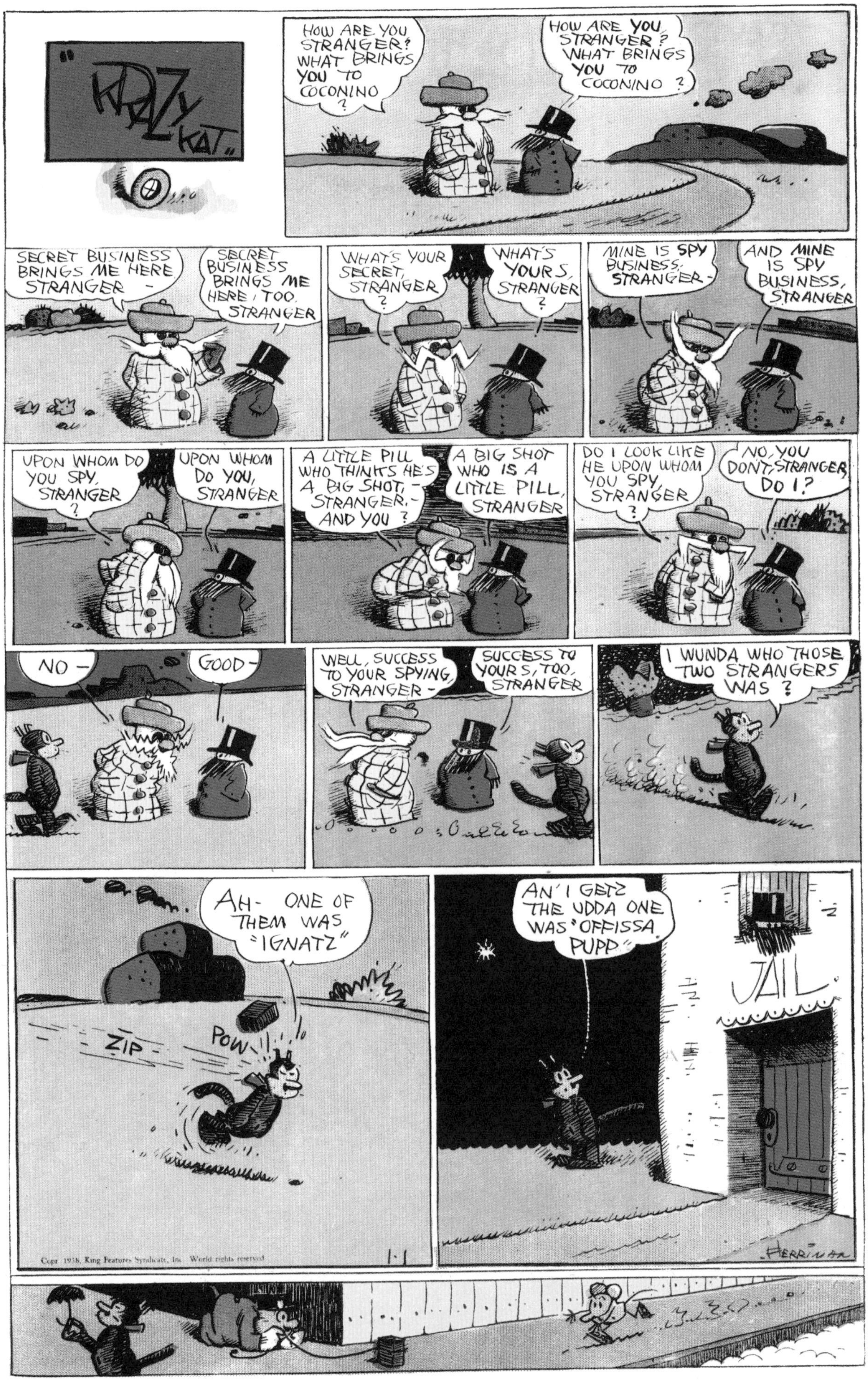
"KRAZY KAT"
HOW ARE YOU STRANGER? WHAT BRINGS YOU TO COCONINO ?
HOW ARE YOU, STRANGER? WHAT BRINGS YOU TO COCONINO ?
SECRET BUSINESS BRINGS ME HERE STRANGER -
SECRET BUSINESS BRINGS ME HERE, TOO, STRANGER
WHAT'S YOUR SECRET, STRANGER ?
WHAT'S YOURS, STRANGER ?
MINE IS SPY BUSINESS, STRANGER -
AND MINE IS SPY BUSINESS, STRANGER
UPON WHOM DO YOU SPY, STRANGER ?
UPON WHOM DO YOU, STRANGER
A LITTLE PILL WHO THINKS HE'S A BIG SHOT, - STRANGER, - AND YOU ?
A BIG SHOT WHO IS A LITTLE PILL, STRANGER
DO I LOOK LIKE HE UPON WHOM YOU SPY, STRANGER ?
NO, YOU DONT, STRANGER, DO I?
NO -
GOOD -
WELL, SUCCESS TO YOUR SPYING, STRANGER -
SUCCESS TO YOURS, TOO, STRANGER
I WUNDA WHO THOSE TWO STRANGERS WAS ?
AH - ONE OF THEM WAS "IGNATZ"
ZIP
POW
AN' I GETZ THE UDDA ONE WAS "OFFISSA PUPP"
JAIL
Copr. 1938, King Features Syndicate, Inc. World rights reserved
HERRIMAN

January 1st, 1939.

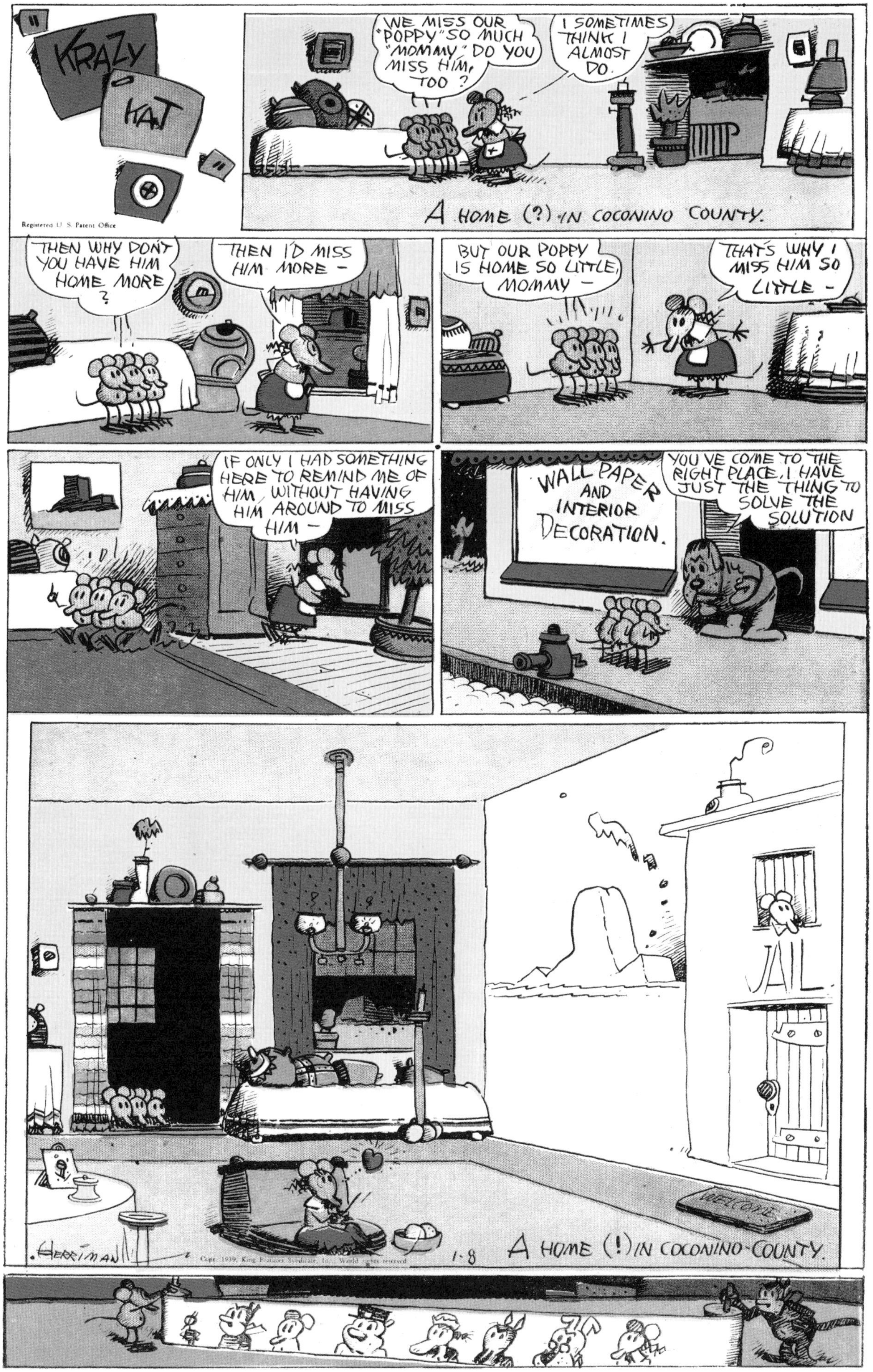
"KRAZY KAT"
Registered U.S. Patent Office
WE MISS OUR "POPPY" SO MUCH "MOMMY," DO YOU MISS HIM, TOO?
I SOMETIMES THINK I ALMOST DO.
A HOME (?) IN COCONINO COUNTY.
THEN WHY DON'T YOU HAVE HIM HOME MORE?
THEN I'D MISS HIM MORE -
BUT OUR POPPY IS HOME SO LITTLE, MOMMY -
THAT'S WHY I MISS HIM SO LITTLE -
IF ONLY I HAD SOMETHING HERE TO REMIND ME OF HIM, WITHOUT HAVING HIM AROUND TO MISS HIM -
WALL PAPER AND INTERIOR DECORATION.
YOU'VE COME TO THE RIGHT PLACE. I HAVE JUST THE THING TO SOLVE THE SOLUTION
JAIL
WELCOME
HERRIMAN
Copr. 1939, King Features Syndicate, Inc., World rights reserved
1-8
A HOME (!) IN COCONINO COUNTY.

January 8th, 1939.

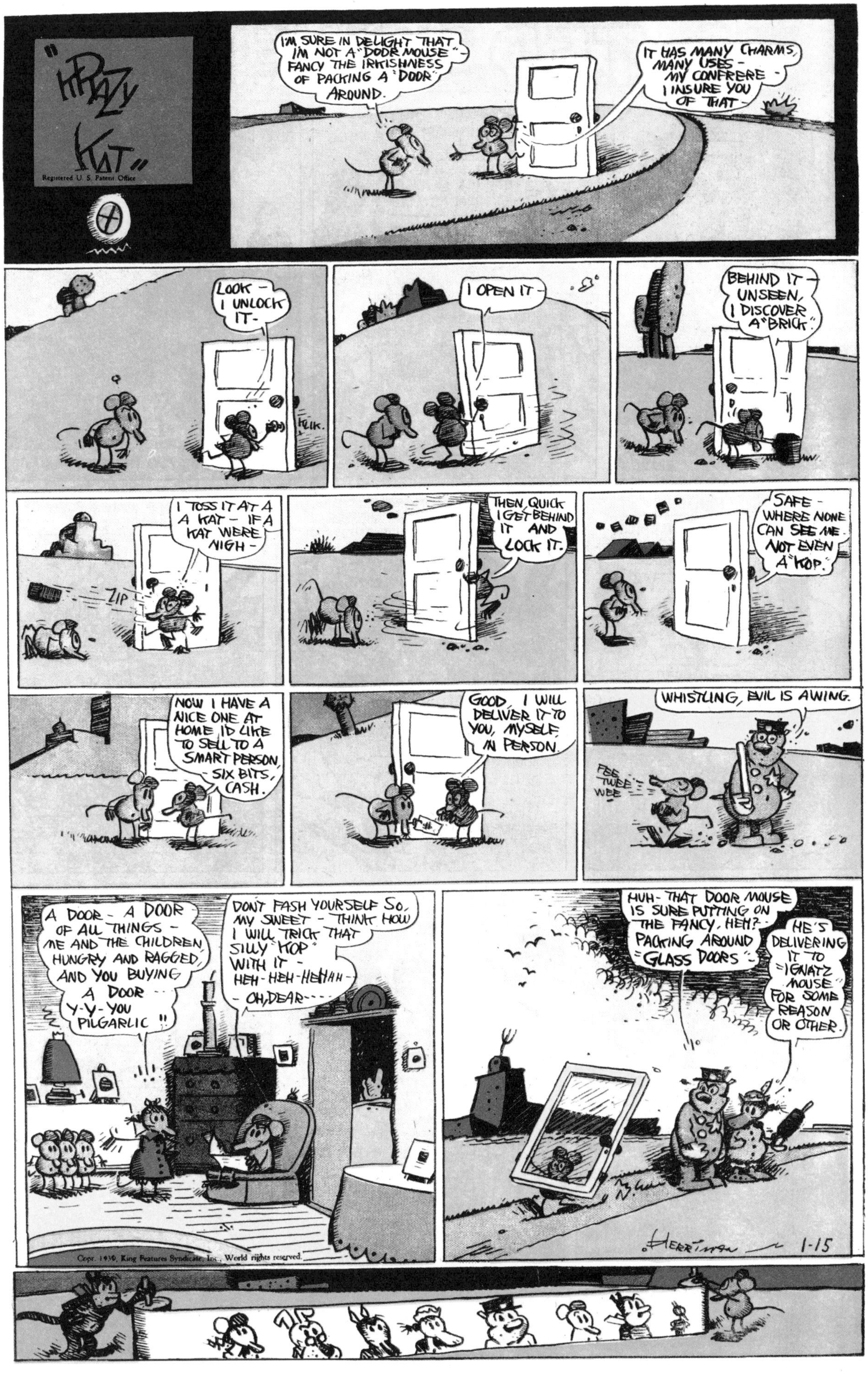
"KRAZY KAT"
Registered U. S. Patent Office
I'M SURE IN DELIGHT THAT I'M NOT A "DOOR MOUSE" - FANCY THE IRKISHNESS OF PACKING A "DOOR" AROUND.
IT HAS MANY CHARMS, MANY USES - MY CONFRERE - I INSURE YOU OF THAT -
LOOK - I UNLOCK IT -
KLIK.
I OPEN IT -
BEHIND IT - UNSEEN, I DISCOVER A "BRICK".
I TOSS IT AT A A KAT - IF A KAT WERE NIGH -
ZIP
THEN, QUICK I GET BEHIND IT AND LOCK IT.
SAFE - WHERE NONE CAN SEE ME. NOT EVEN A "KOP".
NOW I HAVE A NICE ONE AT HOME I'D LIKE TO SELL TO A SMART PERSON - SIX BITS, CASH.
GOOD, I WILL DELIVER IT TO YOU, MYSELF, IN PERSON.
WHISTLING, EVIL IS AWING.
FEE TWEE WEE
A DOOR - A DOOR OF ALL THINGS - ME AND THE CHILDREN, HUNGRY AND RAGGED, AND YOU BUYING A DOOR - Y-Y-YOU PILGARLIC !!
DON'T FASH YOURSELF SO, MY SWEET - THINK HOW I WILL TRICK THAT SILLY "KOP" WITH IT - HEH-HEH-HEHAH - OH, DEAR -
HUH - THAT DOOR MOUSE IS SURE PUTTING ON THE FANCY, HEH? - PACKING AROUND GLASS DOORS -
HE'S DELIVERING IT TO IGNATZ MOUSE FOR SOME REASON OR OTHER.
Copr. 1939, King Features Syndicate, Inc., World rights reserved.
HERRIMAN 1-15

January 15th, 1939.

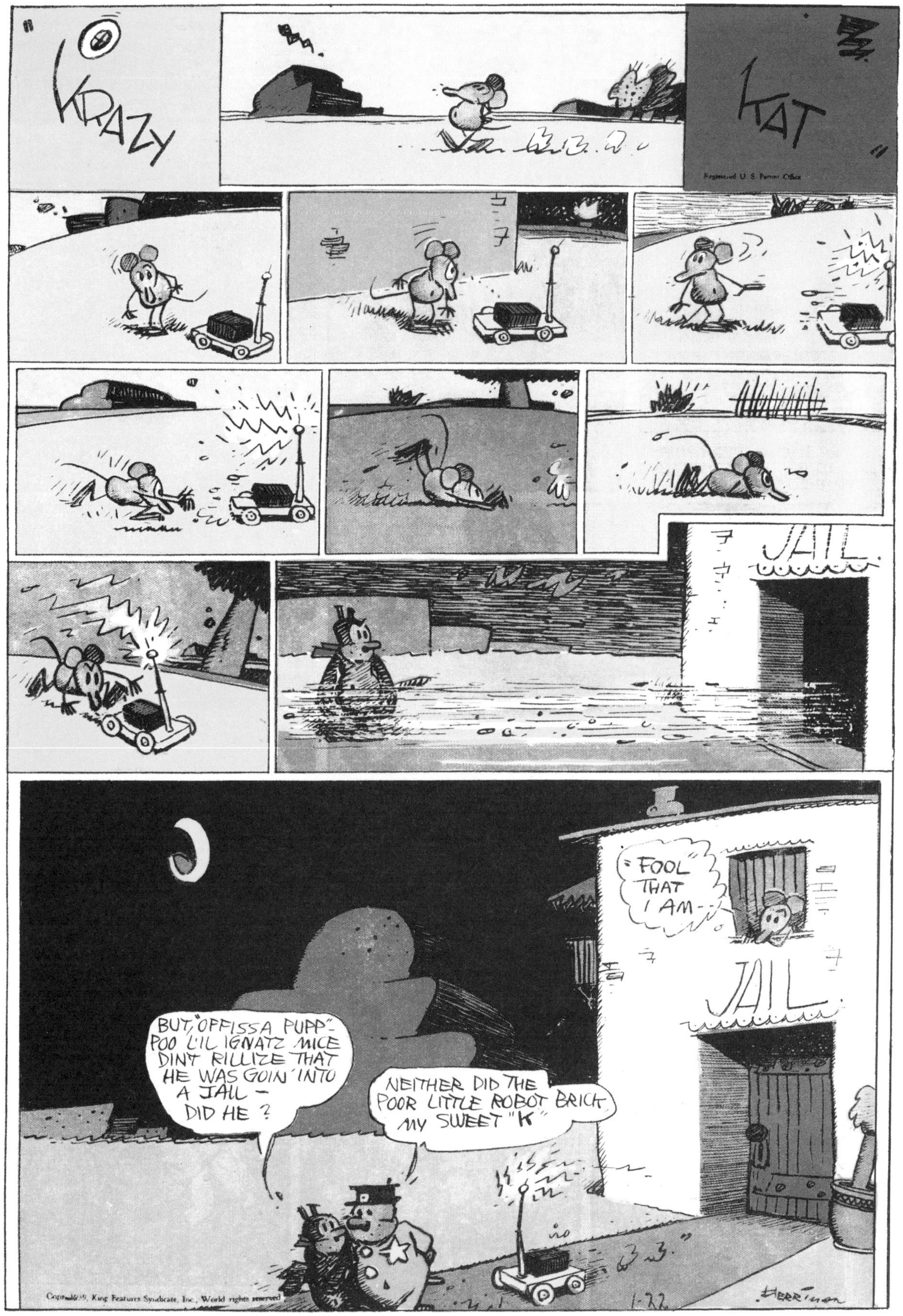
KRAZY
KAT
Registered U.S. Patent Office
JAIL
FOOL THAT I AM--
JAIL
BUT, "OFFISSA PUPP" POO L'IL IGNATZ MICE DIN'T RILLIZE THAT HE WAS GOIN' INTO A JAIL - DID HE ?
NEITHER DID THE POOR LITTLE ROBOT BRICK, MY SWEET "K"
King Features Syndicate, Inc., World rights reserved
1-22
HERRIMAN

January 22nd, 1940.

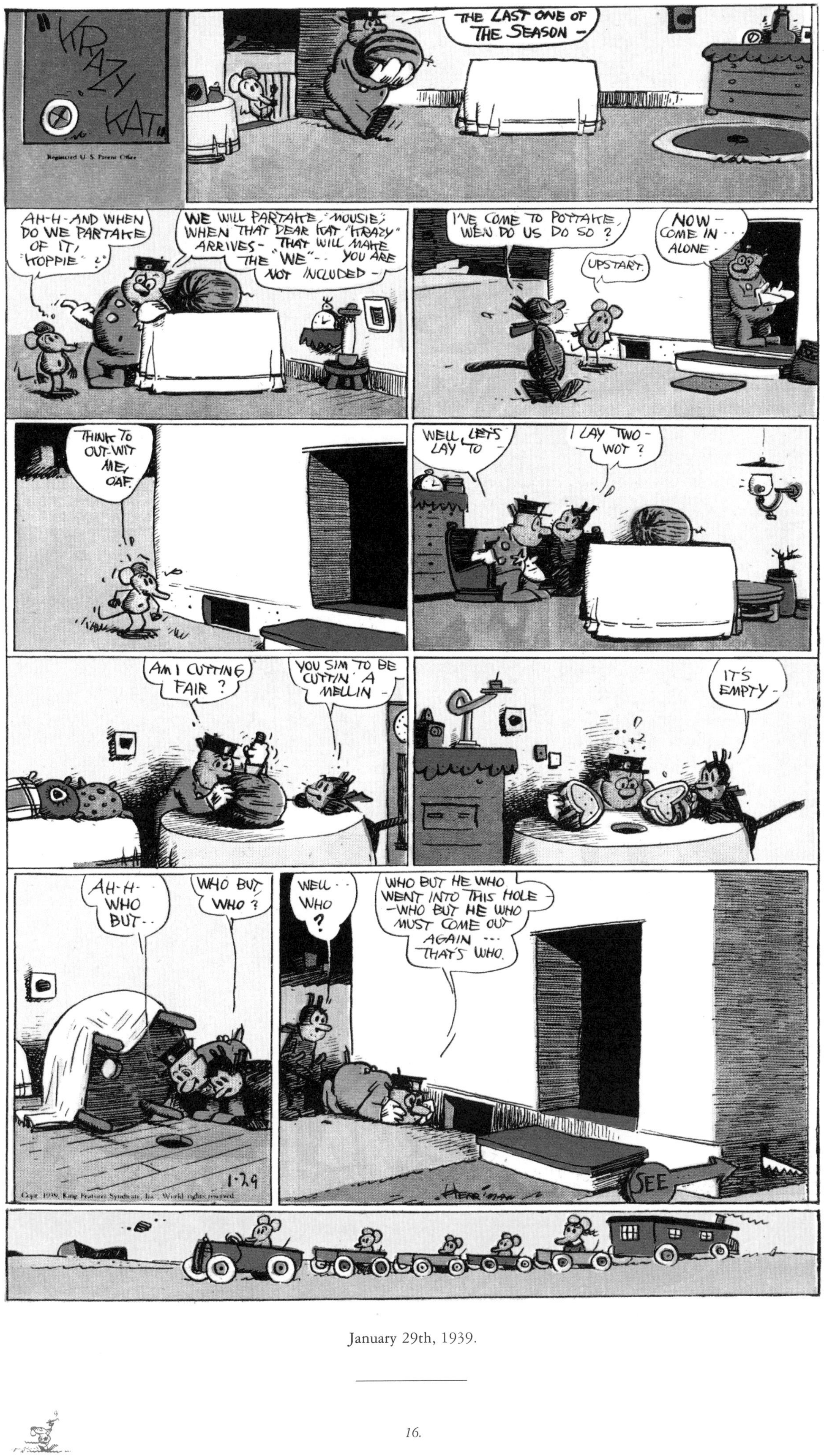
"KRAZY KAT"
Registered U. S. Patent Office
THE LAST ONE OF THE SEASON -
AH-H- AND WHEN DO WE PARTAKE OF IT, "KOPPIE" ?
WE WILL PARTAKE, "MOUSIE," WHEN THAT DEAR KAT "KRAZY" ARRIVES - THAT WILL MAKE THE "WE" - - YOU ARE NOT INCLUDED -
I'VE COME TO POTTAKE, WEN DO US DO SO ?
UPSTART.
NOW - COME IN - - ALONE -
THINK TO OUT-WIT ME, OAF.
WELL, LET'S LAY TO -
LAY TWO - WOT ?
AM I CUTTING FAIR ?
YOU SIM TO BE CUTTIN' A MELLIN -
IT'S EMPTY -
AH-H- WHO BUT - -
WHO BUT, WHO ?
WELL - - WHO ?
WHO BUT HE WHO WENT INTO THIS HOLE - WHO BUT HE WHO MUST COME OUT AGAIN - - - THAT'S WHO.
1-29
Copr. 1939, King Features Syndicate, Inc., World rights reserved
HERRIMAN
SEE

January 29th, 1939.

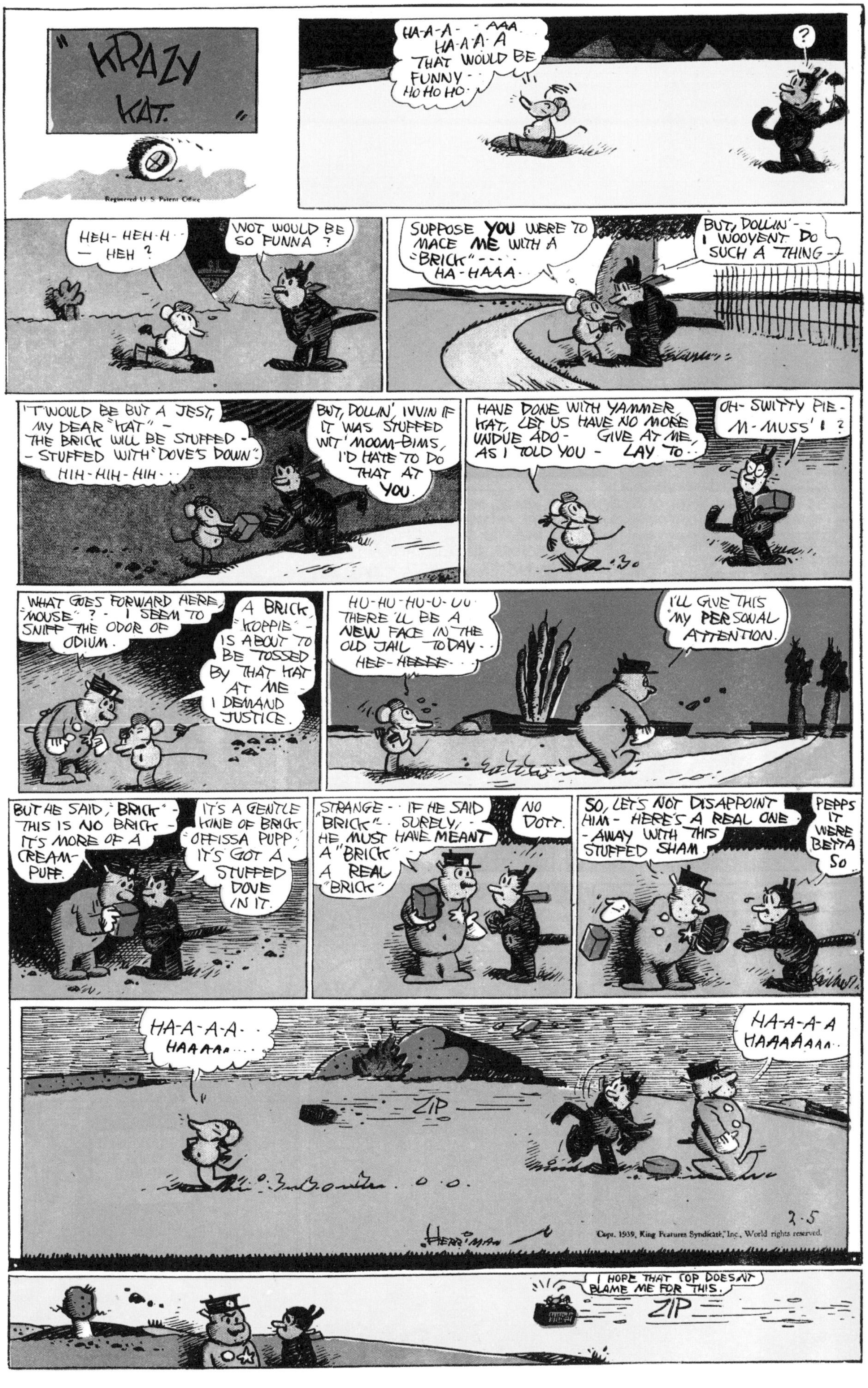
"KRAZY KAT."
Registered U. S. Patent Office
HA-A-A- -AAA. HA-A-A-A THAT WOULD BE FUNNY- HO HO HO-
?
HEH-HEH-H- —HEH ?
WOT WOULD BE SO FUNNA ?
SUPPOSE YOU WERE TO MACE ME WITH A "BRICK"---- HA-HAAA
BUT, DOLLIN'-- I WOOYENT DO SUCH A THING-
'T WOULD BE BUT A JEST, MY DEAR "KAT" - THE BRICK WILL BE STUFFED - - STUFFED WITH "DOVE'S DOWN" HIH-HIH-HIH...
BUT, DOLLIN', IVVIN IF IT WAS STUFFED WIT' MOOM-BIMS, I'D HATE TO DO THAT AT YOU.
HAVE DONE WITH YAMMER, KAT, LET US HAVE NO MORE UNDUE ADO- GIVE AT ME, AS I TOLD YOU - LAY TO.
OH- SWITTY PIE- M-MUSS'! ?
WHAT GOES FORWARD HERE, MOUSE ? - I SEEM TO SNIFF THE ODOR OF ODIUM.
A BRICK "KOPPIE" IS ABOUT TO BE TOSSED BY THAT KAT AT ME - I DEMAND JUSTICE.
HU-HU-HU-U-UU THERE'LL BE A NEW FACE IN THE OLD JAIL TODAY- HEE-HEEEE-
I'LL GIVE THIS MY PERSONAL ATTENTION.
BUT HE SAID, "BRICK" - THIS IS NO BRICK - IT'S MORE OF A CREAM-PUFF.
IT'S A GENTLE KINE OF BRICK OFFISSA PUPP. IT'S GOT A STUFFED DOVE IN IT.
"STRANGE- - IF HE SAID "BRICK"- SURELY, HE MUST HAVE MEANT A "BRICK" A REAL "BRICK".
NO DOTT.
SO, LET'S NOT DISAPPOINT HIM- HERE'S A REAL ONE - AWAY WITH THIS STUFFED SHAM
PEPPS IT WERE BETTA SO
HA-A-A-A- HAAAAA....
ZIP
HA-A-A-A HAAAAAAA..
HERRIMAN
2-5
Copr. 1939, King Features Syndicate, Inc., World rights reserved.
I HOPE THAT COP DOESN'T BLAME ME FOR THIS.
ZIP

February 5th, 1939.

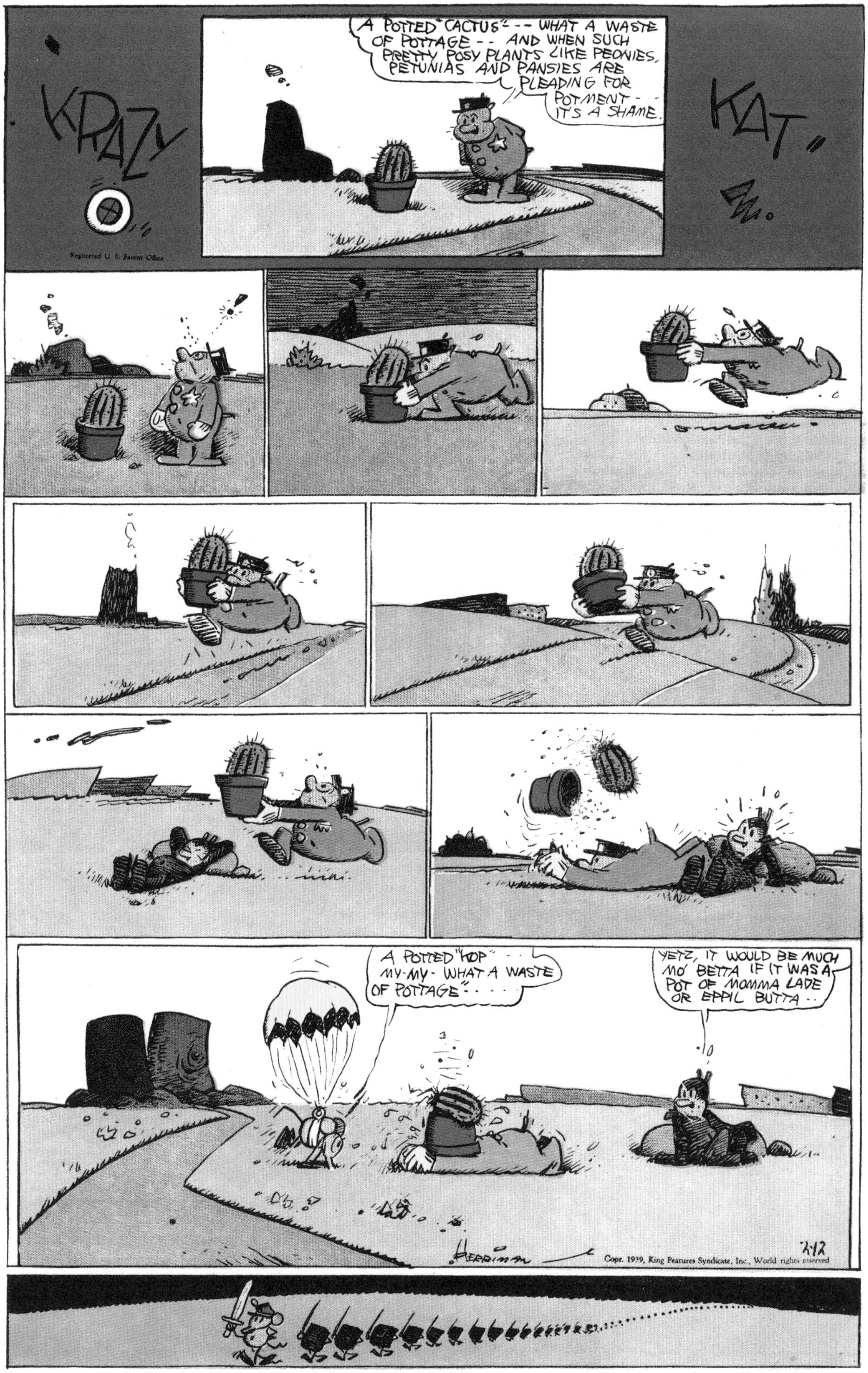
KRAZY KAT
Registered U. S. Patent Office
A POTTED "CACTUS" -- WHAT A WASTE OF POTTAGE -- AND WHEN SUCH PRETTY POSY PLANTS LIKE PEONIES, PETUNIAS AND PANSIES ARE PLEADING FOR POTMENT -- IT'S A SHAME.
A POTTED "KOP" -- MY-MY- WHAT A WASTE OF POTTAGE" - - -
YETZ, IT WOULD BE MUCH MO' BETTA IF IT WAS A POT OF MOMMA LADE OR EPPIL BUTTA - -
HERRIMAN
2-12
Copr. 1939, King Features Syndicate, Inc., World rights reserved

February 12th, 1939.

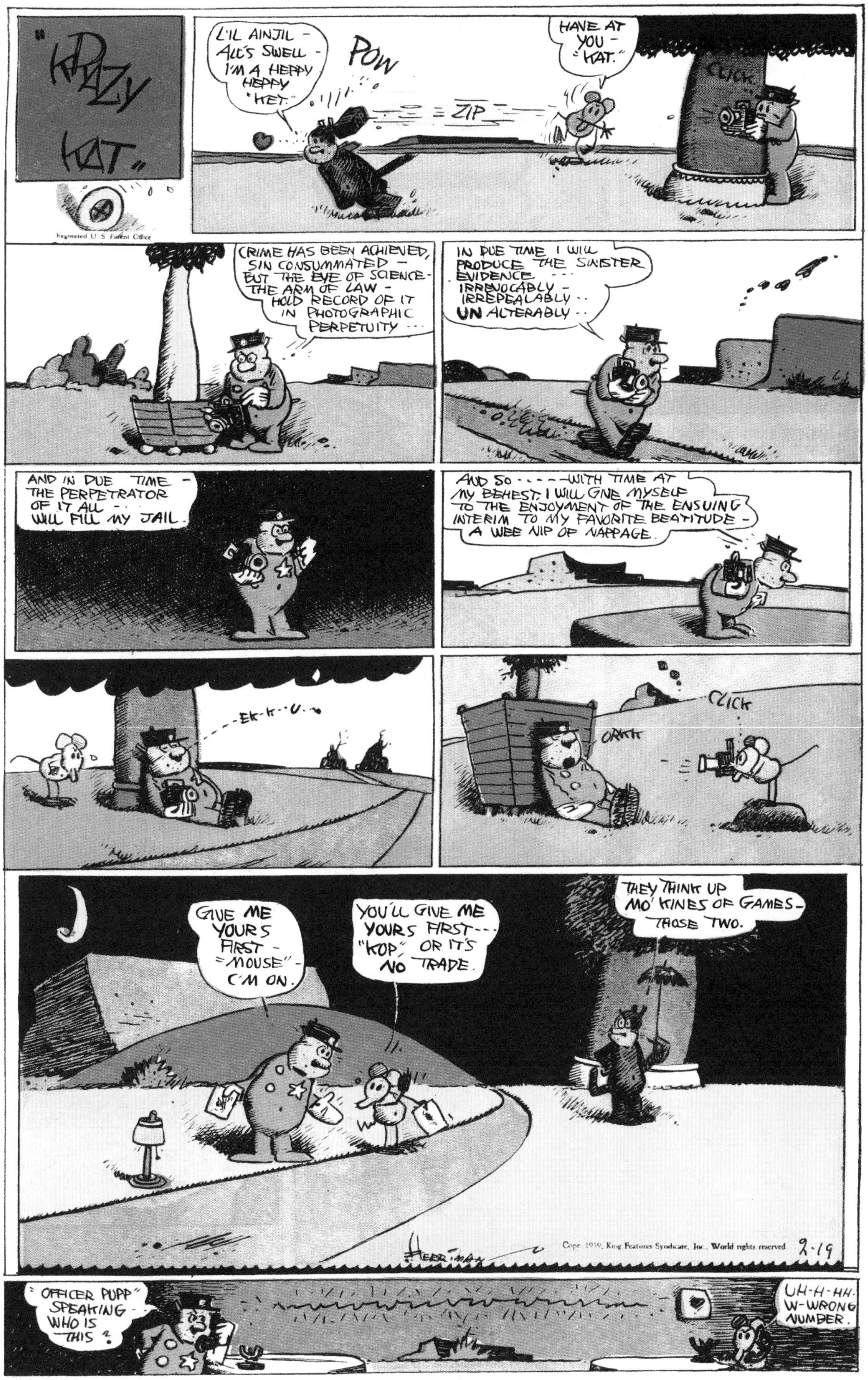
"KRAZY KAT"
Registered U. S. Patent Office
L'IL AINJIL - ALL'S SWELL - I'M A HEPPY HEPPY "KET."
POW
ZIP
HAVE AT YOU - "KAT."
CLICK
CRIME HAS BEEN ACHIEVED, SIN CONSUMMATED - BUT THE EYE OF SCIENCE - THE ARM OF LAW - HOLD RECORD OF IT IN PHOTOGRAPHIC PERPETUITY - - -
IN DUE TIME I WILL PRODUCE THE SINISTER EVIDENCE - - - IRREVOCABLY - IRREPEALABLY - - UN ALTERABLY - -
AND IN DUE TIME THE PERPETRATOR OF IT ALL - - WILL FILL MY JAIL.
AND SO - - - - WITH TIME AT MY BEHEST, I WILL GIVE MYSELF TO THE ENJOYMENT OF THE ENSUING INTERIM TO MY FAVORITE BEATITUDE - A WEE NIP OF NAPPAGE.
EK-K-U
CLICK
GIVE ME YOURS FIRST - "MOUSE" - C'M ON.
YOU'LL GIVE ME YOURS FIRST - - - "KOP," OR IT'S NO TRADE.
THEY THINK UP MO' KINES OF GAMES - THOSE TWO.
HERRIMAN
Copr. 1939, King Features Syndicate, Inc., World rights reserved.
2-19
"OFFICER PUPP" SPEAKING - WHO IS THIS ?
UH-H-HH W-WRONG NUMBER.

February 19th, 1939.

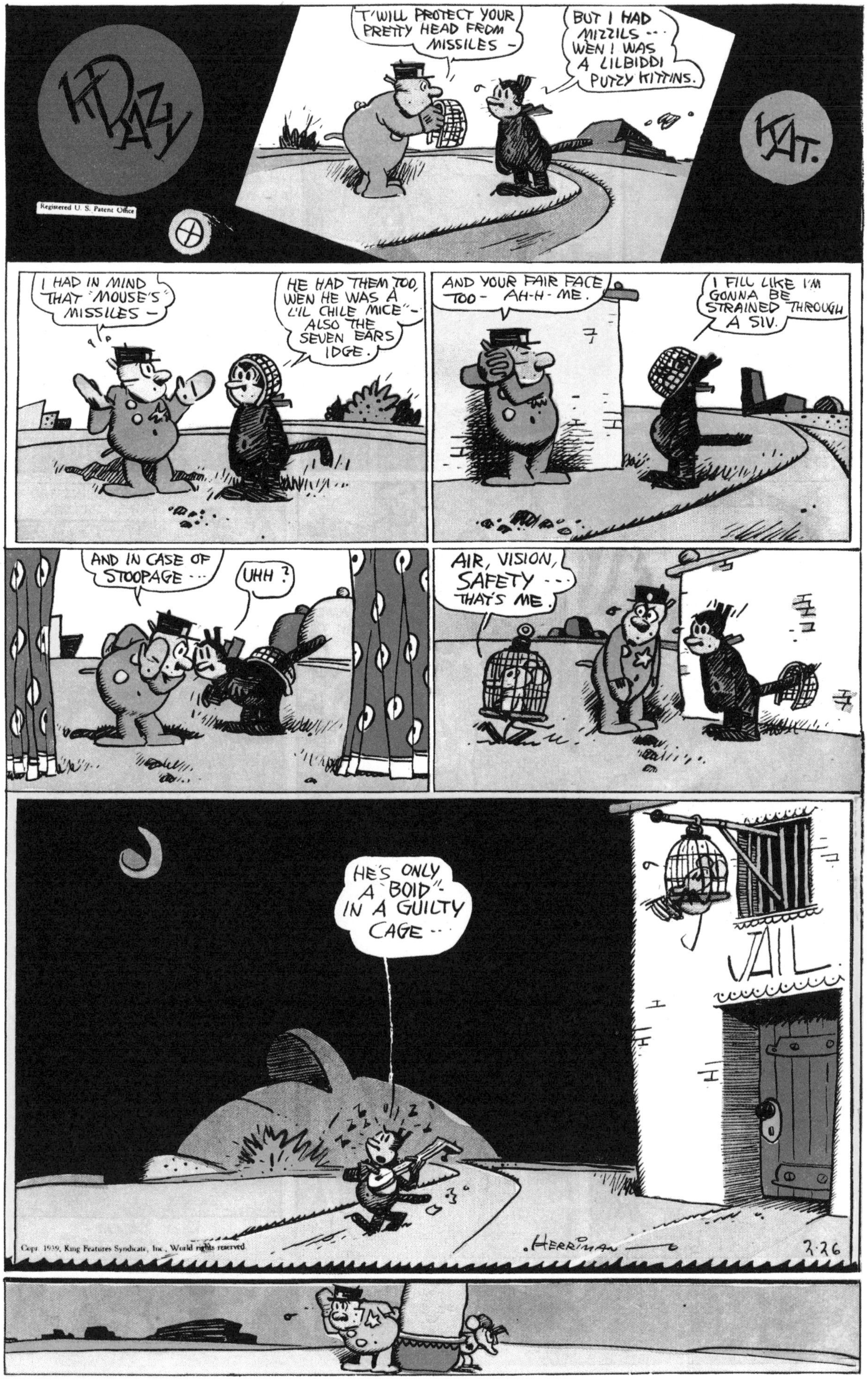
KRAZY
KAT.
Registered U. S. Patent Office
T'WILL PROTECT YOUR PRETTY HEAD FROM MISSILES -
BUT I HAD MIZZILS -- WEN I WAS A LILBIDDI PUTZY KITTINS.
I HAD IN MIND THAT "MOUSE'S" MISSILES -
HE HAD THEM TOO, WEN HE WAS A L'IL CHILE MICE - ALSO THE SEVEN EARS IDGE.
AND YOUR FAIR FACE TOO - AH-H- ME.
I FILL LIKE I'M GONNA BE STRAINED THROUGH A SIV.
AND IN CASE OF STOOPAGE ---
UHH ?
AIR, VISION, SAFETY --- THAT'S ME.
HE'S ONLY A "BOID" IN A GUILTY CAGE --
JAIL
Copr. 1939, King Features Syndicate, Inc., World rights reserved.
HERRIMAN
2-26

February 26th, 1939.

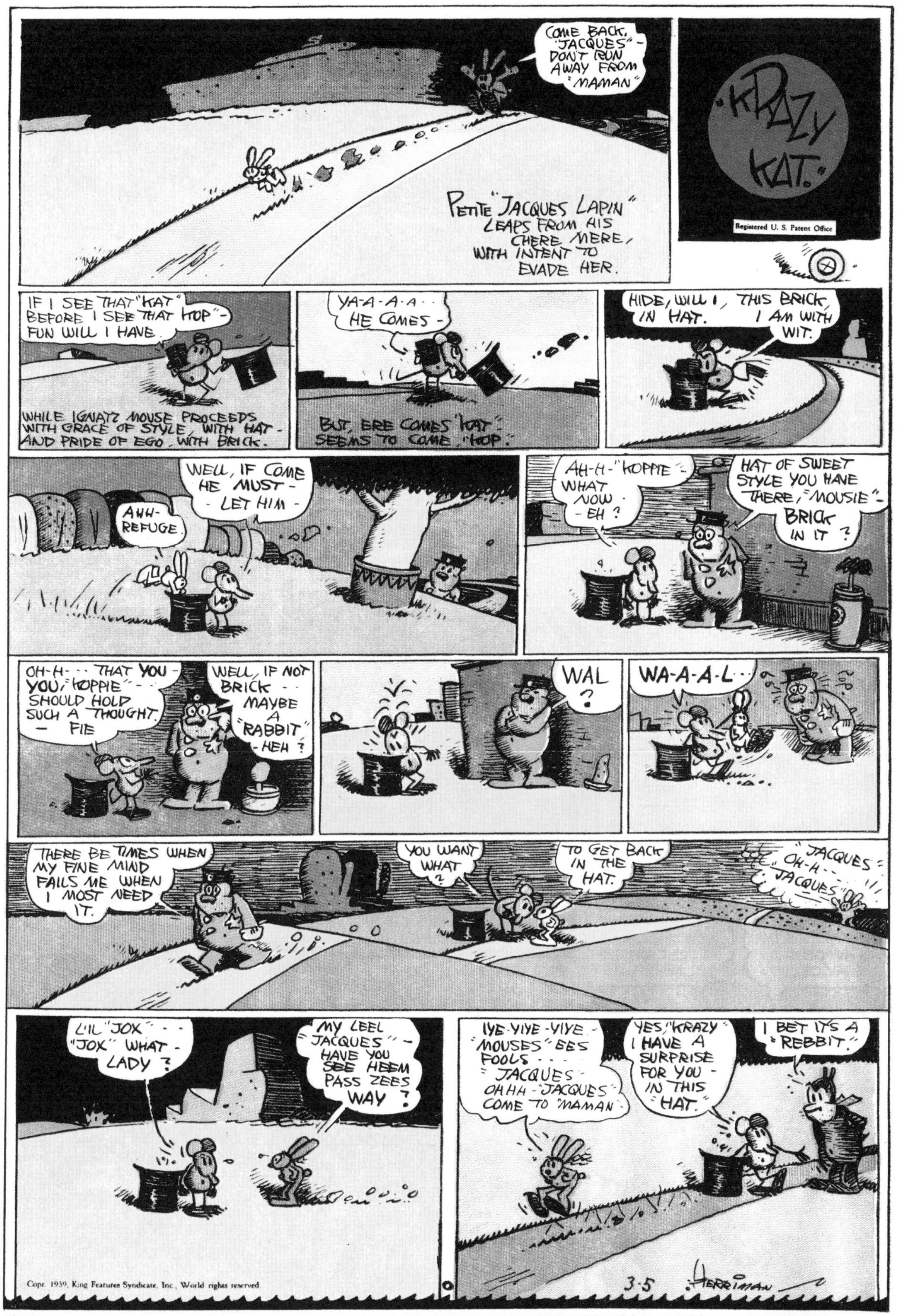
COME BACK, "JACQUES" - DON'T RUN AWAY FROM "MAMAN"
"KRAZY KAT."
Registered U. S. Patent Office
PETITE "JACQUES LAPIN" LEAPS FROM HIS CHERE MERE, WITH INTENT TO EVADE HER.
IF I SEE THAT "KAT" BEFORE I SEE THAT "KOP" - FUN WILL I HAVE.
WHILE IGNATZ MOUSE PROCEEDS WITH GRACE OF STYLE, WITH HAT - AND PRIDE OF EGO, WITH BRICK.
YA-A-A-A - - HE COMES -
BUT, ERE COMES "KAT" SEEMS TO COME "KOP".
HIDE, WILL I, IN HAT.
THIS BRICK, I AM WITH WIT.
AHH - REFUGE
WELL, IF COME HE MUST - - LET HIM -
AH-H- "KOPPIE" - WHAT NOW - - EH ?
HAT OF SWEET STYLE YOU HAVE THERE, "MOUSIE" - BRICK IN IT ?
OH-H- - - THAT YOU - YOU, "KOPPIE" - - SHOULD HOLD SUCH A THOUGHT. - FIE
WELL, IF NOT BRICK - - MAYBE A "RABBIT" - HEH ?
WAL ?
WA-A-A-L - -
THERE BE TIMES WHEN MY FINE MIND FAILS ME WHEN I MOST NEED IT.
YOU WANT WHAT ?
TO GET BACK IN THE HAT.
"JACQUES" OH-H- - "JACQUES"
L'IL "JOX" - - "JOX" WHAT - LADY ?
MY LEEL "JACQUES" - HAVE YOU SEE HEEM PASS ZEES WAY ?
IYE-YIYE-YIYE - "MOUSES" EES FOOLS - "JACQUES" - OH HH - "JACQUES" - COME TO "MAMAN"
YES, "KRAZY" I HAVE A SURPRISE FOR YOU - IN THIS "HAT."
I BET IT'S A "REBBIT."
Copr. 1939, King Features Syndicate, Inc., World rights reserved
3-5
HERRIMAN

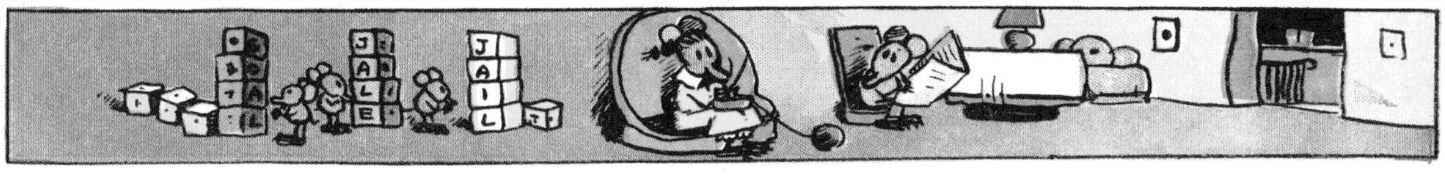
JAIL
JAIL
JAIL

March 5th, 1939.

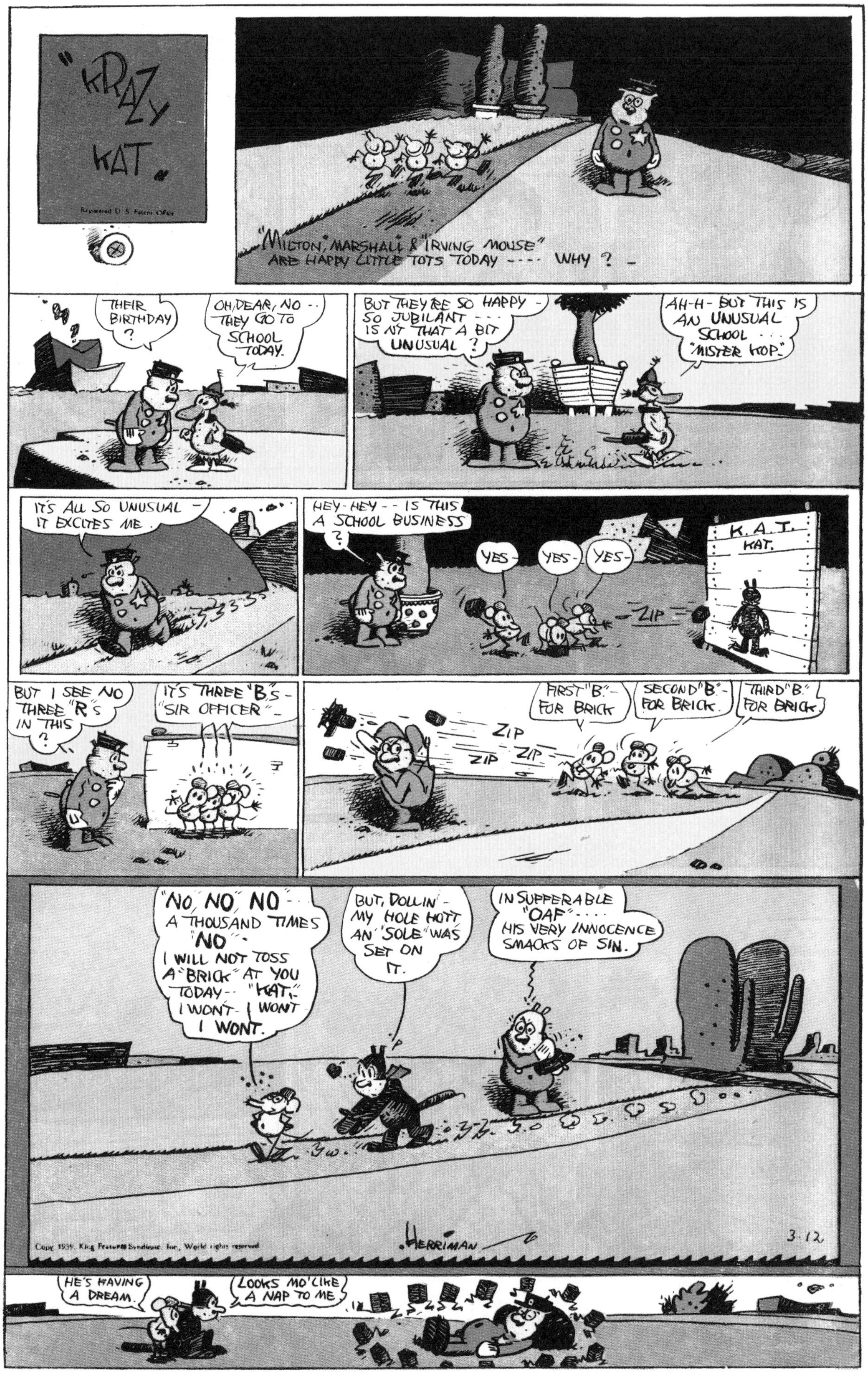
"KRAZY KAT."
Registered U.S. Patent Office
"MILTON," MARSHALL & "IRVING MOUSE" ARE HAPPY LITTLE TOTS TODAY ---- WHY ? -
THEIR BIRTHDAY ?
OH, DEAR, NO - THEY GO TO SCHOOL TODAY.
BUT THEY'RE SO HAPPY - SO JUBILANT --- IS N'T THAT A BIT UNUSUAL ?
AH-H - BUT THIS IS AN UNUSUAL SCHOOL ... "MISTER KOP."
IT'S ALL SO UNUSUAL - IT EXCITES ME.
HEY-HEY - - IS THIS A SCHOOL BUSINESS ?
YES-
YES-
YES-
ZIP
K.A.T. KAT.
BUT I SEE NO THREE "R"S IN THIS ?
IT'S THREE "B"S - "SIR OFFICER" -
FIRST "B" - FOR BRICK
SECOND "B" - FOR BRICK.
THIRD "B". FOR BRICK.
ZIP
ZIP
ZIP
"NO, NO, NO - A THOUSAND TIMES "NO" - I WILL NOT TOSS A "BRICK" AT YOU TODAY - "KAT," - I WONT - I WONT I WONT.
BUT, DOLLIN - MY HOLE HOTT AN' "SOLE" WAS SET ON IT.
INSUFFERABLE "OAF" ... HIS VERY INNOCENCE SMACKS OF SIN.
Copr. 1939, King Features Syndicate, Inc., World rights reserved
HERRIMAN
3-12
HE'S HAVING A DREAM.
LOOKS MO' LIKE A NAP TO ME.

March 12th, 1939.

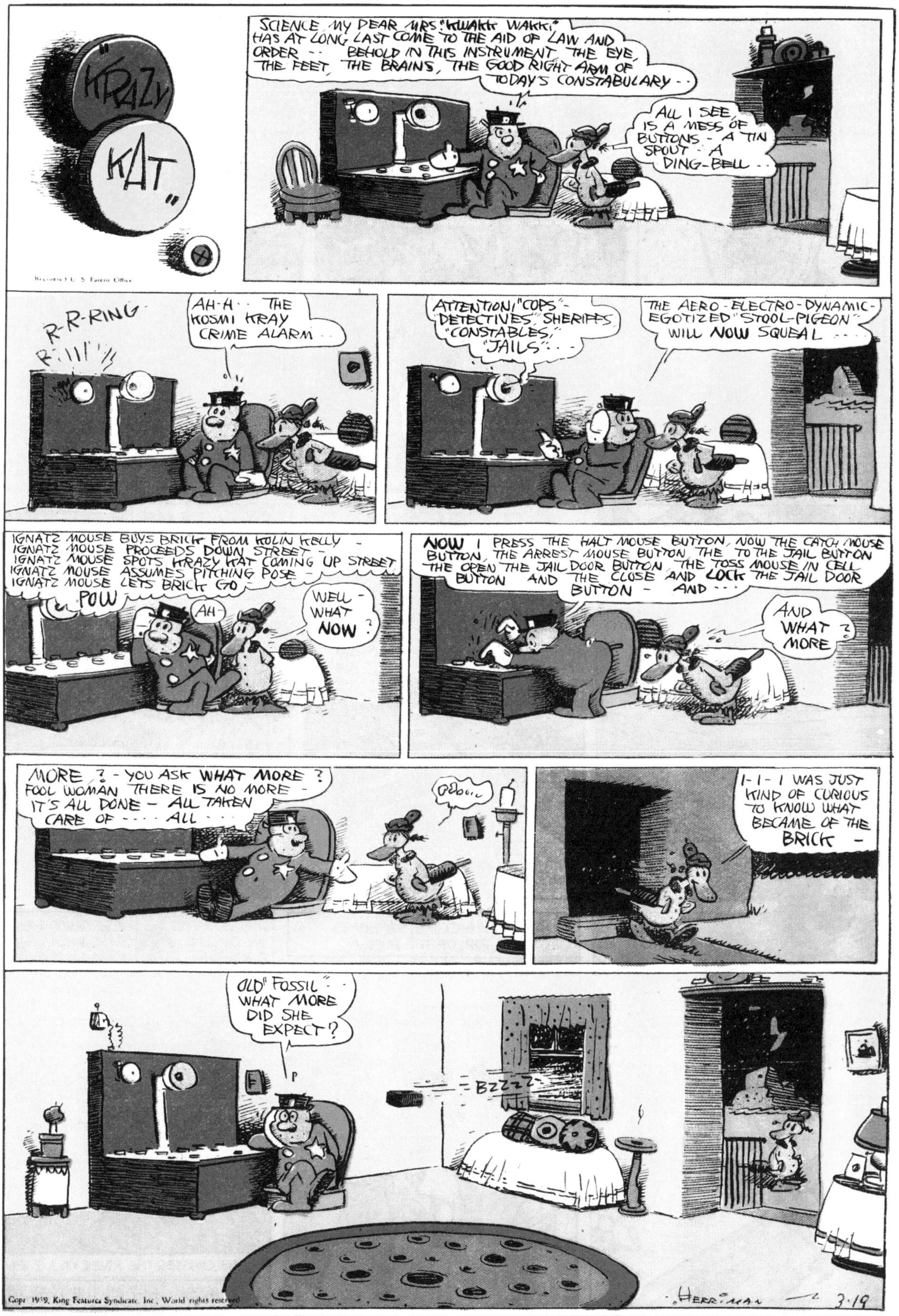
"KRAZY KAT"
Registered U. S. Patent Office
SCIENCE, MY DEAR MRS. "KWAKK WAKK," HAS AT LONG LAST COME TO THE AID OF LAW AND ORDER -- BEHOLD IN THIS INSTRUMENT THE EYE, THE FEET, THE BRAINS, THE GOOD RIGHT ARM OF TODAY'S CONSTABULARY --
ALL I SEE, IS A MESS OF BUTTONS - A TIN SPOUT - A DING-BELL --
R-R-RING
AH-H -- THE KOSMI KRAY CRIME ALARM --
ATTENTION! "COPS" - "DETECTIVES" "SHERIFFS" "CONSTABLES," "JAILS" --
THE AERO-ELECTRO-DYNAMIC-EGOTIZED "STOOL-PIGEON" WILL NOW SQUEAL ---
IGNATZ MOUSE BUYS BRICK FROM KOLIN KELLY - IGNATZ MOUSE PROCEEDS DOWN STREET - IGNATZ MOUSE SPOTS KRAZY KAT COMING UP STREET IGNATZ MOUSE ASSUMES PITCHING POSE - IGNATZ MOUSE LETS BRICK GO -
POW
AH-
WELL - WHAT NOW?
NOW I PRESS THE HALT MOUSE BUTTON, NOW THE CATCH MOUSE BUTTON, THE ARREST MOUSE BUTTON, THE TO THE JAIL BUTTON, THE OPEN THE JAIL DOOR BUTTON, THE TOSS MOUSE IN CELL BUTTON AND THE CLOSE AND LOCK THE JAIL DOOR BUTTON - AND ---
AND WHAT MORE?
MORE ? - YOU ASK WHAT MORE ? FOOL WOMAN THERE IS NO MORE - IT'S ALL DONE - ALL TAKEN CARE OF ---- ALL ---
I-I-I WAS JUST KIND OF CURIOUS TO KNOW WHAT BECAME OF THE BRICK -
OLD "FOSSIL" - WHAT MORE DID SHE EXPECT?
BZZZZ
Copr 1939, King Features Syndicate, Inc., World rights reserved
HERRIMAN 3-19
LOVE LETTER FROM ANCIENT EGYPT
MUSEUM

March 19th, 1939.

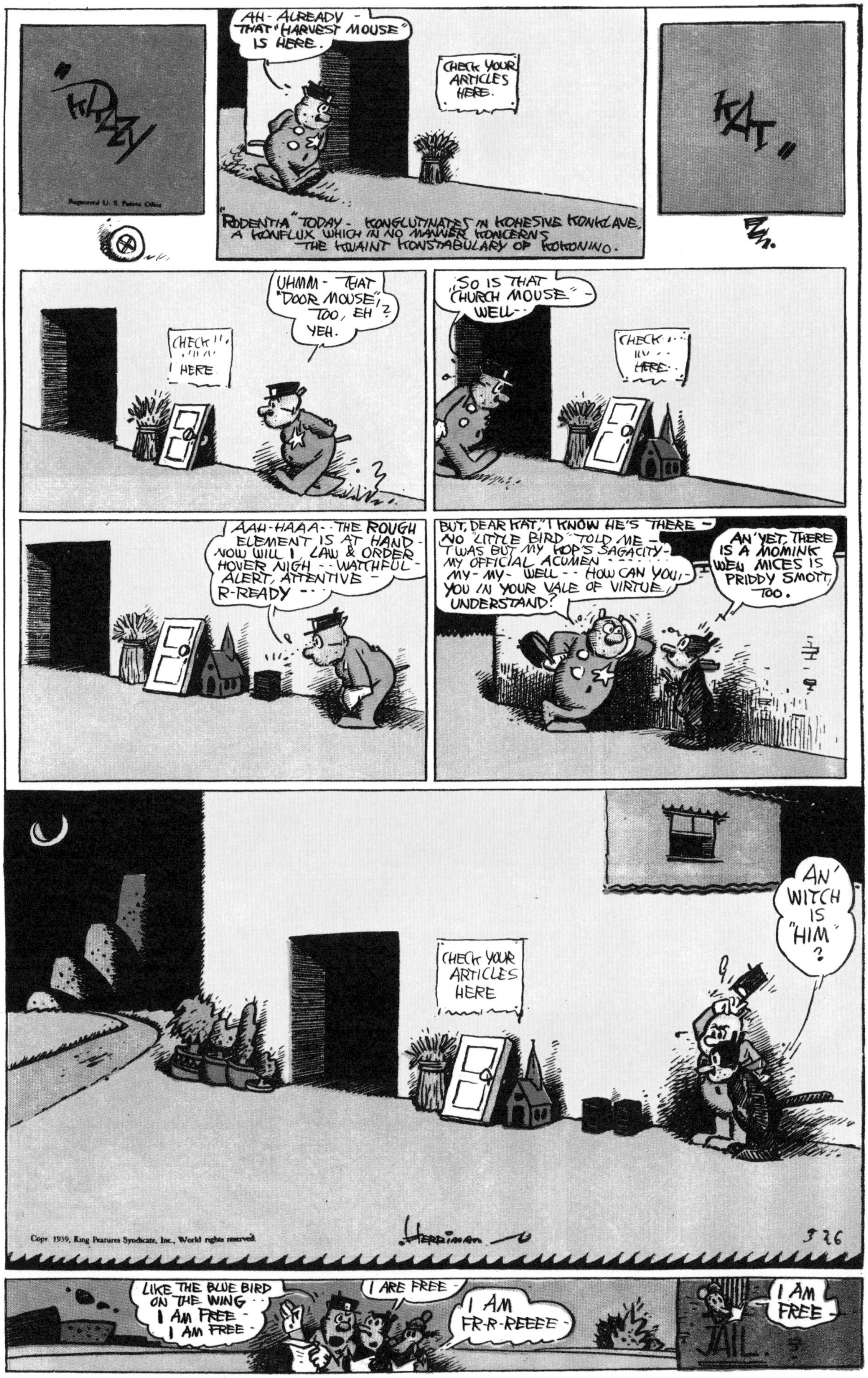
"KRAZY
Registered U. S. Patent Office
KAT"
AH-ALREADY - THAT "HARVEST MOUSE" IS HERE.
CHECK YOUR ARTICLES HERE.
"RODENTIA" TODAY - KONGLUTINATES IN KOHESIVE KONKLAVE, A KONFLUX WHICH IN NO MANNER KONCERNS THE KWAINT KONSTABULARY OF KOKONINO.
UHMM - THAT "DOOR MOUSE", TOO, EH? YEH.
CHECK HERE
SO IS THAT "CHURCH MOUSE" - WELL -
CHECK HERE
AAH-HAAA - THE ROUGH ELEMENT IS AT HAND - NOW WILL I, LAW & ORDER HOVER NIGH - WATCHFUL - ALERT, ATTENTIVE - R-READY - -
BUT, DEAR KAT, I KNOW HE'S THERE - NO "LITTLE BIRD" TOLD ME - 'TWAS BUT MY KOP'S SAGACITY - MY OFFICIAL ACUMEN - MY-MY- WELL - - HOW CAN YOU, YOU IN YOUR VALE OF VIRTUE, UNDERSTAND?
AN' YET, THERE IS A MOMINK WEN MICES IS PRIDDY SMOTT, TOO.
CHECK YOUR ARTICLES HERE
AN' WITCH IS "HIM"?
Copr. 1939, King Features Syndicate, Inc., World rights reserved.
Herriman
3 26
LIKE THE BLUE BIRD ON THE WING I AM FREE I AM FREE -
I ARE FREE -
I AM FR-R-REEEE
JAIL.
I AM FREE -

March 26th, 1939.

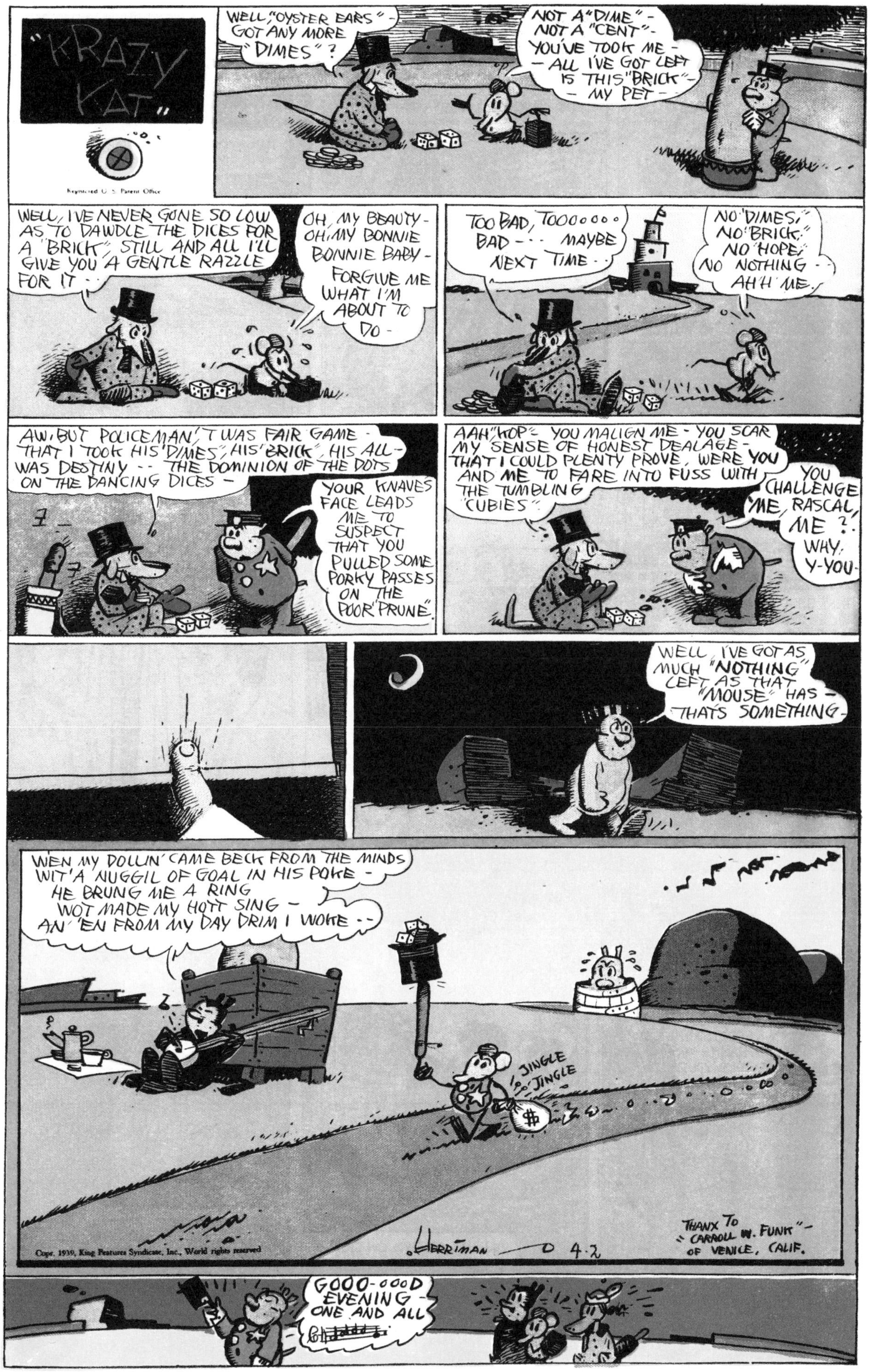
"KRAZY KAT"
Registered U. S. Patent Office
WELL, "OYSTER EARS" - GOT ANY MORE "DIMES"?
NOT A "DIME" - NOT A "CENT" - YOU'VE TOOK ME - ALL I'VE GOT LEFT IS THIS "BRICK" - MY PET -
WELL, I'VE NEVER GONE SO LOW AS TO DAWDLE THE DICES FOR A 'BRICK', STILL AND ALL I'LL GIVE YOU A GENTLE RAZZLE FOR IT -
OH, MY BEAUTY - OH, MY BONNIE BONNIE BABY - FORGIVE ME WHAT I'M ABOUT TO DO -
TOO BAD, TOOOOOOOO BAD - - MAYBE NEXT TIME - -
NO 'DIMES,' NO 'BRICK,' NO 'HOPE,' NO NOTHING - - AH'H ME.
AW, BUT POLICEMAN, 'T WAS FAIR GAME - THAT I TOOK HIS 'DIMES', HIS 'BRICK', HIS ALL - WAS DESTINY - - THE DOMINION OF THE DOTS ON THE DANCING DICES -
YOUR KNAVES FACE LEADS ME TO SUSPECT THAT YOU PULLED SOME PORKY PASSES ON THE 'POOR' PRUNE.
AAH, "KOP" - YOU MALIGN ME - YOU SCAR MY SENSE OF HONEST DEALAGE - THAT I COULD PLENTY PROVE, WERE YOU AND ME TO FARE INTO FUSS WITH THE TUMBLING "CUBIES" -
YOU CHALLENGE 'ME', RASCAL, ME ? - WHY, Y-YOU -
WELL, I'VE GOT AS MUCH "NOTHING" LEFT AS THAT "MOUSE" HAS - THATS SOMETHING -
WEN MY DOLLIN' CAME BECK FROM THE MINDS WIT'A NUGGIL OF GOAL IN HIS POKE - HE BRUNG ME A RING WOT MADE MY HOTT SING - AN' 'EN FROM MY DAY DRIM I WOKE - -
JINGLE JINGLE
Copr. 1939, King Features Syndicate, Inc., World rights reserved
HERRIMAN 4-2
THANX TO CARROLL W. FUNK - OF VENICE, CALIF.
GOOO-OOOD EVENING ONE AND ALL

April 2nd, 1939.

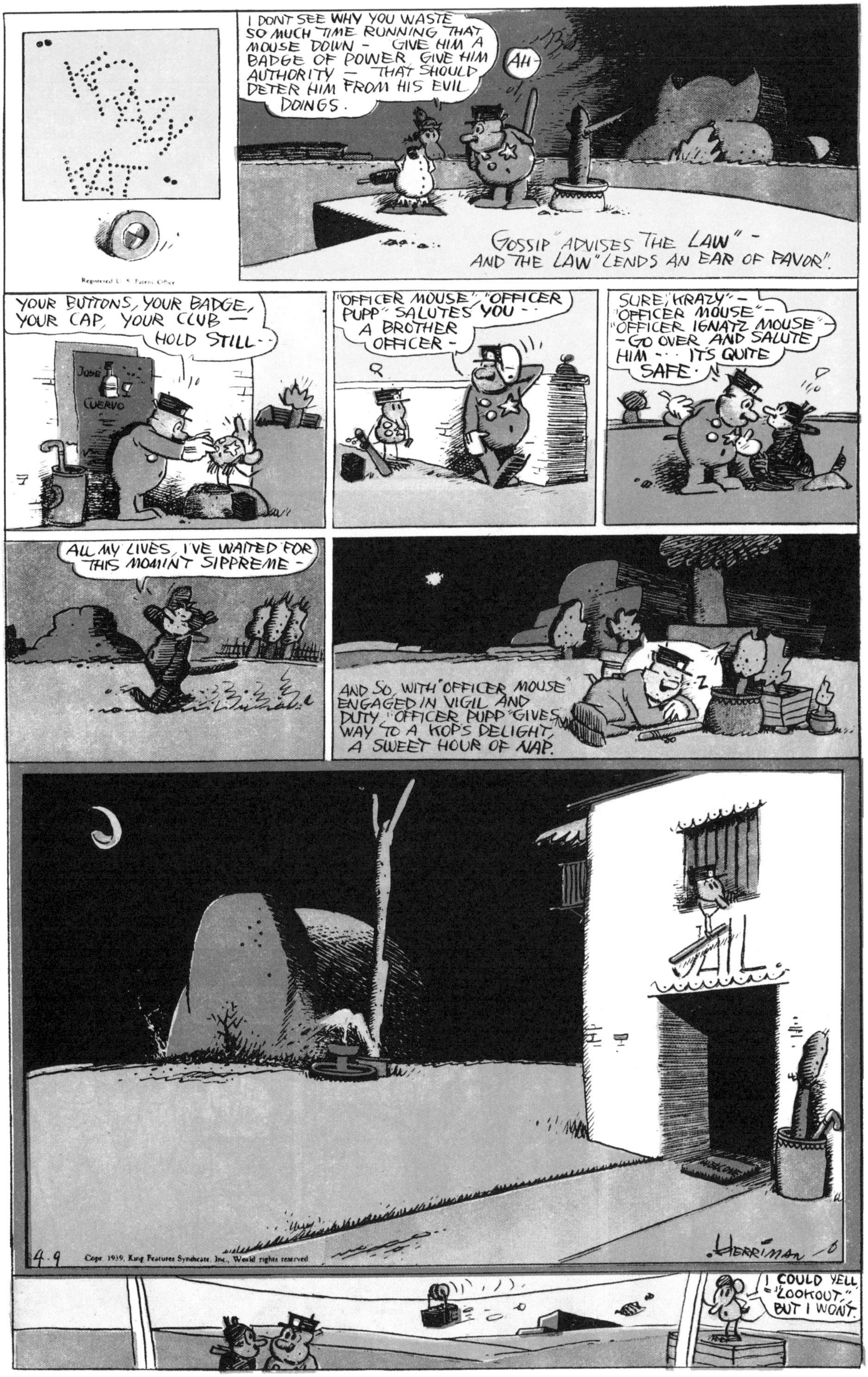
KRAZY KAT
Registered U. S. Patent Office
I DONT SEE WHY YOU WASTE SO MUCH TIME RUNNING THAT MOUSE DOWN - GIVE HIM A BADGE OF POWER GIVE HIM AUTHORITY - THAT SHOULD DETER HIM FROM HIS EVIL DOINGS.
AH
GOSSIP "ADVISES THE LAW" - AND THE LAW "LENDS AN EAR OF FAVOR".
YOUR BUTTONS, YOUR BADGE, YOUR CAP, YOUR CLUB — HOLD STILL - -
JOSE CUERVO
"OFFICER MOUSE", "OFFICER PUPP" SALUTES YOU - - A BROTHER OFFICER -
SURE, "KRAZY" - "OFFICER MOUSE" - "OFFICER IGNATZ MOUSE" - GO OVER AND SALUTE HIM - - - IT'S QUITE SAFE.
ALL MY LIVES, I'VE WAITED FOR THIS MOMINT SIPPREME -
AND SO, WITH "OFFICER MOUSE" ENGAGED IN VIGIL AND DUTY, "OFFICER PUPP" GIVES WAY TO A KOP'S DELIGHT, A SWEET HOUR OF NAP.
JAIL
WELCOME
4-9
Copr. 1939, King Features Syndicate, Inc., World rights reserved
HERRIMAN
I COULD YELL "LOOKOUT," BUT I WONT.

April 9th, 1939.

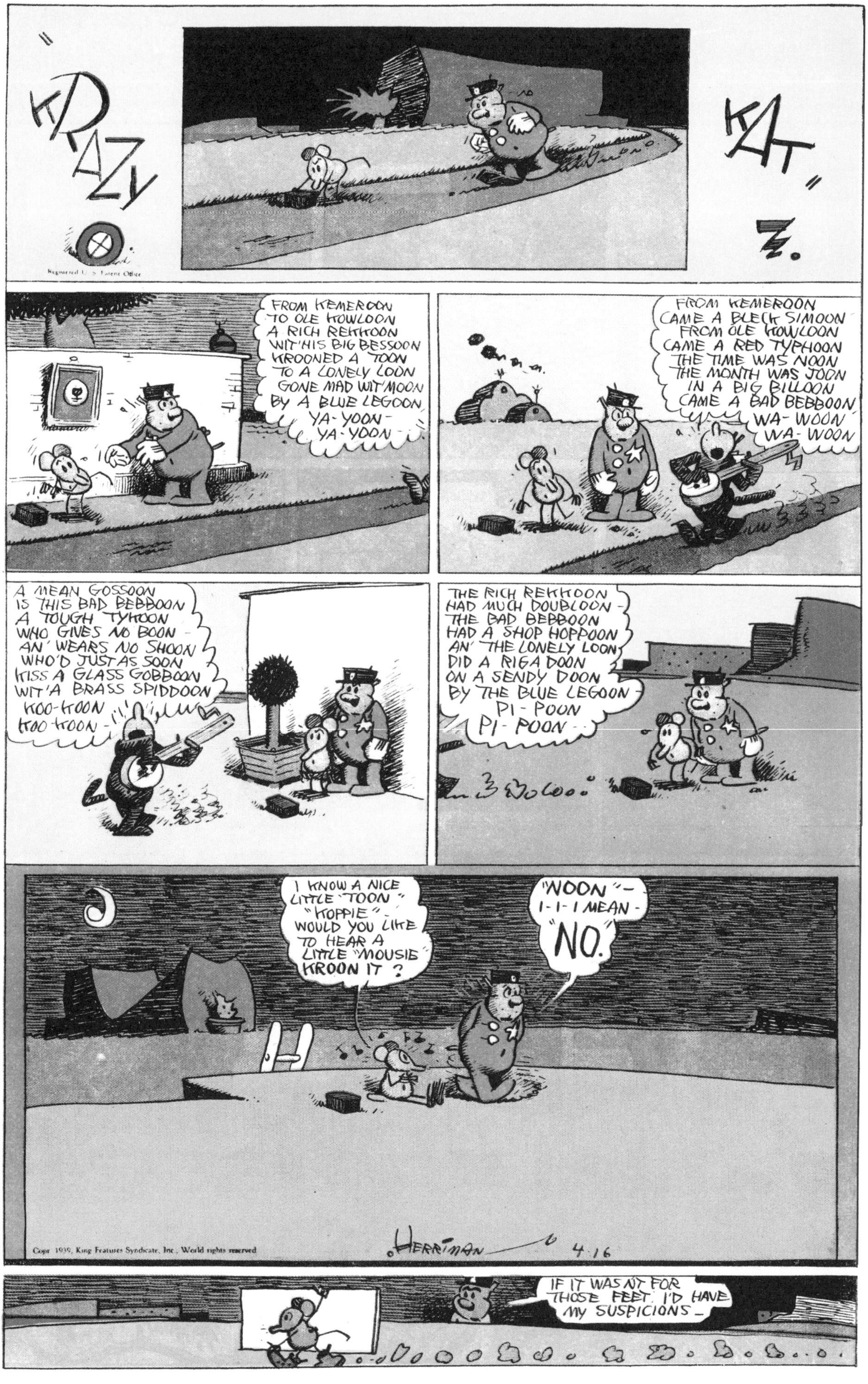
"KRAZY KAT"
Registered U.S. Patent Office
FROM KEMEROON TO OLE KOWLOON A RICH REHTOON WIT'HIS BIG BESSOON KROONED A TOON TO A LONELY LOON GONE MAD WIT'MOON BY A BLUE LEGOON. YA-YOON- YA-YOON-
FROM KEMEROON CAME A BLECK SIMOON FROM OLE KOWLOON CAME A RED TYPHOON THE TIME WAS NOON THE MONTH WAS JOON IN A BIG BILLOON CAME A BAD BEBBOON. WA-WOON WA-WOON
A MEAN GOSSOON IS THIS BAD BEBBOON A TOUGH TYKOON WHO GIVES NO BOON - AN' WEARS NO SHOON WHO'D JUST AS SOON KISS A GLASS GOBBOON WIT'A BRASS SPIDDOON KOO-KOON KOO-KOON -
THE RICH REHTOON HAD MUCH DOUBLOON - THE BAD BEBBOON HAD A SHOP HOPPOON AN' THE LONELY LOON DID A RIGA DOON ON A SENDY DOON BY THE BLUE LEGOON - PI-POON PI-POON -
I KNOW A NICE LITTLE "TOON" "KOPPIE" - WOULD YOU LIKE TO HEAR A LITTLE "MOUSIE KROON IT?
"NOON" - I-I-I MEAN - "NO."
Copr 1939, King Features Syndicate, Inc., World rights reserved
HERRIMAN 4.16
IF IT WAS N'T FOR THOSE FEET. I'D HAVE MY SUSPICIONS -

April 16th, 1939.

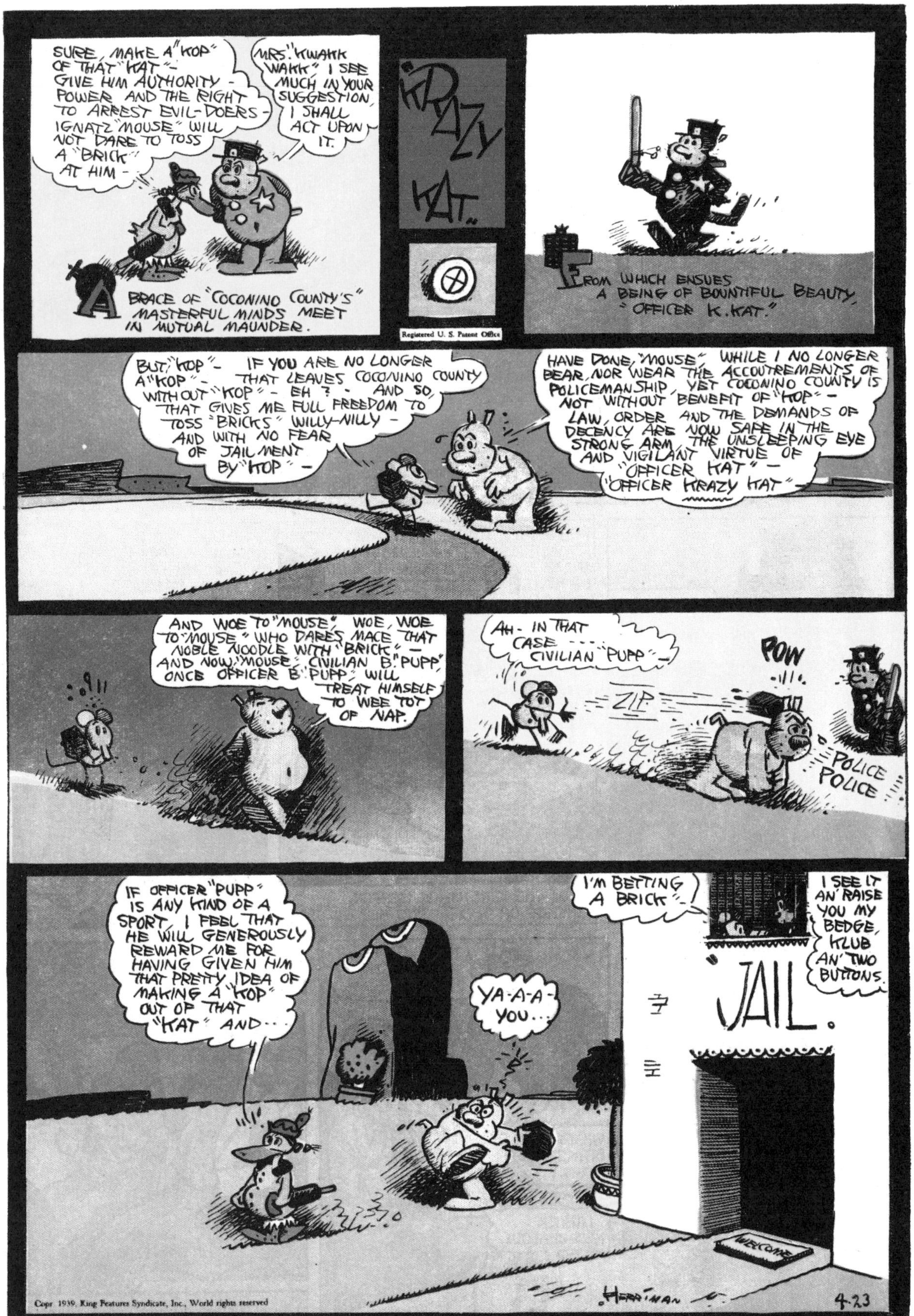
SURE, MAKE A "KOP" OF THAT "KAT" - GIVE HIM AUTHORITY - POWER AND THE RIGHT TO ARREST EVIL-DOERS - IGNATZ "MOUSE" WILL NOT DARE TO TOSS A "BRICK" AT HIM -
MRS. "KWAKK WAKK" I SEE MUCH IN YOUR SUGGESTION, I SHALL ACT UPON IT.
A BRACE OF "COCONINO COUNTY'S" MASTERFUL MINDS MEET IN MUTUAL MAUNDER.
"KRAZY KAT"
Registered U. S. Patent Office
FROM WHICH ENSUES A BEING OF BOUNTIFUL BEAUTY "OFFICER K. KAT."
BUT, "KOP" - IF YOU ARE NO LONGER A "KOP" - THAT LEAVES COCONINO COUNTY WITHOUT "KOP" - EH ? - AND SO, THAT GIVES ME FULL FREEDOM TO TOSS "BRICKS" WILLY-NILLY - AND WITH NO FEAR OF JAILMENT BY "KOP" -
HAVE DONE, "MOUSE", WHILE I NO LONGER BEAR, NOR WEAR THE ACCOUTREMENTS OF POLICEMANSHIP, YET COCONINO COUNTY IS NOT WITHOUT BENEFIT OF "KOP" - LAW, ORDER AND THE DEMANDS OF DECENCY ARE NOW SAFE IN THE STRONG ARM, THE UNSLEEPING EYE AND VIGILANT VIRTUE OF "OFFICER KAT" - "OFFICER KRAZY KAT" -
AND WOE TO "MOUSE", WOE, WOE TO "MOUSE" WHO DARES MACE THAT NOBLE NOODLE WITH "BRICK" - AND NOW, "MOUSE", CIVILIAN B. "PUPP", ONCE OFFICER B. "PUPP", WILL TREAT HIMSELF TO WEE TOT OF NAP.
AH - IN THAT CASE - - - CIVILIAN "PUPP" -
POW
ZIP
POLICE POLICE
IF OFFICER "PUPP" IS ANY KIND OF A SPORT, I FEEL THAT HE WILL GENEROUSLY REWARD ME FOR HAVING GIVEN HIM THAT PRETTY IDEA OF MAKING A "KOP" OUT OF THAT "KAT" AND - -
I'M BETTING A BRICK
I SEE IT AN' RAISE YOU MY BEDGE, KLUB AN' TWO BUTTONS.
"JAIL."
YA-A-A YOU...
WELCOME
HERRIMAN
4-23
Copr 1939, King Features Syndicate, Inc., World rights reserved
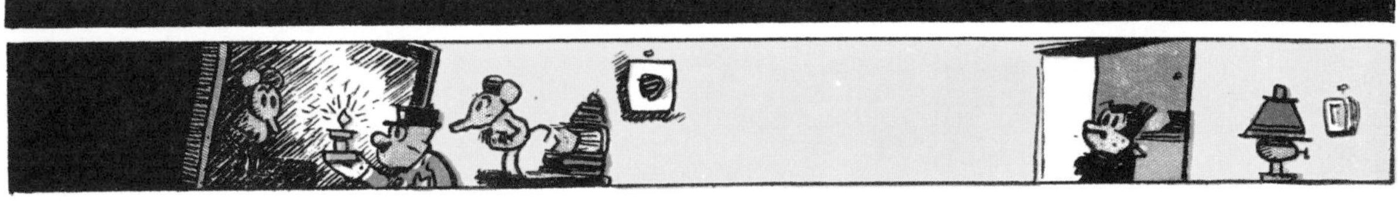

April 23rd, 1939.

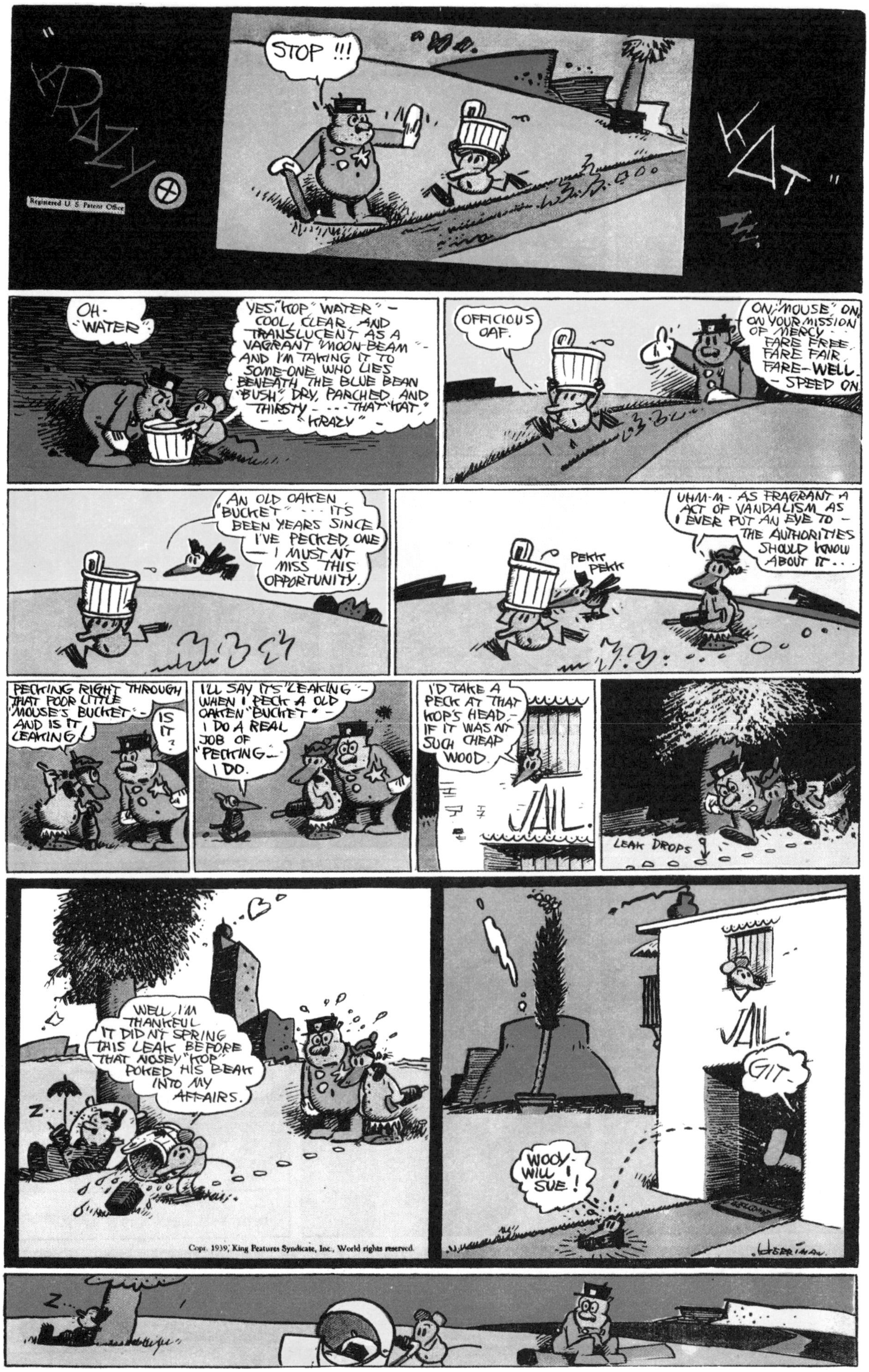
"KRAZY KAT"
Registered U. S. Patent Office
STOP !!!
OH- "WATER"
YES, "KOP" WATER" - COOL, CLEAR, AND TRANSLUCENT AS A VAGRANT "MOON-BEAM" - AND I'M TAKING IT TO SOME-ONE WHO LIES BENEATH THE BLUE BEAN "BUSH", DRY, PARCHED AND THIRSTY - - - THAT "KAT" - - "KRAZY" -
OFFICIOUS OAF.
ON, "MOUSE", ON, ON YOUR MISSION OF MERCY - - FARE FREE, FARE FAIR, FARE-WELL. - SPEED ON
"AN OLD OAKEN "BUCKET" - - - IT'S BEEN YEARS SINCE I'VE PECKED ONE - I MUST N'T MISS THIS OPPORTUNITY.
PEKK PEKK
UHM-M - AS FRAGRANT A ACT OF VANDALISM AS I EVER PUT AN EYE TO - THE AUTHORITIES SHOULD KNOW ABOUT IT . . .
PECKING RIGHT THROUGH THAT POOR LITTLE "MOUSE'S BUCKET" - AND IS IT LEAKING !
IS IT ?
I'LL SAY IT'S "LEAKING" - WHEN I PECK A OLD OAKEN "BUCKET" - I DO A REAL JOB OF "PECKING" - I DO.
I'D TAKE A PECK AT THAT KOP'S HEAD - IF IT WAS N'T SUCH CHEAP WOOD.
JAIL.
LEAK DROPS
WELL, I'M THANKFUL IT DID N'T SPRING THIS LEAK BEFORE THAT NOSEY "KOP" POKED HIS BEAK INTO MY AFFAIRS.
Z...
Copr. 1939, King Features Syndicate, Inc., World rights reserved.
JAIL
GIT.
WOOY - WILL SUE !
HERRIMAN.
Z...

April 30th, 1939.

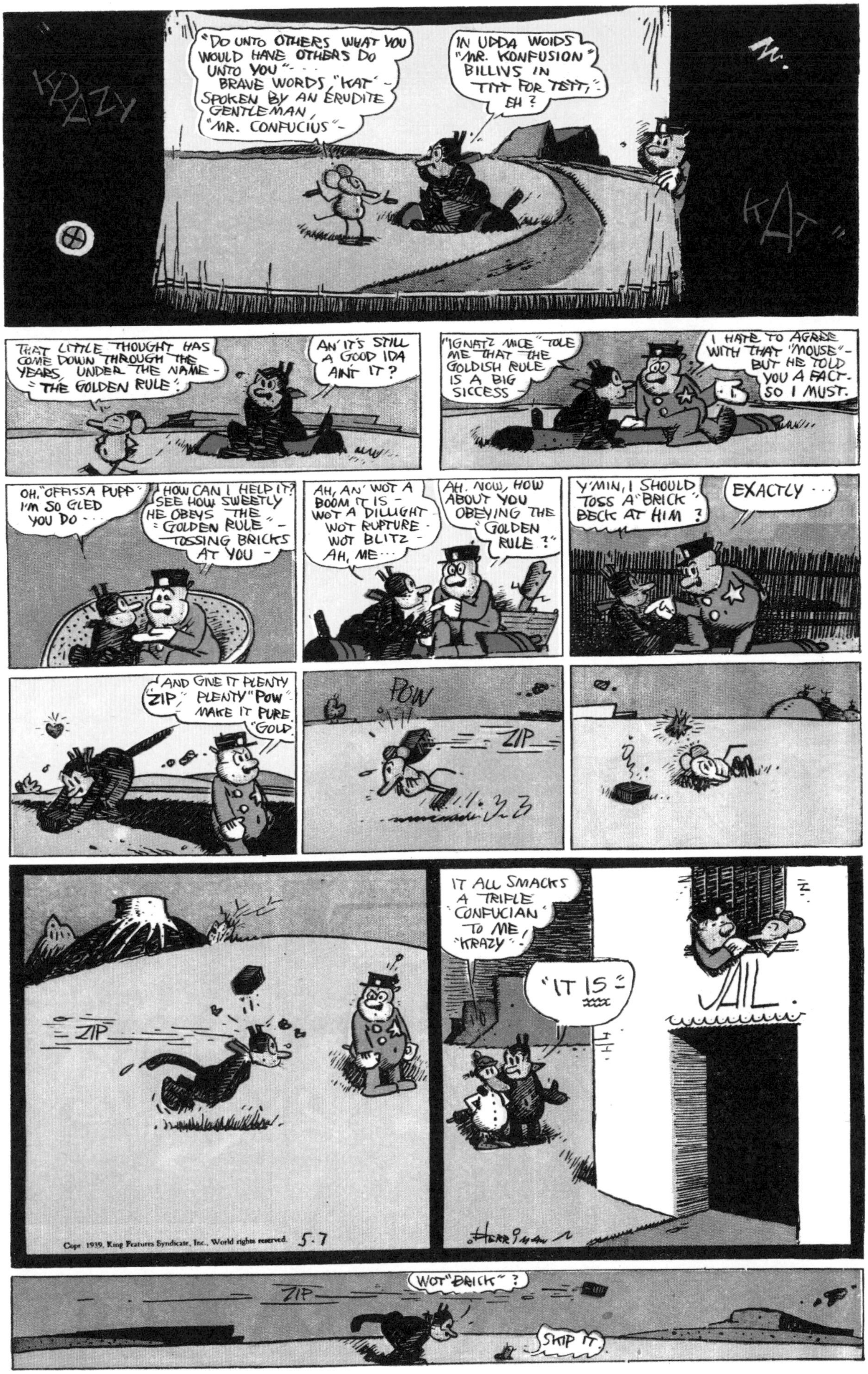
KRAZY
KAT
"DO UNTO OTHERS WHAT YOU WOULD HAVE OTHERS DO UNTO YOU" - BRAVE WORDS, "KAT" - SPOKEN BY AN ERUDITE GENTLEMAN, "MR. CONFUCIUS" -
IN UDDA WOIDS "MR. KONFUSION" BILLIVS IN TITT FOR TETT, EH?
THAT LITTLE THOUGHT HAS COME DOWN THROUGH THE YEARS, UNDER THE NAME - "THE GOLDEN RULE".
AN' IT'S STILL A GOOD IDA AIN'T IT?
"IGNATZ MICE" TOLE ME THAT THE GOLDISH RULE IS A BIG SICCESS
I HATE TO AGREE WITH THAT "MOUSE" - BUT HE TOLD YOU A FACT - SO I MUST.
OH, "OFFISSA PUPP" I'M SO GLED YOU DO...
HOW CAN I HELP IT? SEE HOW SWEETLY HE OBEYS THE "GOLDEN RULE" - TOSSING BRICKS AT YOU -
AH, AN' WOT A BOOM IT IS - WOT A DILLIGHT - WOT RUPTURE - WOT BLITZ - AH, ME...
AH. NOW, HOW ABOUT YOU OBEYING THE "GOLDEN RULE?"
Y'MIN, I SHOULD TOSS A "BRICK" BECK AT HIM?
EXACTLY...
"AND GIVE IT PLENTY "ZIP," PLENTY "POW" - MAKE IT PURE "GOLD"
POW
ZIP
ZIP
IT ALL SMACKS A TRIFLE "CONFUCIAN" TO ME, "KRAZY"
"IT IS"
JAIL.
Copr 1939, King Features Syndicate, Inc., World rights reserved. 5-7
HERRIMAN
ZIP
WOT "BRICK"?
SKIP IT.

May 7th, 1939.

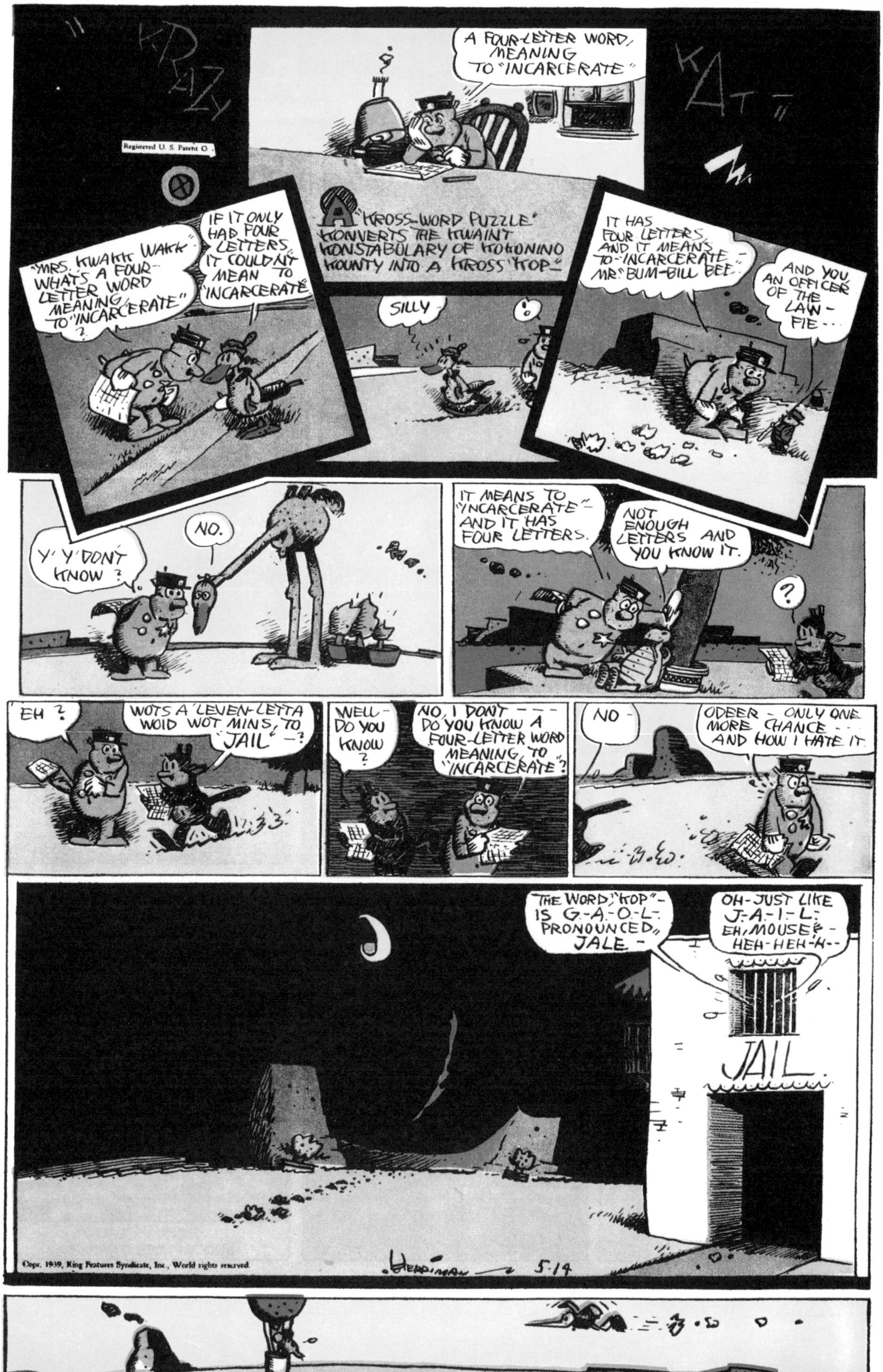
"KRAZY KAT"
Registered U. S. Patent O.
A FOUR-LETTER WORD, MEANING TO "INCARCERATE"
A "KROSS-WORD PUZZLE" KONVERTS THE KWAINT KONSTABULARY OF KOKONINO KOUNTY INTO A KROSS "KOP"—
"MRS. KWAKK WAKK WHAT'S A FOUR-LETTER WORD MEANING TO "INCARCERATE"?
IF IT ONLY HAD FOUR LETTERS, IT COULDN'T MEAN TO "INCARCERATE"
SILLY
IT HAS FOUR LETTERS, AND IT MEANS TO "INCARCERATE" MR. BUM-BILL BEE
AND YOU, AN OFFICER OF THE LAW—FIE—
Y' Y' DON'T KNOW?
NO.
IT MEANS TO "INCARCERATE"—AND IT HAS FOUR LETTERS.
NOT ENOUGH LETTERS AND YOU KNOW IT.
?
EH?
WOTS A 'LEVEN-LETTA WOID WOT MINS, TO "JAIL"—?
WELL—DO YOU KNOW?
NO, I DON'T——DO YOU KNOW A FOUR-LETTER WORD MEANING, TO "INCARCERATE"?
NO—
ODEER—ONLY ONE MORE CHANCE——AND HOW I HATE IT.
"THE WORD, "KOP"—IS G-A-O-L-PRONOUNCED, "JALE—
OH—JUST LIKE J-A-I-L; EH, MOUSE?—HEH-HEH-H—
JAIL
Copr. 1939, King Features Syndicate, Inc., World rights reserved.
HERRIMAN 5-14

May14th, 1939.

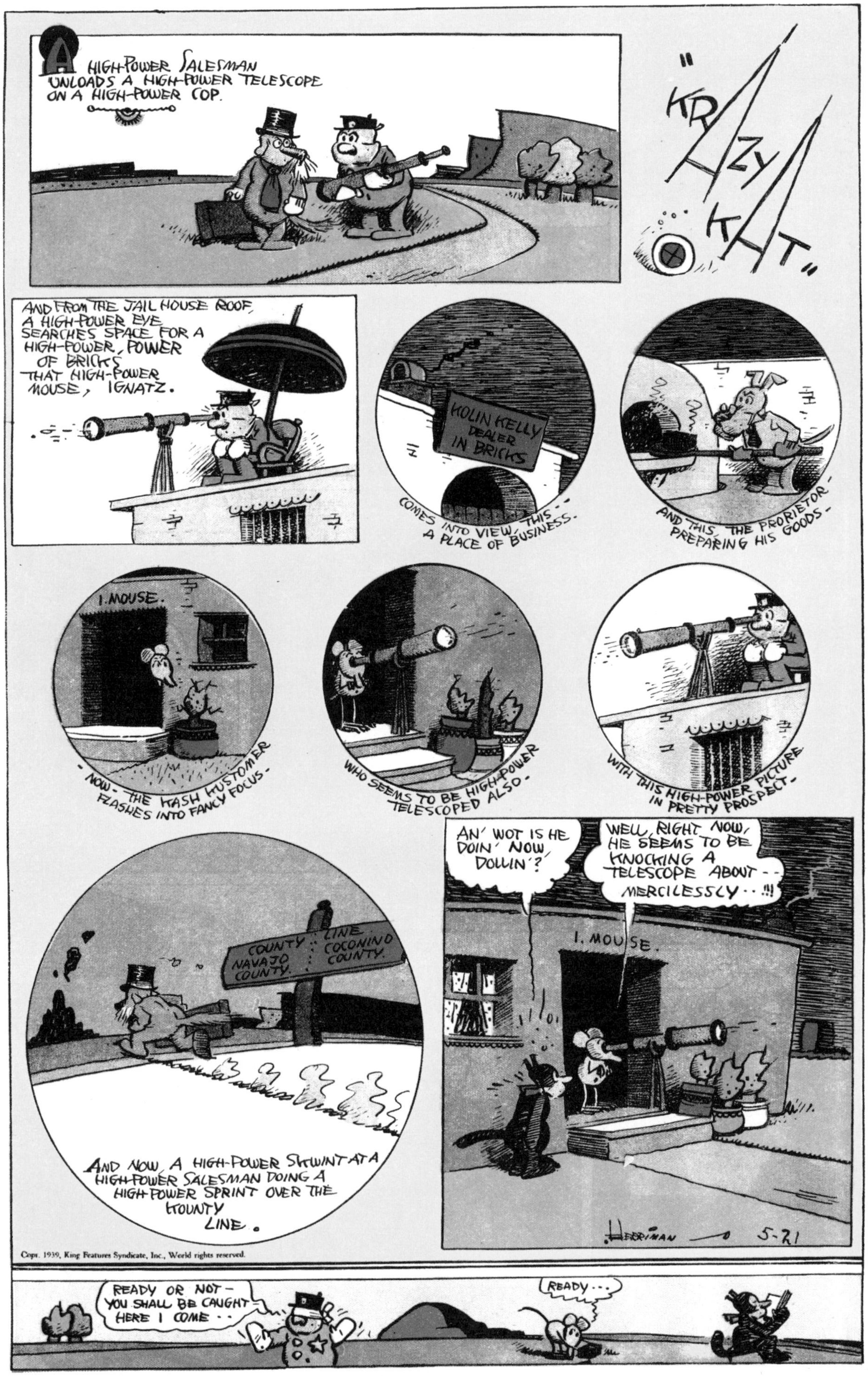
"KRAZY KAT"
A HIGH-POWER SALESMAN UNLOADS A HIGH-POWER TELESCOPE ON A HIGH-POWER COP.
AND FROM THE JAIL HOUSE ROOF, A HIGH-POWER EYE SEARCHES SPACE FOR A HIGH-POWER, POWER OF BRICKS THAT HIGH-POWER MOUSE, IGNATZ.
KOLIN KELLY DEALER IN BRICKS
COMES INTO VIEW, THIS - A PLACE OF BUSINESS.
AND THIS, THE PRORIETOR - PREPARING HIS GOODS -
I. MOUSE.
- NOW - THE KASH KUSTOMER FLASHES INTO FANCY FOCUS -
WHO SEEMS TO BE HIGH-POWER TELESCOPED ALSO -
WITH THIS HIGH-POWER PICTURE IN PRETTY PROSPECT -
COUNTY LINE
NAVAJO COUNTY
COCONINO COUNTY
AND NOW, A HIGH-POWER SKWINT AT A HIGH-POWER SALESMAN DOING A HIGH-POWER SPRINT OVER THE KOUNTY LINE.
AN' WOT IS HE DOIN' NOW, DOLLIN'?
WELL, RIGHT NOW, HE SEEMS TO BE KNOCKING A TELESCOPE ABOUT - - MERCILESSLY - - !!!
I. MOUSE.
HERRIMAN 5-21
Copr. 1939, King Features Syndicate, Inc., World rights reserved.
READY OR NOT - YOU SHALL BE CAUGHT - HERE I COME - -
READY - - -

May 21st, 1939.

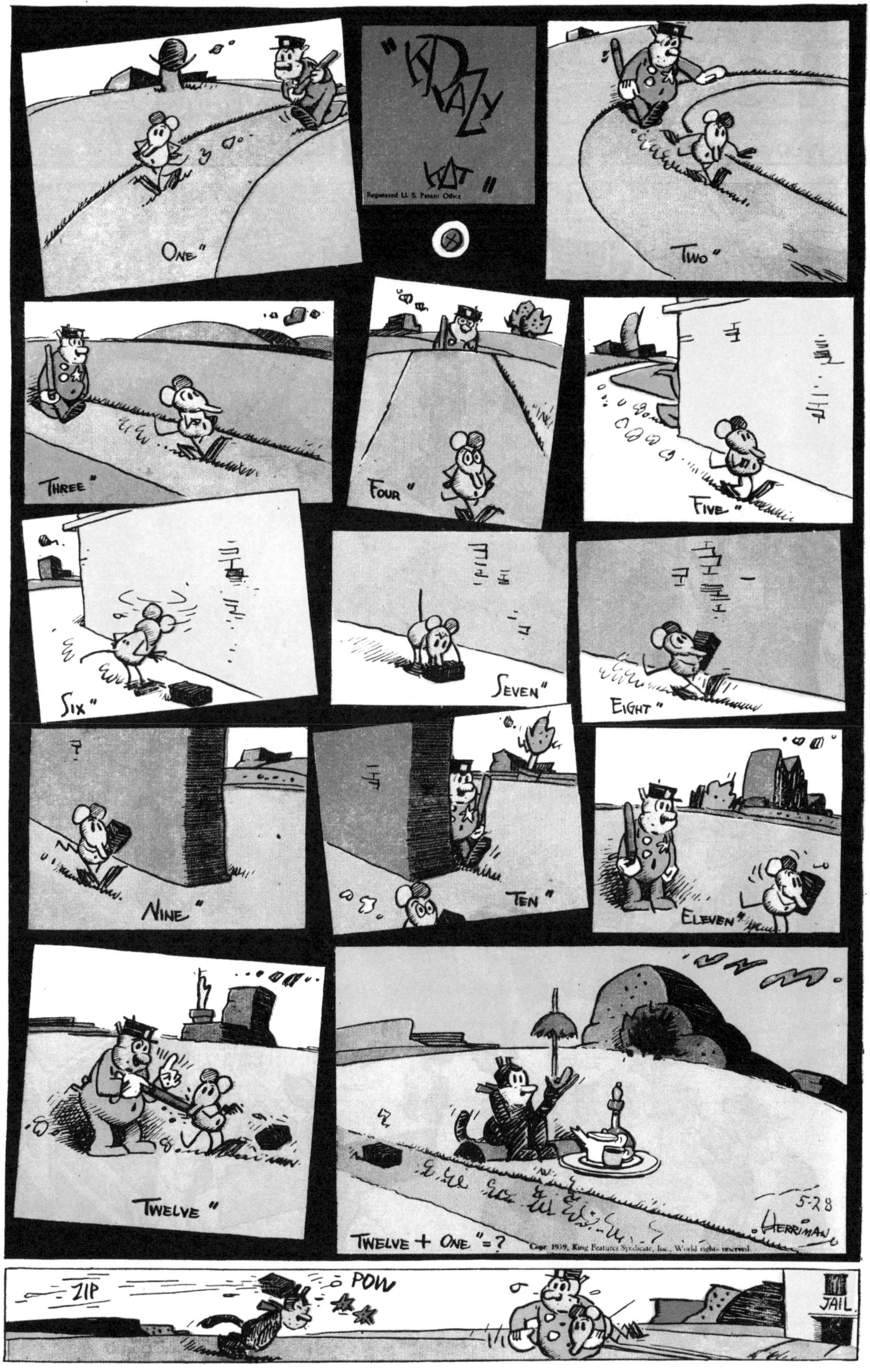
"Krazy Kat"
Registered U. S. Patent Office
One"
Two"
Three"
Four"
Five"
Six"
Seven"
Eight"
Nine"
Ten"
Eleven"
Twelve"
Twelve + One"=?
5-28
Herriman
Copr. 1939, King Features Syndicate, Inc., World rights reserved.
ZIP
POW
JAIL

May 28th, 1939.

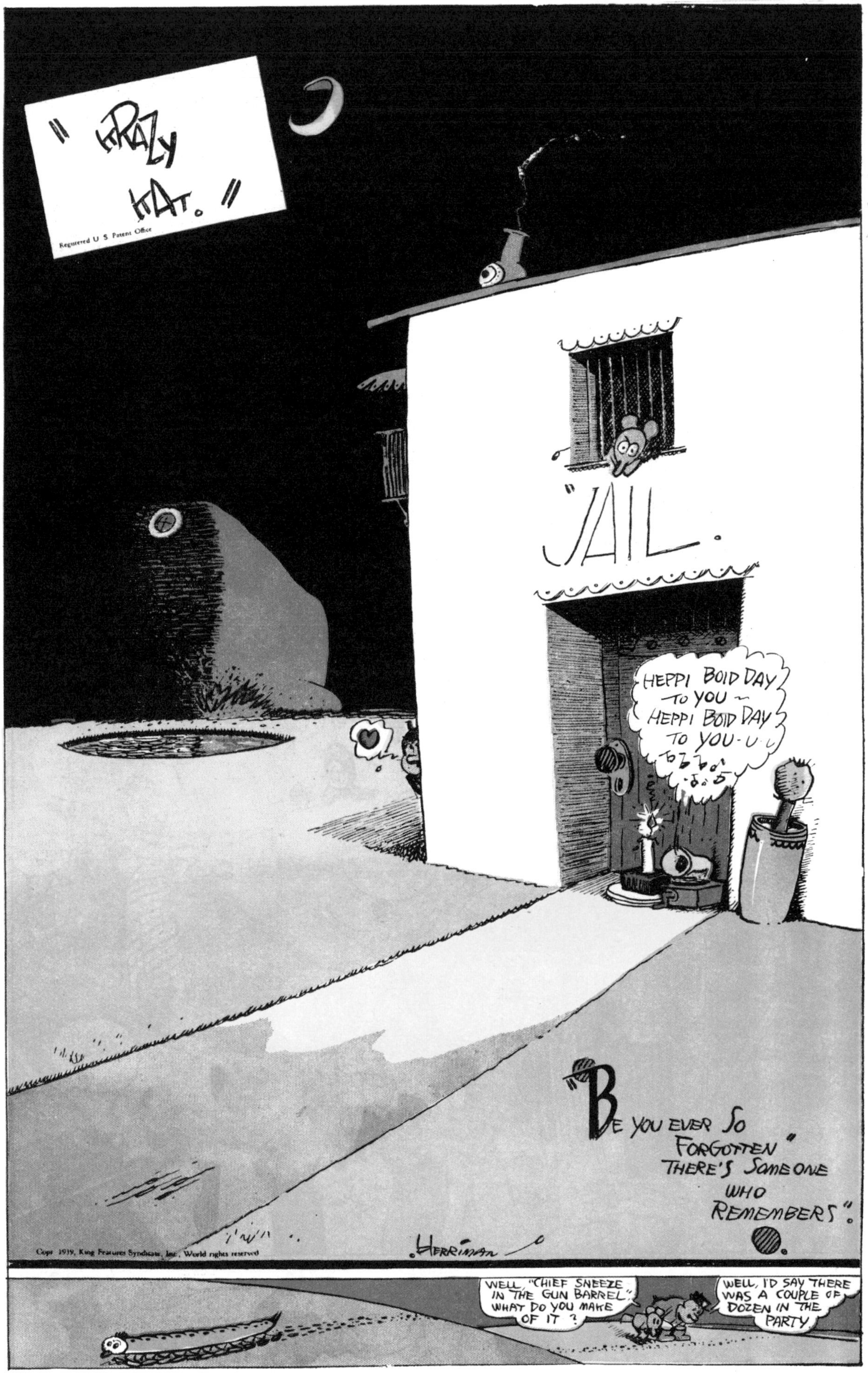
"KRAZY KAT."
Registered U S Patent Office
"JAIL."
HEPPI BOID DAY TO YOU ~ HEPPI BOID DAY TO YOU-U-U
"Be you ever so forgotten" there's some one who remembers".
Copr 1939, King Features Syndicate, Inc., World rights reserved
Herriman
WELL, "CHIEF SNEEZE IN THE GUN BARREL", WHAT DO YOU MAKE OF IT ?
WELL, I'D SAY THERE WAS A COUPLE OF DOZEN IN THE PARTY

June 4th, 1939.

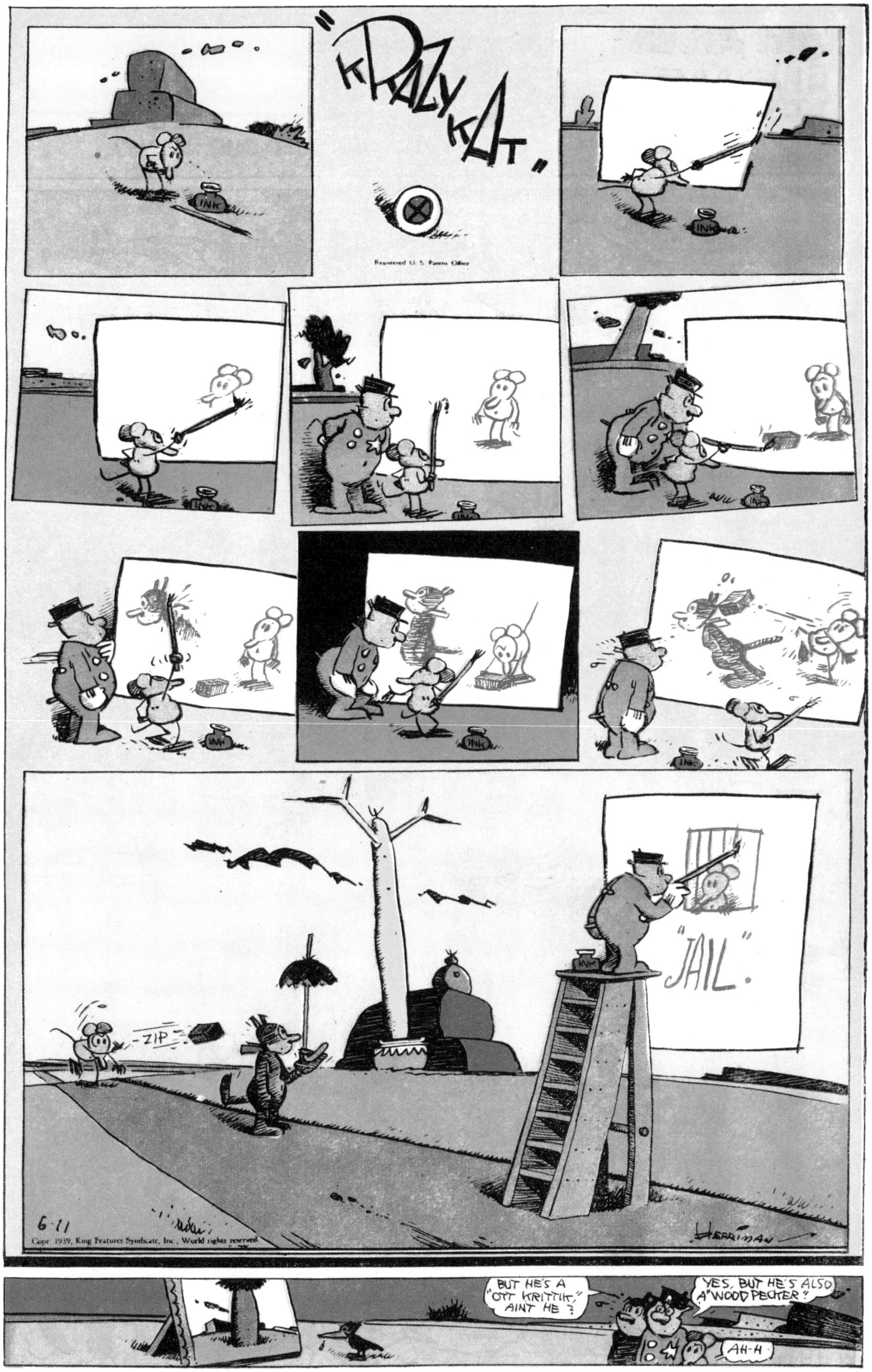
"KRAZY KAT"
Registered U. S. Patent Office
INK
INK
INK
INK
INK
INK
INK
INK
-ZIP
INK
"JAIL".
6-11
Copr 1939, King Features Syndicate, Inc., World rights reserved
HERRIMAN
BUT HE'S A "OTT KRITTIK," AINT HE ?
YES, BUT HE'S ALSO A "WOOD PECKER"!
AH-H

June 11th, 1939.

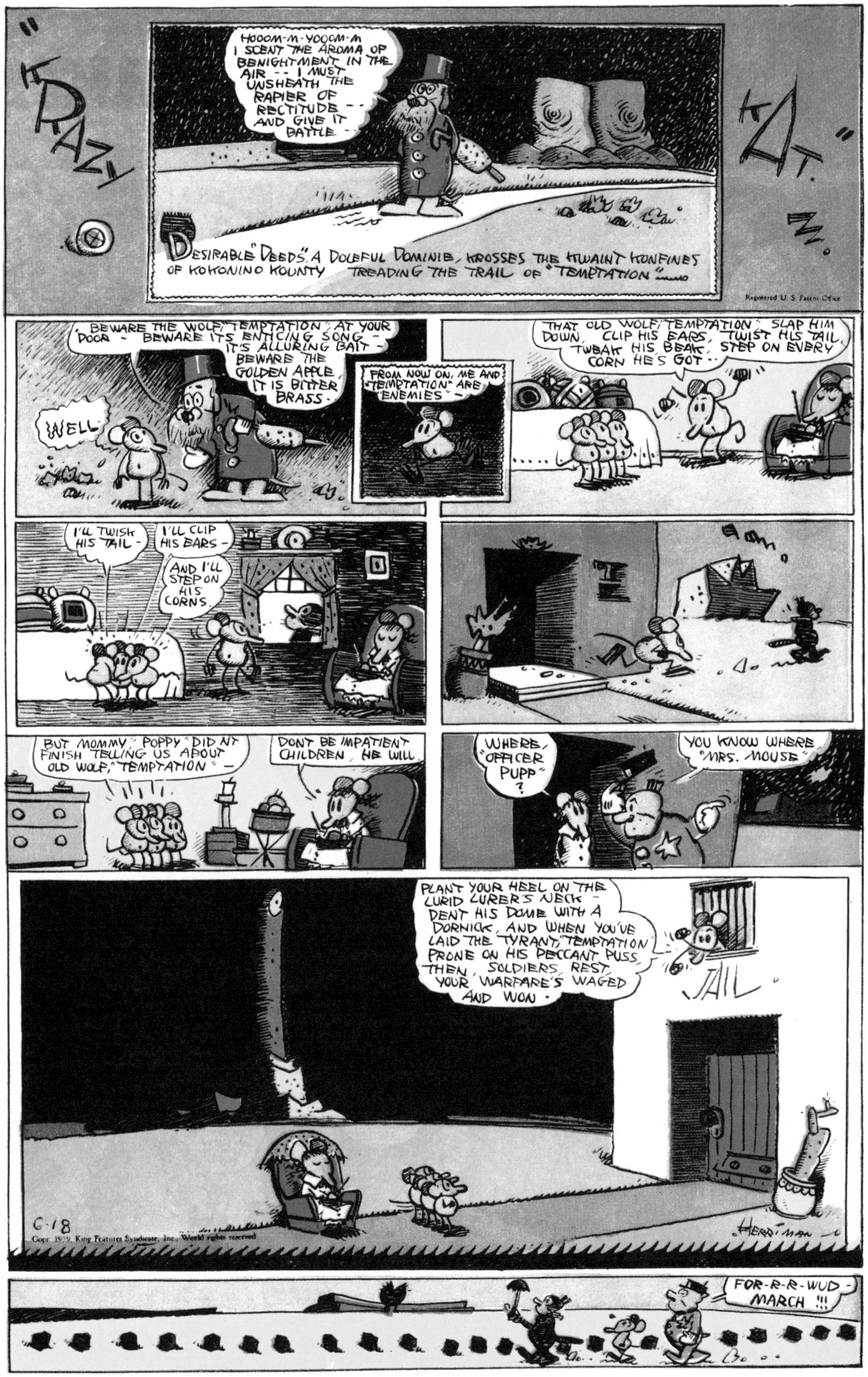
"KRAZY KAT."
HOOOM-M-YOOOM-M I SCENT THE AROMA OF BENIGHTMENT IN THE AIR -- I MUST UNSHEATH THE RAPIER OF RECTITUDE -- AND GIVE IT BATTLE --
DESIRABLE "DEEDS" A DOLEFUL DOMINIE, KROSSES THE KWAINT KONFINES OF KOKONINO KOUNTY TREADING THE TRAIL OF "TEMPTATION"
Registered U. S. Patent Office
BEWARE THE WOLF, "TEMPTATION" AT YOUR DOOR - BEWARE ITS ENTICING SONG - IT'S ALLURING BAIT - BEWARE THE GOLDEN APPLE, IT IS BITTER BRASS -
WELL
FROM NOW ON, ME AND "TEMPTATION" ARE "ENEMIES" -
THAT OLD WOLF, "TEMPTATION" SLAP HIM DOWN, CLIP HIS EARS, TWIST HIS TAIL, TWEAK HIS BEAK, STEP ON EVERY CORN HE'S GOT --
I'LL TWISH HIS TAIL -
I'LL CLIP HIS EARS -
AND I'LL STEP ON HIS CORNS.
BUT MOMMY "POPPY" DID NT FINISH TELLING US ABOUT OLD WOLF, "TEMPTATION" -
DONT BE IMPATIENT CHILDREN, HE WILL.
WHERE, "OFFICER PUPP" ?
YOU KNOW WHERE "MRS. MOUSE"
PLANT YOUR HEEL ON THE LURID LURER'S NECK - DENT HIS DOME WITH A DORNICK, AND WHEN YOU'VE LAID THE TYRANT, "TEMPTATION" PRONE ON HIS PECCANT PUSS THEN, SOLDIERS, REST, YOUR WARFARE'S WAGED AND WON -
JAIL
6-18
Copr. 1939, King Features Syndicate, Inc., World rights reserved
HERRIMAN
FOR-R-R-WUD-MARCH !!!

June 18th, 1939.

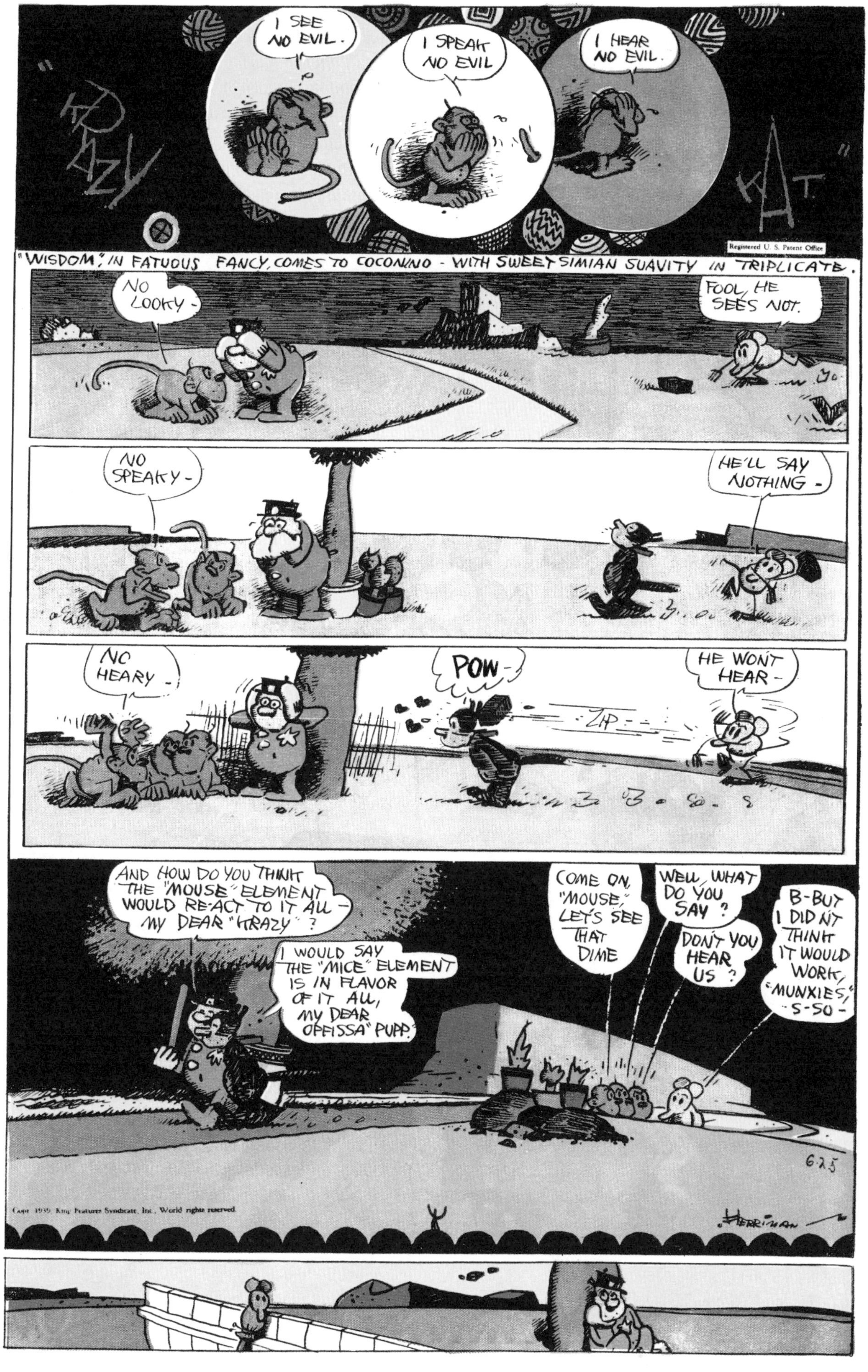
"KRAZY KAT"
I SEE NO EVIL.
I SPEAK NO EVIL
I HEAR NO EVIL.
Registered U. S. Patent Office
"WISDOM," IN FATUOUS FANCY, COMES TO COCONINO - WITH SWEET SIMIAN SUAVITY IN TRIPLICATE.
NO LOOKY -
FOOL, HE SEES NOT.
NO SPEAKY -
HE'LL SAY NOTHING -
NO HEARY -
POW -
ZIP
HE WON'T HEAR -
AND HOW DO YOU THINK THE "MOUSE" ELEMENT WOULD RE-ACT TO IT ALL - MY DEAR "KRAZY" ?
I WOULD SAY THE "MICE" ELEMENT IS IN FLAVOR OF IT ALL, MY DEAR "OFFISSA" PUPP.
COME ON, "MOUSE," LET'S SEE THAT DIME
WELL, WHAT DO YOU SAY ?
DON'T YOU HEAR US ?
B-BUT I DID N'T THINK IT WOULD WORK, "MUNXIES," - S-SO -
6-25
Copr. 1939, King Features Syndicate, Inc., World rights reserved.
HERRIMAN

June 25th, 1939.

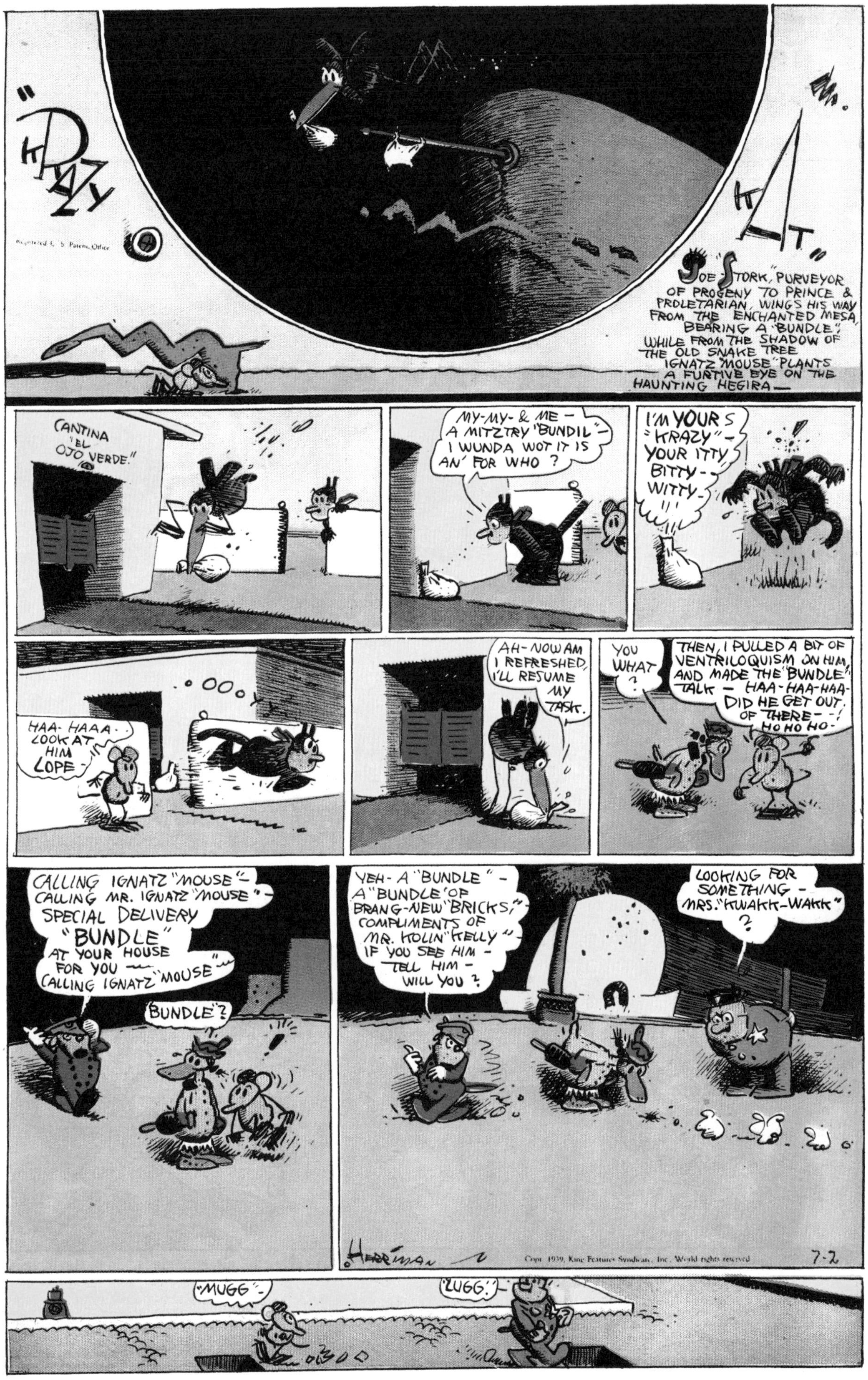
"Krazy Kat"
Registered U. S. Patent Office
"Joe Stork," purveyor of progeny to prince & proletarian, wings his way from the enchanted mesa, bearing a "bundle", while from the shadow of the old snake tree Ignatz "Mouse" plants a furtive eye on the haunting hegira—
Cantina "El Ojo Verde."
My-my- & me- a mitztry "bundil"- I wunda wot it is an' for who?
I'm your s "Krazy"- your itty bitty- witty- !!!
Haa-haaa- look at him lope-
Ah- now am I refreshed, I'll resume my task.
You what?
Then, I pulled a bit of ventriloquism on him, and made the "bundle" talk - haa-haa-haa did he get out of there--!
Ho ho ho-
Calling Ignatz "Mouse"- calling Mr. Ignatz "Mouse"- special delivery "Bundle" at your house for you — calling Ignatz "Mouse"-
"Bundle"?
Yeh- a "bundle"- a "bundle" of brang-new "bricks," compliments of Mr. Kolin "Kelly"- if you see him- tell him- will you?
Looking for something- Mrs. "Kwakk-Wakk"?
Herriman
Copr. 1939, King Features Syndicate, Inc. World rights reserved
7-2
"Mugg"
"Zugg."

July 2nd, 1939.

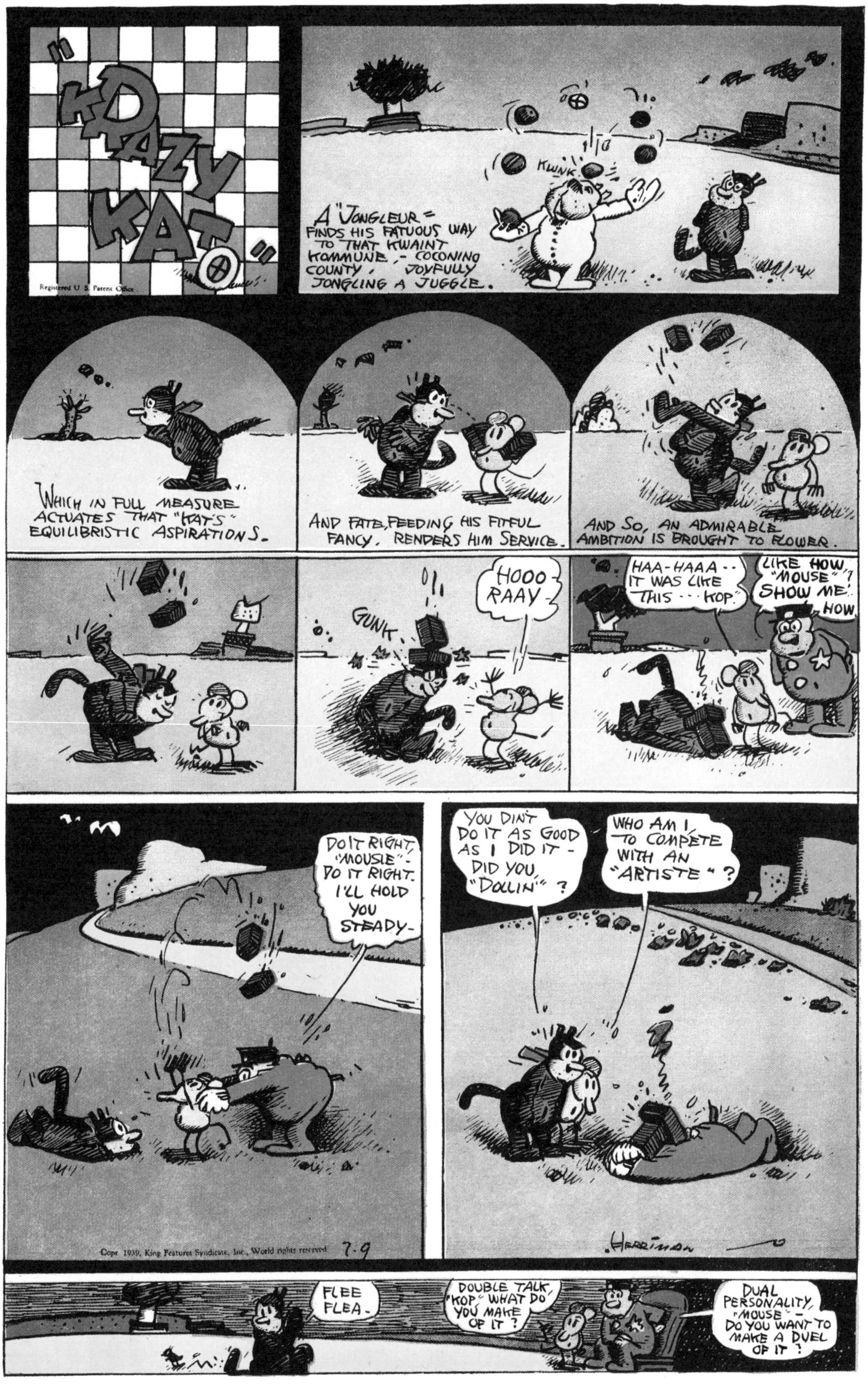
"KRAZY KAT"
Registered U. S. Patent Office
KLUNK
A "JONGLEUR" FINDS HIS FATUOUS WAY TO THAT KWAINT KOMMUNE, - COCONINO COUNTY, JOYFULLY JONGLING A JUGGLE.
WHICH IN FULL MEASURE ACTUATES THAT "KAT'S" EQUILIBRISTIC ASPIRATIONS.
AND FATE, FEEDING HIS FITFUL FANCY, RENDERS HIM SERVICE.
AND SO, AN ADMIRABLE AMBITION IS BROUGHT TO FLOWER.
GUNK
HOOO RAAY
HAA-HAAA - IT WAS LIKE THIS - - KOP.
LIKE HOW, "MOUSE"? SHOW ME HOW
DO IT RIGHT, "MOUSE" - DO IT RIGHT. I'LL HOLD YOU STEADY -
Copr 1939, King Features Syndicate, Inc., World rights reserved
7.9
YOU DIN'T DO IT AS GOOD AS I DID IT - DID YOU, "DOLLIN"?
WHO AM I, TO COMPETE WITH AN "ARTISTE"?
HERRIMAN
FLEE FLEA.
DOUBLE TALK, "KOP" WHAT DO YOU MAKE OF IT?
DUAL PERSONALITY, "MOUSE" - DO YOU WANT TO MAKE A DUEL OF IT?

July 9th, 1939.

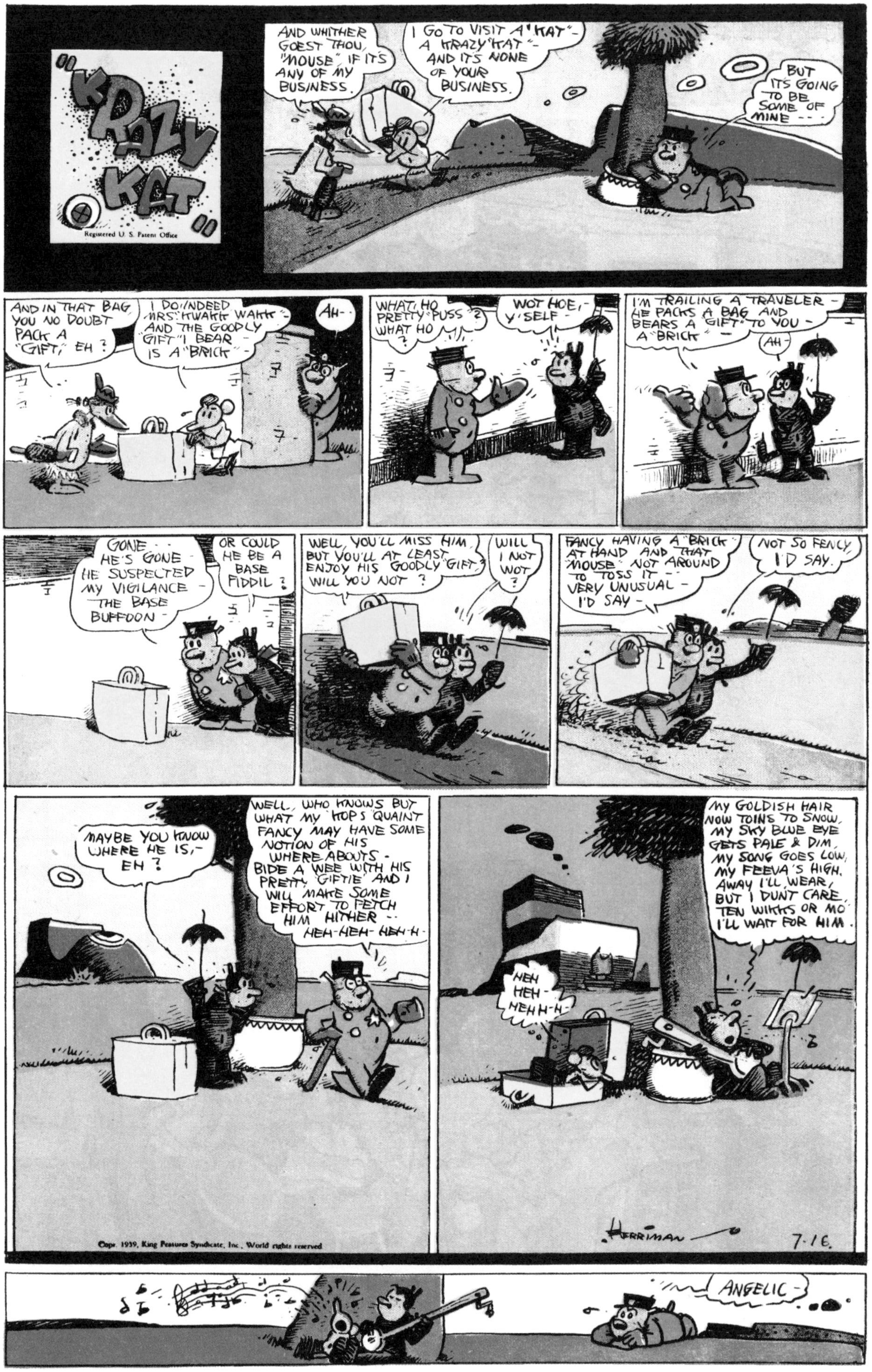
"KRAZY KAT"
Registered U. S. Patent Office
AND WHITHER GOEST THOU, "MOUSE," IF IT'S ANY OF MY BUSINESS.
I GO TO VISIT A "KAT" - A "KRAZY" "KAT" - AND ITS NONE OF YOUR BUSINESS.
BUT ITS GOING TO BE SOME OF MINE - - -
AND IN THAT BAG YOU NO DOUBT PACK A "GIFT," EH ?
I DO, INDEED MRS. KWAKK WAKK AND THE GOODLY "GIFT" I BEAR IS A "BRICK" -
AH - -
WHAT, HO PRETTY PUSS ? WHAT HO ?
WOT HOE, Y'SELF -
I'M TRAILING A TRAVELER - HE PACKS A BAG AND BEARS A "GIFT" TO YOU - A "BRICK" -
AH
GONE - - HE'S GONE HE SUSPECTED MY VIGILANCE - THE BASE BUFFOON -
OR COULD HE BE A BASE FIDDIL ?
WELL, YOU'LL MISS HIM, BUT YOU'LL AT LEAST ENJOY HIS GOODLY "GIFT," WILL YOU NOT ?
WILL I NOT WOT ?
FANCY HAVING A "BRICK" AT HAND AND THAT "MOUSE" NOT AROUND TO TOSS IT - - VERY UNUSUAL - I'D SAY -
NOT SO FENCY, I'D SAY.
MAYBE YOU KNOW WHERE HE IS, - EH ?
WELL, WHO KNOWS BUT WHAT MY "HOP'S" QUAINT FANCY MAY HAVE SOME NOTION OF HIS WHERE ABOUTS - BIDE A WEE WITH HIS PRETTY "GIFTIE" AND I WILL MAKE SOME EFFORT TO FETCH HIM HITHER
HEH-HEH- HEH-H-
HEH HEH HEH-H-H-
MY GOLDISH HAIR NOW TOINS TO SNOW, MY SKY BLUE EYE GETS PALE & DIM, MY SONG GOES LOW, MY FEEVA'S HIGH, AWAY I'LL WEAR, BUT I DUNT CARE, TEN WIKKS OR MO' I'LL WAIT FOR HIM.
Copr. 1939, King Features Syndicate, Inc., World rights reserved
HERRIMAN
7-16.
ANGELIC -

July 16th, 1939.

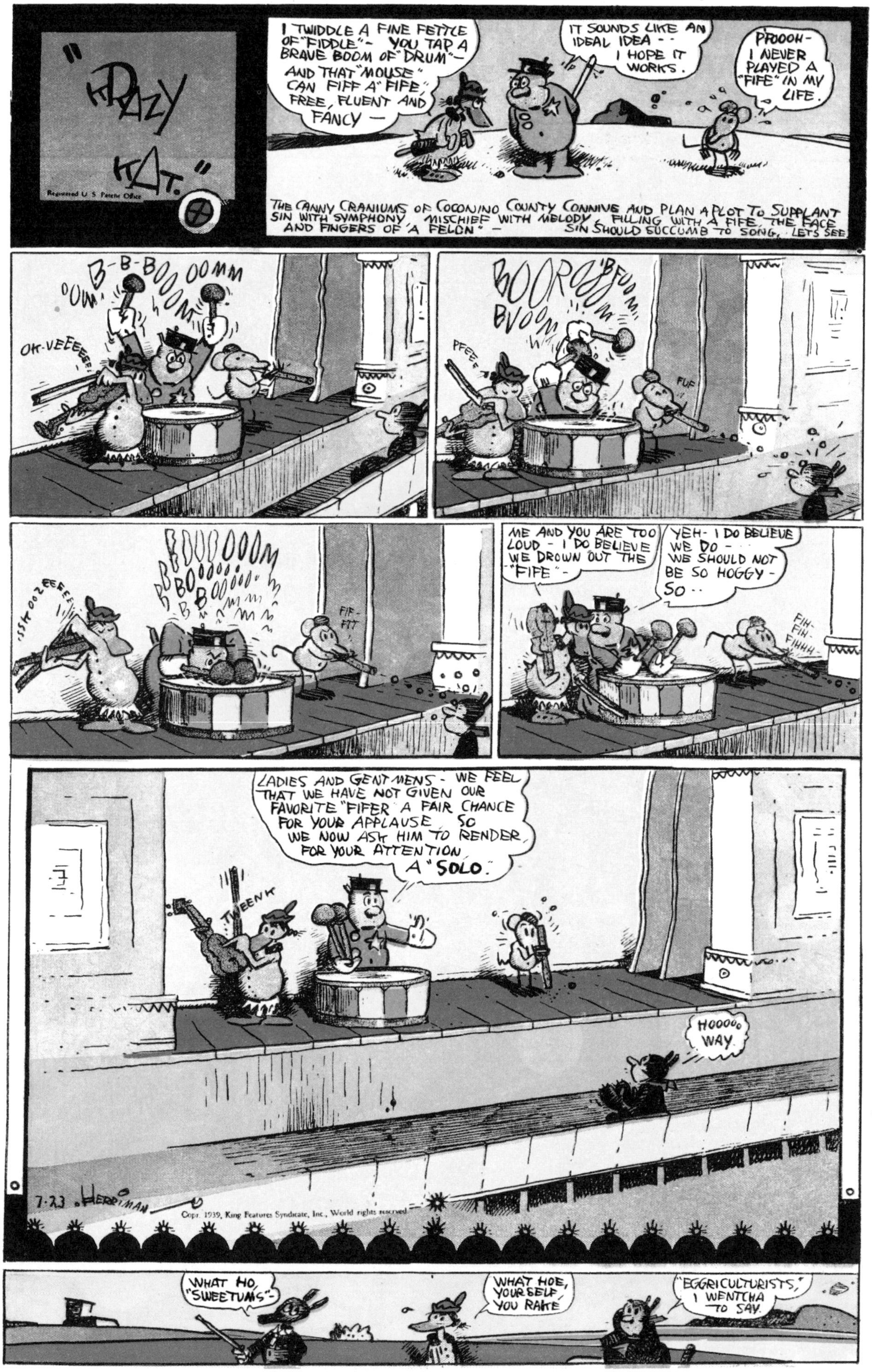
"KRAZY KAT."
Registered U. S. Patent Office
I TWIDDLE A FINE FETTLE OF "FIDDLE" - YOU TAP A BRAVE BOOM OF "DRUM" - AND THAT "MOUSE" CAN FIFF A "FIFE", FREE, FLUENT AND FANCY -
IT SOUNDS LIKE AN IDEAL IDEA - - I HOPE IT WORKS.
PFOOOH - I NEVER PLAYED A "FIFE" IN MY LIFE.
THE CANNY CRANIUMS OF COCONINO COUNTY CONNIVE AND PLAN A PLOT TO SUPPLANT SIN WITH SYMPHONY, MISCHIEF WITH MELODY, FILLING WITH A FIFE, THE FACE AND FINGERS OF A FELON - SIN SHOULD SUCCUMB TO SONG, LETS SEE.
B-B-BOOOOMM
OH-VEEEEEE
BOOROOM BVOOM
PFEEE
FUF
BOOOOOOM
FIF-FIT
ME AND YOU ARE TOO LOUD - I DO BELIEVE WE DROWN OUT THE "FIFE" -
YEH - I DO BELIEVE WE DO - - WE SHOULD NOT BE SO HOGGY - SO - -
FIH-FIH-FIHHH-
LADIES AND GENT MENS - WE FEEL THAT WE HAVE NOT GIVEN OUR FAVORITE "FIFER" A FAIR CHANCE FOR YOUR APPLAUSE SO WE NOW ASK HIM TO RENDER, FOR YOUR ATTENTION, A "SOLO".
TWEENK
HOOOOO WAY.
7-23 HERRIMAN
Copr. 1939, King Features Syndicate, Inc., World rights reserved
WHAT HO, "SWEETUMS" -
WHAT HOE, YOURSELF, YOU RAKE
"EGGRICULTURISTS," I WENTCHA TO SAY.

July 23rd, 1939.

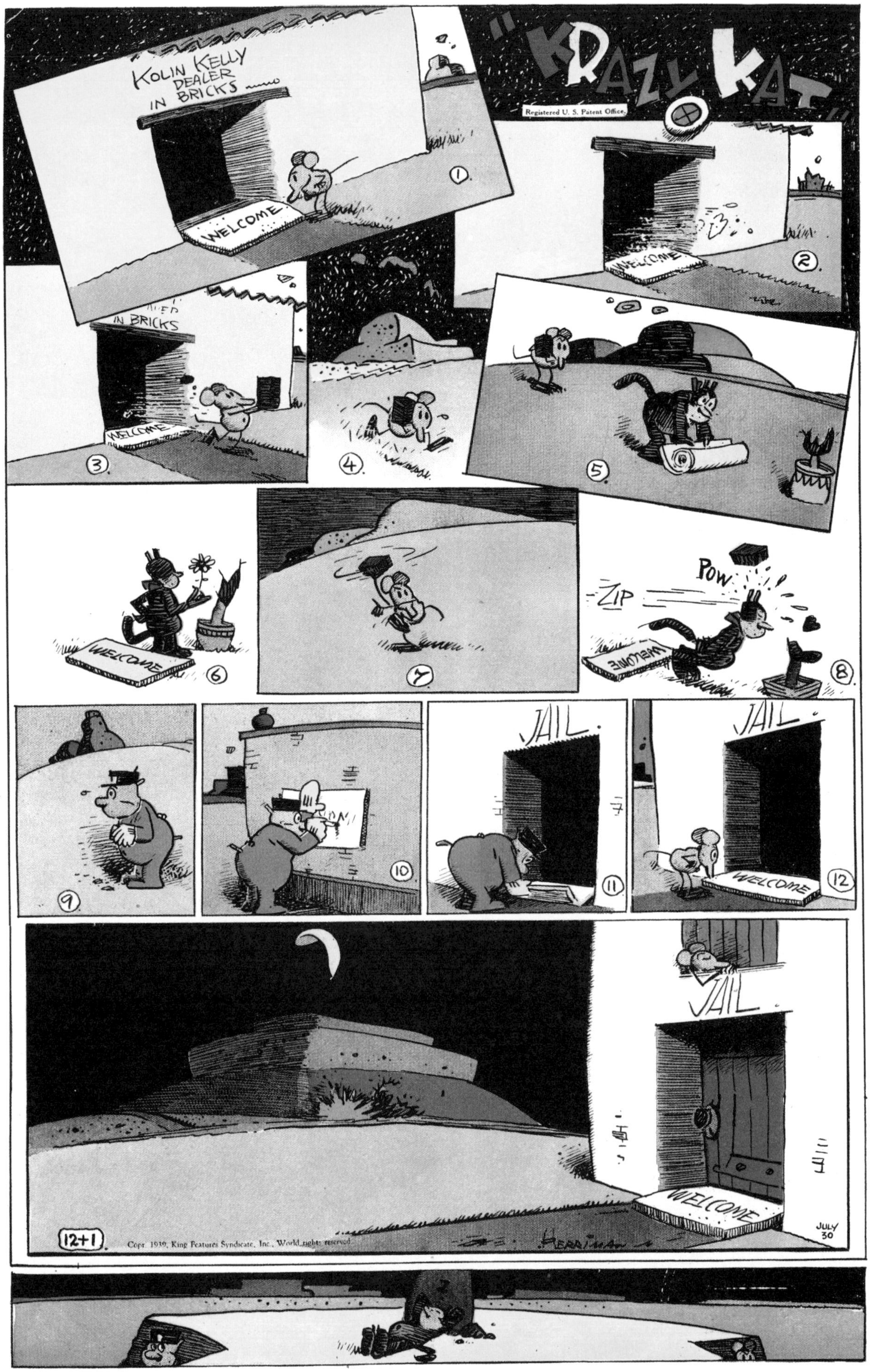
"KRAZY KAT"
Registered U. S. Patent Office.
KOLIN KELLY DEALER IN BRICKS
WELCOME
IN BRICKS
WELCOME
WELCOME
POW
ZIP
WELCOME
JAIL
JAIL
WELCOME
JAIL
WELCOME
12+1
Copr. 1939, King Features Syndicate, Inc., World rights reserved.
HERRIMAN
JULY 30

July 30th, 1939.

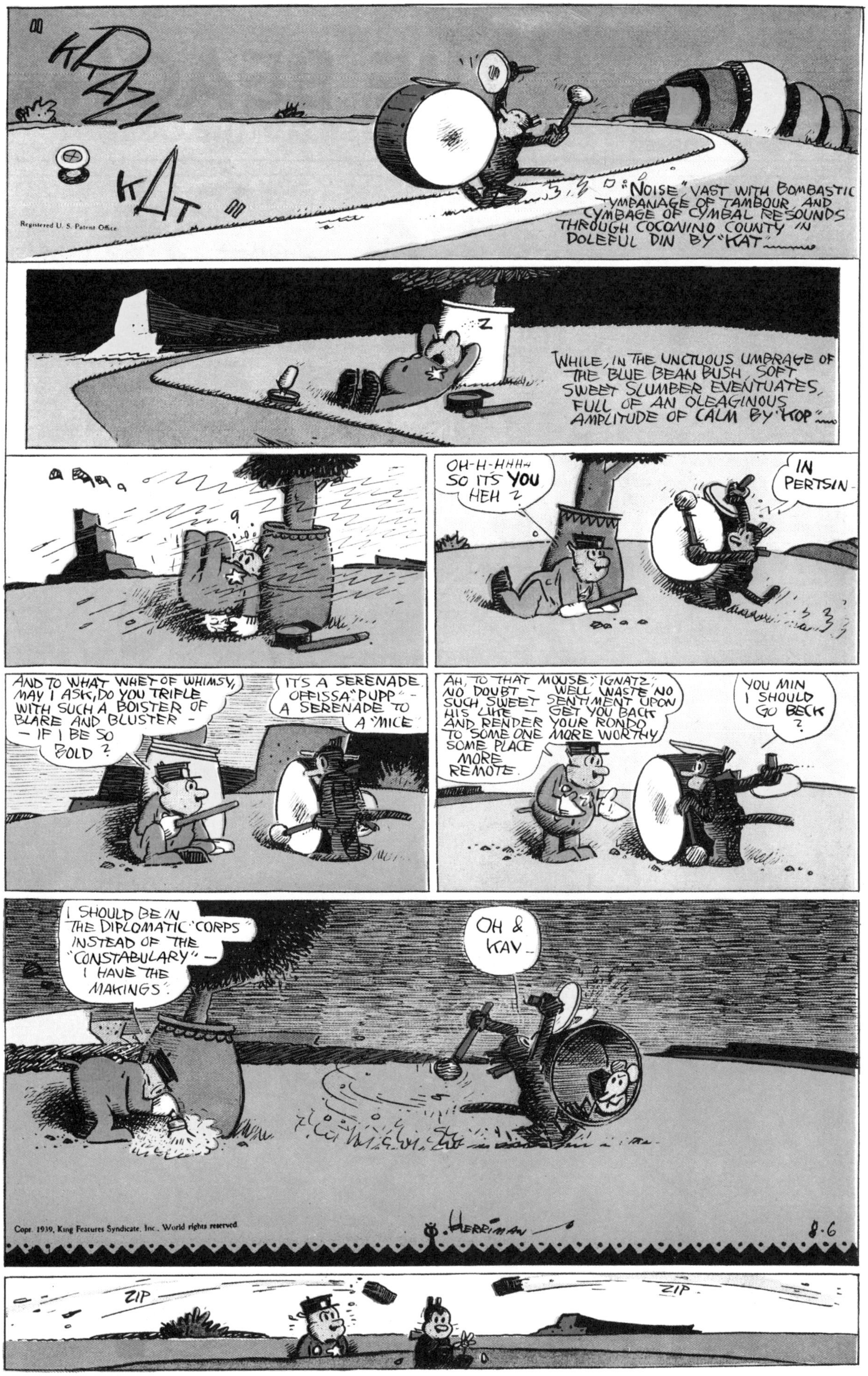

KRAZY KAT
Registered U. S. Patent Office
"Noise" vast with bombastic tympanage of tambour, and cymbage of cymbal resounds through Coconino County in doleful din by "Kat"
While, in the unctuous umbrage of the blue bean bush, soft sweet slumber eventuates, full of an oleaginous amplitude of calm by "Kop"
Oh-h-hhhh so it's you heh?
In pertsin
And to what whet of whimsy, may I ask, do you trifle with such a boister of blare and bluster – if I be so bold?
It's a serenade Offissa "Pupp" – a serenade to a "mice"
Ah, to that mouse, Ignatz, no doubt – well waste no such sweet sentiment upon his like – get you back and render your rondo to some one more worthy some place more remote
You min I should go beck?
I should be in the Diplomatic "Corps" instead of the "Constabulary" – I have the makings
Oh & kay
Copr. 1939, King Features Syndicate, Inc., World rights reserved.
Herriman
8-6
ZIP
ZIP

August 6th, 1939.

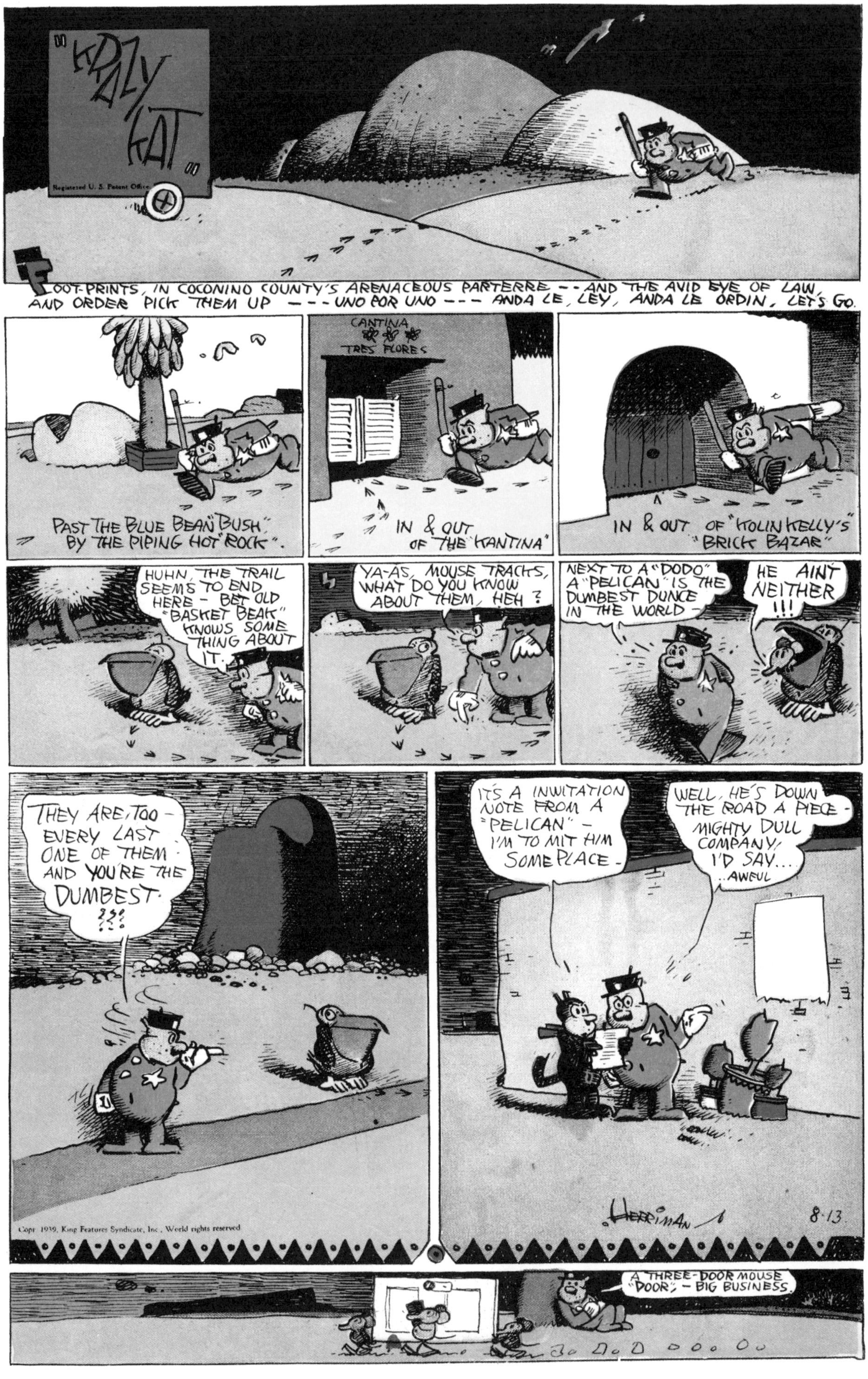
"KRAZY KAT"
Registered U. S. Patent Office
FOOT-PRINTS, IN COCONINO COUNTY'S ARENACEOUS PARTERRE -- AND THE AVID EYE OF LAW, AND ORDER PICK THEM UP --- UNO POR UNO --- ANDA LE LEY, ANDA LE ORDIN, LET'S GO.
PAST THE BLUE BEAN BUSH" BY THE PIPING HOT ROCK".
CANTINA TRES FLORES
IN & OUT OF THE "KANTINA"
IN & OUT OF "KOLIN KELLY'S" "BRICK BAZAR"
HUHN, THE TRAIL SEEMS TO END HERE - BET OLD "BASKET BEAK" KNOWS SOME THING ABOUT IT.
YA-AS, MOUSE TRACKS, WHAT DO YOU KNOW ABOUT THEM, HEH?
NEXT TO A "DODO" A "PELICAN" IS THE DUMBEST DUNCE IN THE WORLD -
HE AINT NEITHER !!!
THEY ARE, TOO - EVERY LAST ONE OF THEM AND YOU'RE THE DUMBEST.
IT'S A INWITATION NOTE FROM A "PELICAN" - I'M TO MIT HIM SOME PLACE -
WELL, HE'S DOWN THE ROAD A PIECE - MIGHTY DULL COMPANY, I'D SAY... ...AWFUL
HERRIMAN 8-13.
Copr 1939, King Features Syndicate, Inc., World rights reserved
A THREE-DOOR MOUSE "DOOR" - BIG BUSINESS.

August 13th, 1939.

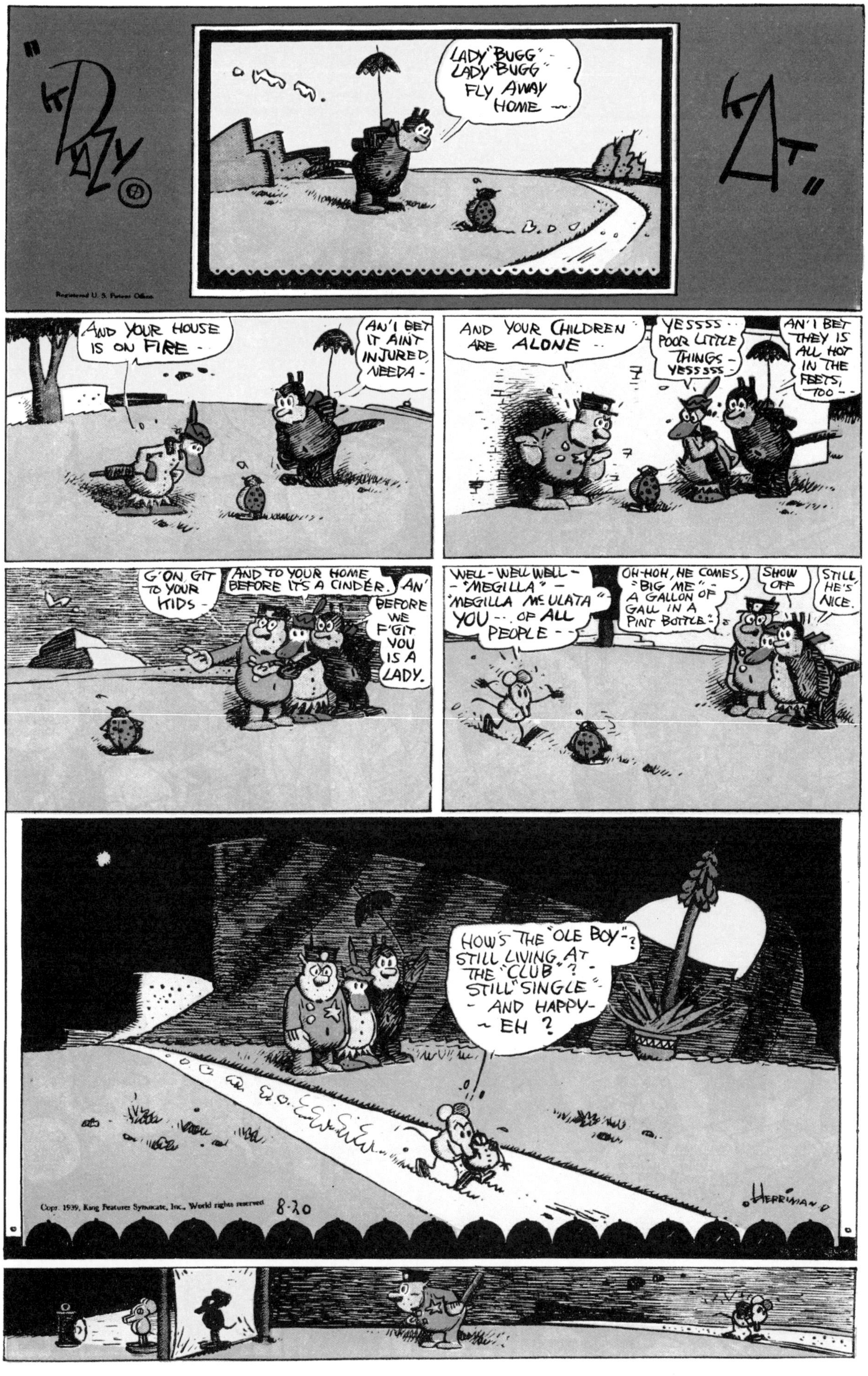
"KRAZY KAT"
LADY "BUGG" LADY "BUGG" FLY AWAY HOME
Registered U. S. Patent Office.
AND YOUR HOUSE IS ON FIRE
AN' I BET IT AINT INJURED, NEEDA
AND YOUR CHILDREN ARE ALONE
YESSSS POOR LITTLE THINGS YESSSSS
AN' I BET THEY IS ALL HOT IN THE FEETS, TOO
G'ON GIT TO YOUR KIDS
AND TO YOUR HOME, BEFORE ITS A CINDER.
AN' BEFORE WE F'GIT YOU IS A LADY.
WELL-WELL WELL - "MEGILLA" - "MEGILLA McULATA" YOU - OF ALL PEOPLE
OH-HOH, HE COMES, "BIG ME" A GALLON OF GALL IN A PINT BOTTLE.
SHOW OFF
STILL, HE'S NICE.
HOW'S THE "OLE BOY"? STILL LIVING AT THE "CLUB"? STILL "SINGLE" - AND HAPPY - EH?
Copr. 1939, King Features Syndicate, Inc., World rights reserved
8-20
HERRIMAN

August 20th, 1939.

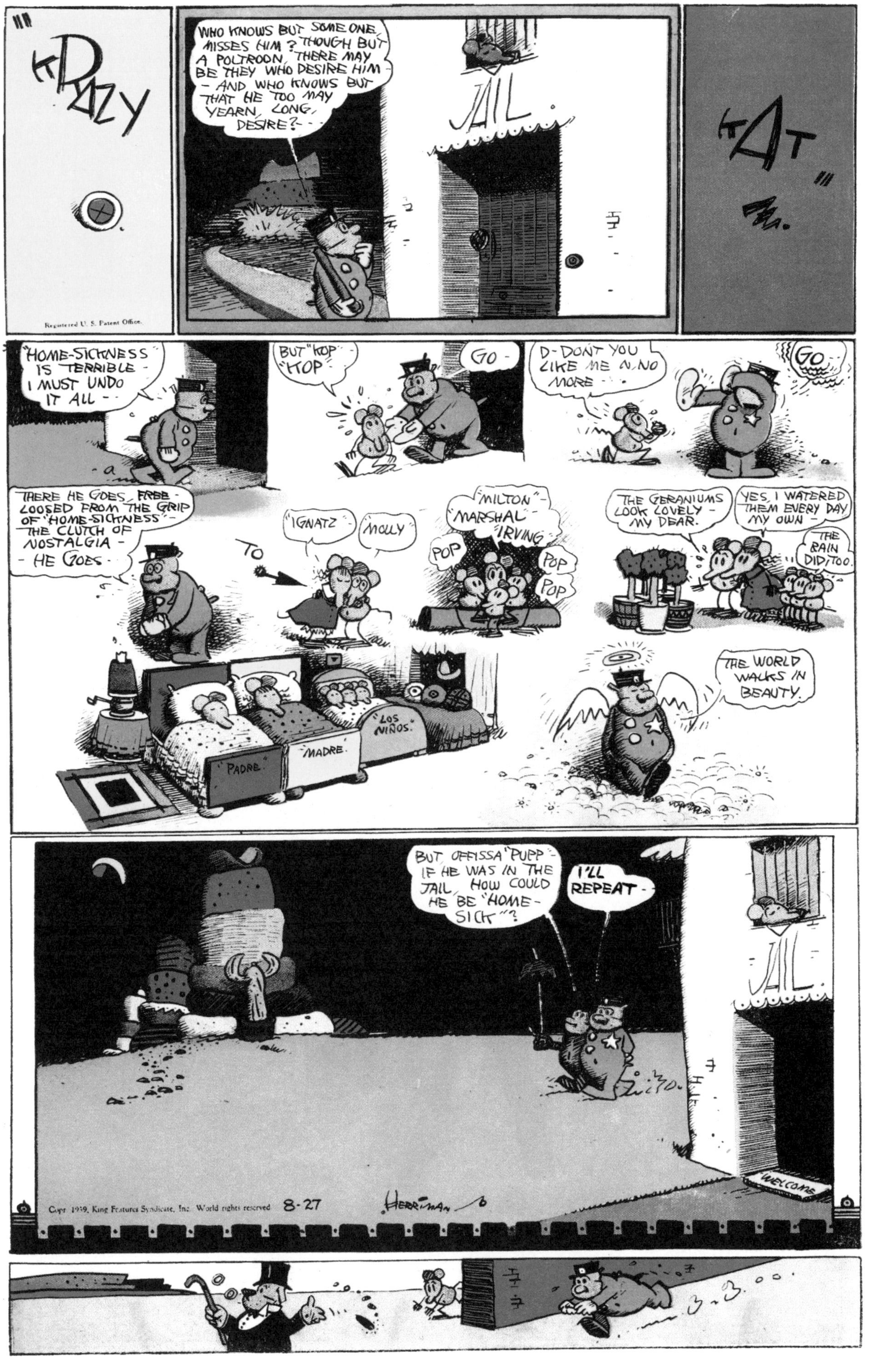
"KRAZY
KAT"
Registered U. S. Patent Office.
WHO KNOWS BUT SOME ONE MISSES HIM? THOUGH BUT A POLTROON, THERE MAY BE THEY WHO DESIRE HIM - AND WHO KNOWS BUT THAT HE TOO MAY YEARN, LONG, DESIRE? -
JAIL
"HOME-SICKNESS IS TERRIBLE - I MUST UNDO IT ALL - -
BUT "KOP" KOP
GO -
D-DON'T YOU LIKE ME N-NO MORE -
GO -
THERE HE GOES, FREE - LOOSED FROM THE GRIP OF "HOME-SICKNESS" - THE CLUTCH OF NOSTALGIA - HE GOES -
TO
IGNATZ
MOLLY
MILTON
MARSHAL
IRVING
POP
POP
POP
THE GERANIUMS LOOK LOVELY - MY DEAR.
YES, I WATERED THEM EVERY DAY MY OWN
THE RAIN DID, TOO.
PADRE
MADRE
LOS NIÑOS
THE WORLD WALKS IN BEAUTY.
BUT OFFISSA "PUPP" IF HE WAS IN THE JAIL, HOW COULD HE BE "HOME-SICK"?
I'LL REPEAT -
JAIL
WELCOME
Copr 1939, King Features Syndicate, Inc. World rights reserved
8-27
HERRIMAN

August 27th, 1939.

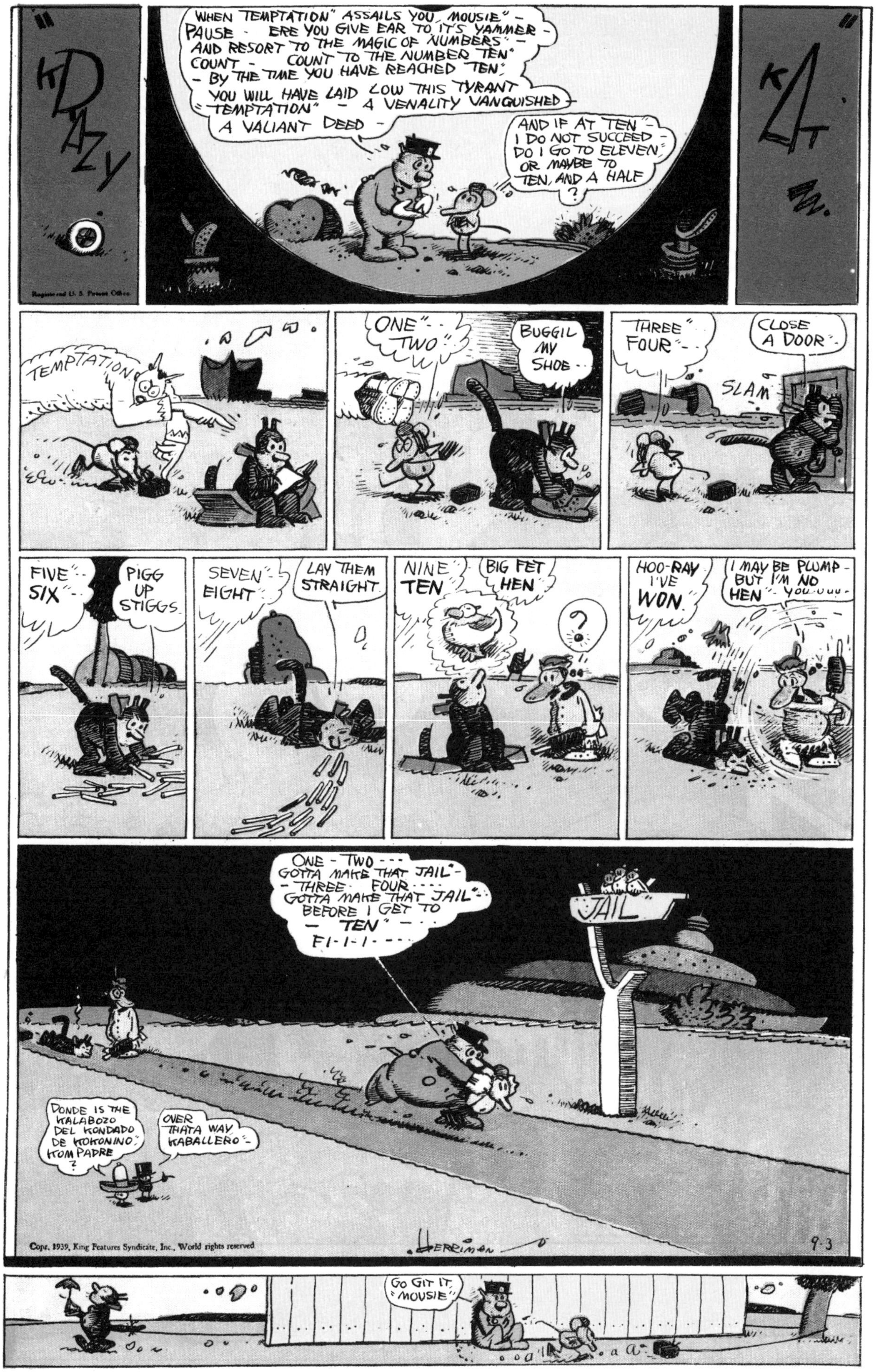
"KRAZY" "KAT"
Registered U. S. Patent Office.
WHEN "TEMPTATION" ASSAILS YOU, "MOUSIE" - PAUSE - ERE YOU GIVE EAR TO IT'S YAMMER - AND RESORT TO THE MAGIC OF "NUMBERS" - COUNT - COUNT TO THE NUMBER "TEN" - BY THE TIME YOU HAVE REACHED "TEN" YOU WILL HAVE LAID LOW THIS TYRANT "TEMPTATION" - A VENALITY VANQUISHED - A VALIANT DEED -
AND IF AT TEN I DO NOT SUCCEED - DO I GO TO ELEVEN, OR MAYBE TO TEN, AND A HALF ?
TEMPTATION
"ONE" - "TWO"
BUGGIL MY SHOE
"THREE" FOUR
CLOSE A DOOR
SLAM
FIVE SIX
PIGG UP STIGGS
SEVEN EIGHT
LAY THEM STRAIGHT
NINE TEN
BIG FET HEN
?
HOO-RAY I'VE WON.
I MAY BE PLUMP - BUT I'M NO HEN
ONE - TWO - - - GOTTA MAKE THAT "JAIL" - - THREE FOUR - - - GOTTA MAKE THAT "JAIL" - BEFORE I GET TO - "TEN" - - F1-1-1 - - -
JAIL
DONDE IS THE KALABOZO DEL KONDADO DE KOKONINO, KOMPADRE ?
OVER THATA WAY, KABALLERO -
Copr. 1939, King Features Syndicate, Inc., World rights reserved
HERRIMAN
9-3
GO GIT IT, "MOUSIE"

September 3rd, 1939.

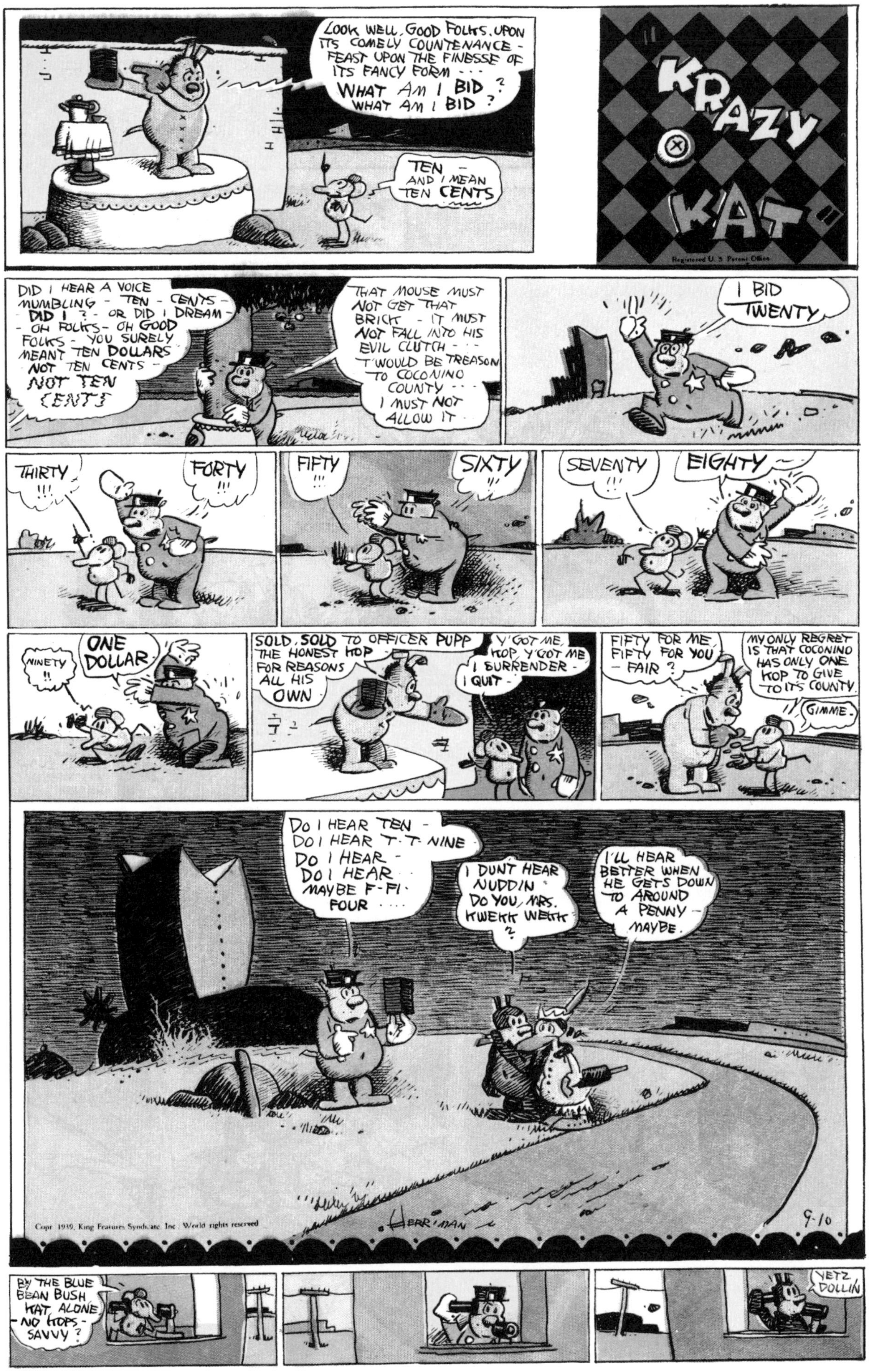
LOOK WELL, GOOD FOLKS, UPON ITS COMELY COUNTENANCE - FEAST UPON THE FINESSE OF ITS FANCY FORM --- WHAT AM I BID ? WHAT AM I BID ?
TEN - AND I MEAN TEN CENTS
KRAZY KAT
Registered U.S. Patent Office
DID I HEAR A VOICE MUMBLING - TEN - CENTS - DID I ? - OR DID I DREAM - OH FOLKS - OH GOOD FOLKS - YOU SURELY MEANT TEN DOLLARS - NOT TEN CENTS - NOT TEN CENTS
THAT MOUSE MUST NOT GET THAT BRICK - IT MUST NOT FALL INTO HIS EVIL CLUTCH - - 'T WOULD BE TREASON TO COCONINO COUNTY --- I MUST NOT ALLOW IT -
I BID TWENTY
THIRTY !!!
FORTY !!!
FIFTY !!!
SIXTY !!!
SEVENTY !!!
EIGHTY
NINETY !!
ONE DOLLAR
SOLD, SOLD TO OFFICER PUPP THE HONEST KOP - FOR REASONS ALL HIS OWN
Y' GOT ME, KOP, Y' GOT ME I SURRENDER - I QUIT -
FIFTY FOR ME, FIFTY FOR YOU - FAIR ?
MY ONLY REGRET IS THAT COCONINO HAS ONLY ONE KOP TO GIVE TO ITS COUNTY.
GIMME.
DO I HEAR TEN - DO I HEAR T-T-NINE - DO I HEAR - DO I HEAR - MAYBE F-FI- FOUR ....
I DUNT HEAR NUDDIN DO YOU, MRS. KWEKK WEKK ?
I'LL HEAR BETTER WHEN HE GETS DOWN TO AROUND A PENNY - MAYBE.
Copr 1939, King Features Syndicate, Inc. World rights reserved
HERRIMAN
9-10
BY THE BLUE BEAN BUSH KAT, ALONE - NO KOPS - SAVVY ?
YETZ DOLLIN

September 10th, 1939.

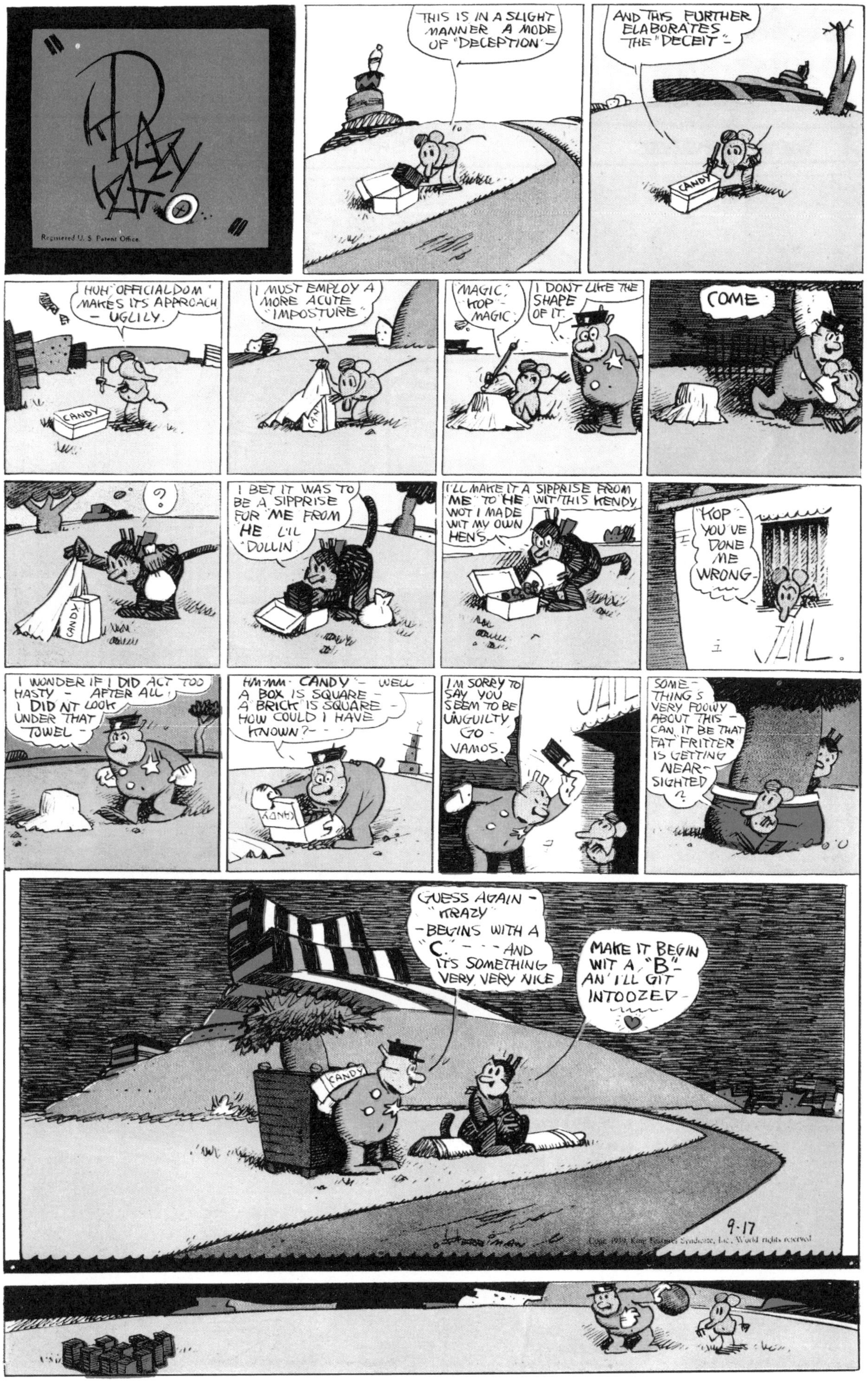
Krazy Kat
Registered U. S. Patent Office.
THIS IS IN A SLIGHT MANNER A MODE OF "DECEPTION" –
AND THIS FURTHER ELABORATES THE "DECEIT" –
CANDY
HUH, OFFICIALDOM MAKES ITS APPROACH – UGLILY.
CANDY
I MUST EMPLOY A MORE ACUTE "IMPOSTURE" –
"MAGIC" "KOP" "MAGIC"
I DONT LIKE THE SHAPE OF IT.
COME
?
CANDY
I BET IT WAS TO BE A SIPPRISE FUR ME FROM HE L'IL "DULLIN"
I'LL MAKE IT A SIPPRISE FROM ME TO HE WIT THIS KENDY WOT I MADE WIT MY OWN HENS.
"KOP – YOU VE DONE ME WRONG –
JAIL.
I WONDER IF I DID ACT TOO HASTY – AFTER ALL, I DID NT LOOK UNDER THAT TOWEL –
HM-M-M- CANDY – WELL A BOX IS SQUARE – A BRICK IS SQUARE – HOW COULD I HAVE KNOWN? –
I'M SORRY TO SAY YOU SEEM TO BE UNGUILTY. GO – VAMOS.
JAIL
SOME-THING'S VERY FOOWY ABOUT THIS – CAN IT BE THAT FAT FRITTER IS GETTING NEAR-SIGHTED ?
GUESS AGAIN – "KRAZY" – BEGINS WITH A "C." – – – AND IT'S SOMETHING VERY, VERY NICE
MAKE IT BEGIN WIT A "B" – AN' I'LL GIT INTOOZED –
CANDY
9-17
Herriman

September 17th, 1939.

"KRAZY KAT"
Registered U.S. Patent Office.
THE FREEDOM OF THE SEA IS MINE "KOPPIE" - MINE, AND MY BONNY "BRICK" - A MURRAIN UPON YOU - YOU AND YOUR OFFICIOUS OAFISHNESS - GOO-BYE!!!
YOU-YOU-YOU-
HERE AM I, PROUDLY ACCOUTERED IN THE RAIMENT OF LAW AND ORDER, BEAMINGLY BADGED, BRASSLY BUTTONED, STOUTLY OAK-STAFFED BEHATTED IN THE COGENT CHAPEAU OF CONSTABULISTIC COHESION - -
AND YET, UPON THE WAVES MY POWER FAILS, MY HIGH OFFICE FALTERS - SIN SNEERS AT ME
PIPE DOWN, POLICEMAN, THAT'S A "ADMIRAL'S" JOB - -
OF COURSE, IT IS, SIR, AND ARE YOU A "ADMIRAL"?
WHO DO YOU S'POSE HAS BEEN RUNNING THE "KOKONINO KNAVEY" ALL THESE YEARS?
OH, SIR, OUT THERE UPON THE BILLOWS WHICH YOU RULE IS A "MOUSE" A "MOUSE" WITH "BRICK" -
AVAST THERE, "KOP" - ARE YOU SURE YOU MEAN WITH "BRICK"?
"BRICK," I DO INDEED MEAN "BRICK," IMPLEMENT OF SIN, DISORDER AND CALAMITY -
AT LAST - AT LAST -
AHOY LAND THE "FLAG SHIP" - "YOUR ADMIRAL" IS COMING ABOARD!!!
BEAR DOWN ON IT, Y' SWAB - THERE'S A FIGHTING FERRY, A SUB-SCOW, AND A GRAVY-BOAT TO POLISH YET - GIT INTO ACTION -
HI, "KELLY" A HOD OF "BRICKS" FOR THE "ADMIRAL"
"EDMIRIL MICE" - I BETCHA.
I GOT A BEAD ON 'IM, AD.
K.K.
9-24
HERRIMAN
MY MAGIC WAND WILL NOW PRODUCE A "BRICK."
NO, NO - NO -

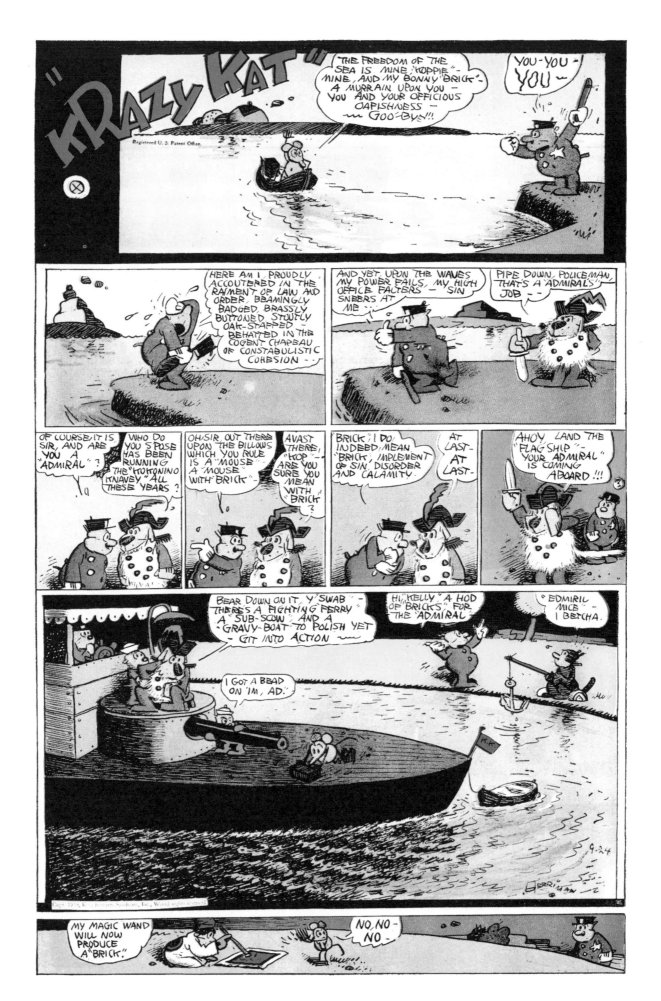

September 24th, 1939.

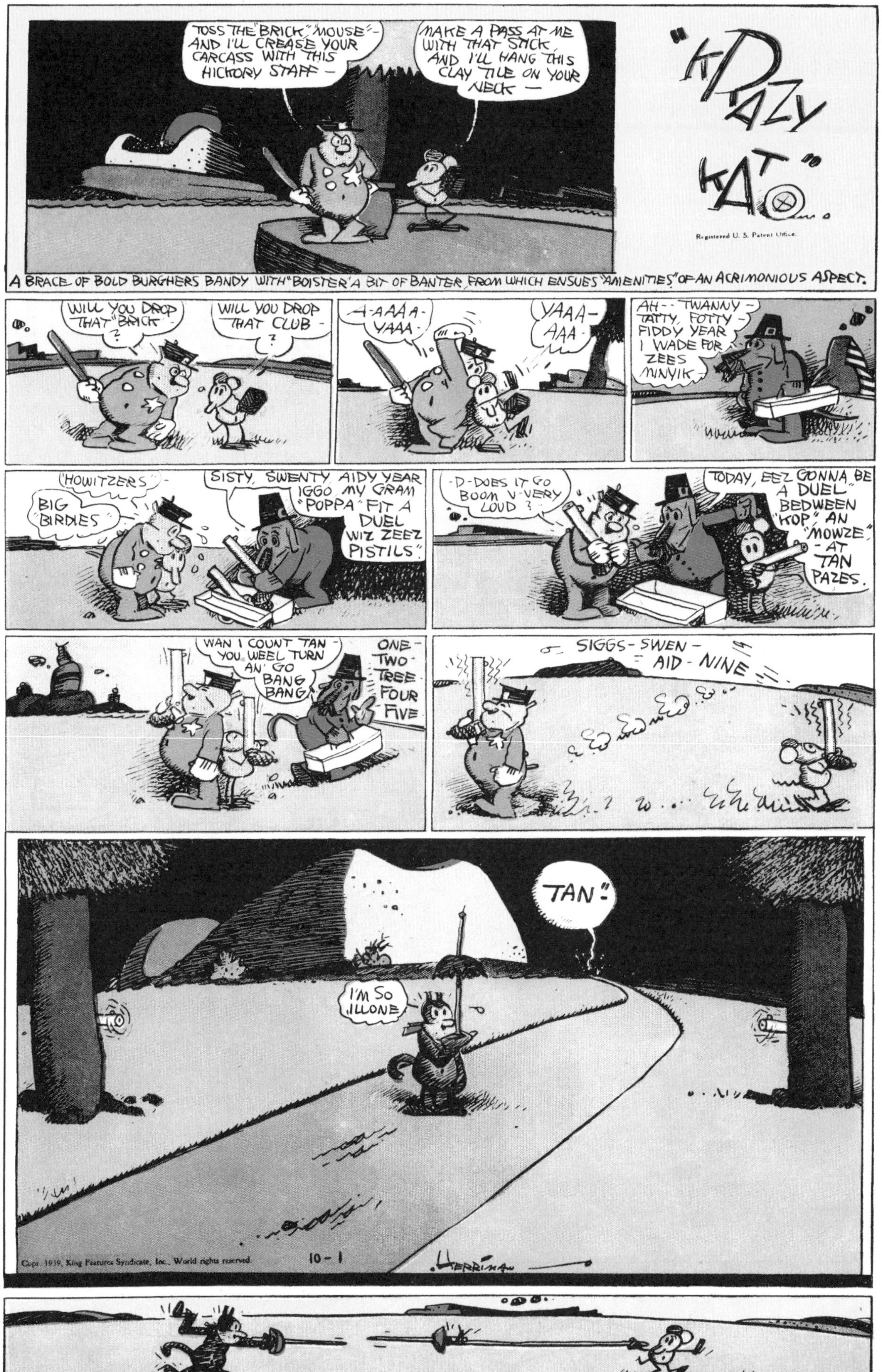
"KRAZY KAT"
Registered U. S. Patent Office.
TOSS THE "BRICK," MOUSE – AND I'LL CREASE YOUR CARCASS WITH THIS HICKORY STAFF –
MAKE A PASS AT ME WITH THAT STICK, AND I'LL HANG THIS CLAY TILE ON YOUR NECK –
A BRACE OF BOLD BURGHERS BANDY WITH "BOISTER" A BIT OF BANTER, FROM WHICH ENSUES "AMENITIES" OF AN ACRIMONIOUS ASPECT.
WILL YOU DROP THAT "BRICK" ?
WILL YOU DROP THAT CLUB – ?
A-AAAA-YAAA-
YAAA-AAA-
AH – TWANNY – TATTY, FOTTY – FIDDY YEAR I WADE FOR ZEES MINYIK
"HOWITZERS" –
BIG BIRDIES
SISTY, SWENTY AIDY YEAR IGGO MY GRAM "POPPA" FIT A DUEL WIZ ZEEZ PISTILS".
D-DOES IT GO BOOM V-VERY LOUD ?
TODAY, EEZ GONNA BE A DUEL BEDWEEN "KOP," AN "MOWZE" – AT TAN PAZES.
WAN I COUNT TAN – YOU WEEL TURN AN' GO BANG BANG
ONE – TWO – TREE – FOUR – FIVE
SIGGS – SWEN – AID – NINE
"TAN" –
I'M SO ILLONE
Copr. 1939, King Features Syndicate, Inc., World rights reserved.
10-1
HERRIMAN

October 1st, 1939.

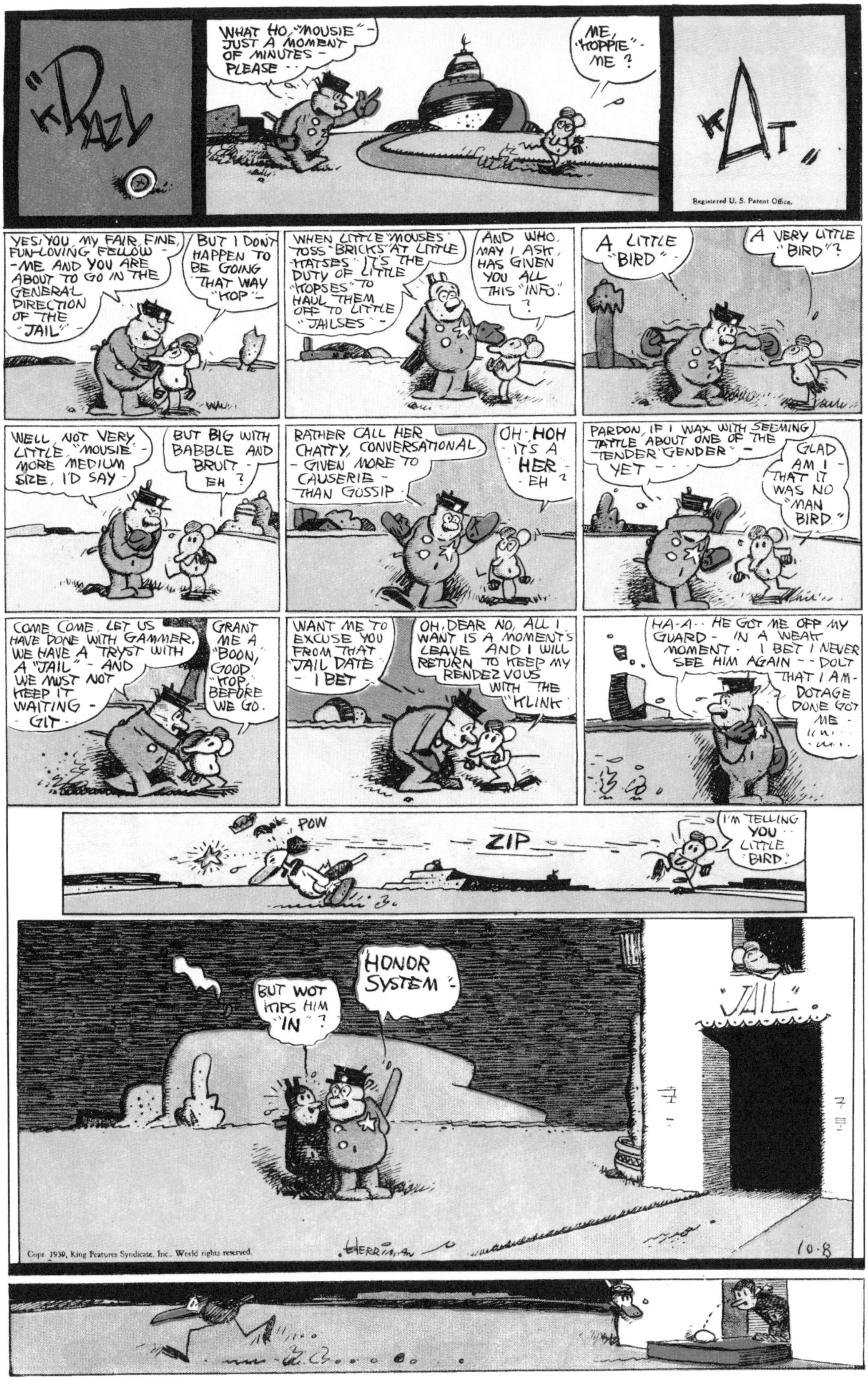
"KRAZY KAT"
WHAT HO, "MOUSIE" - JUST A MOMENT OF MINUTES - PLEASE - -
ME, "KOPPIE" - ME ?
Registered U. S. Patent Office.
YES; YOU, MY FAIR, FINE, FUN-LOVING FELLOW - - ME AND YOU ARE ABOUT TO GO IN THE GENERAL DIRECTION OF THE "JAIL" -
BUT I DON'T HAPPEN TO BE GOING THAT WAY "KOP" -
WHEN LITTLE "MOUSES" TOSS "BRICKS" AT LITTLE "KATSES" IT'S THE DUTY OF LITTLE "KOPSES" TO HAUL THEM OFF TO LITTLE "JAILSES" -
AND WHO, MAY I ASK, HAS GIVEN YOU ALL THIS "INFO." ?
A LITTLE "BIRD" -
A VERY LITTLE "BIRD" ?
WELL, NOT VERY LITTLE, "MOUSIE" - MORE MEDIUM SIZE, I'D SAY -
BUT BIG WITH BABBLE AND BRUIT - EH ?
RATHER CALL HER CHATTY, CONVERSATIONAL - GIVEN MORE TO CAUSERIE - THAN GOSSIP -
OH - HOH - IT'S A HER - EH ?
PARDON, IF I WAX WITH SEEMING TATTLE ABOUT ONE OF THE TENDER GENDER - YET - - -
GLAD AM I - THAT IT WAS NO "MAN BIRD."
COME COME, LET US HAVE DONE WITH GAMMER. WE HAVE A TRYST WITH A "JAIL" - AND WE MUST NOT KEEP IT WAITING - - GIT -
GRANT ME A "BOON," GOOD "KOP," BEFORE WE GO.
WANT ME TO EXCUSE YOU FROM THAT "JAIL DATE" - I BET -
OH, DEAR NO, ALL I WANT IS A MOMENT'S LEAVE AND I WILL RETURN TO KEEP MY RENDEZVOUS WITH THE "KLINK"
HA-A - - HE GOT ME OFF MY GUARD - IN A WEAK MOMENT - I BET I NEVER SEE HIM AGAIN - - DOLT THAT I AM - DOTAGE DONE GOT ME -
POW
ZIP
I'M TELLING YOU - LITTLE "BIRD"
BUT WOT KEEPS HIM "IN" ?
HONOR SYSTEM
"JAIL"
Copr. 1939, King Features Syndicate, Inc., World rights reserved.
HERRIMAN
10-8

October 8th, 1939.

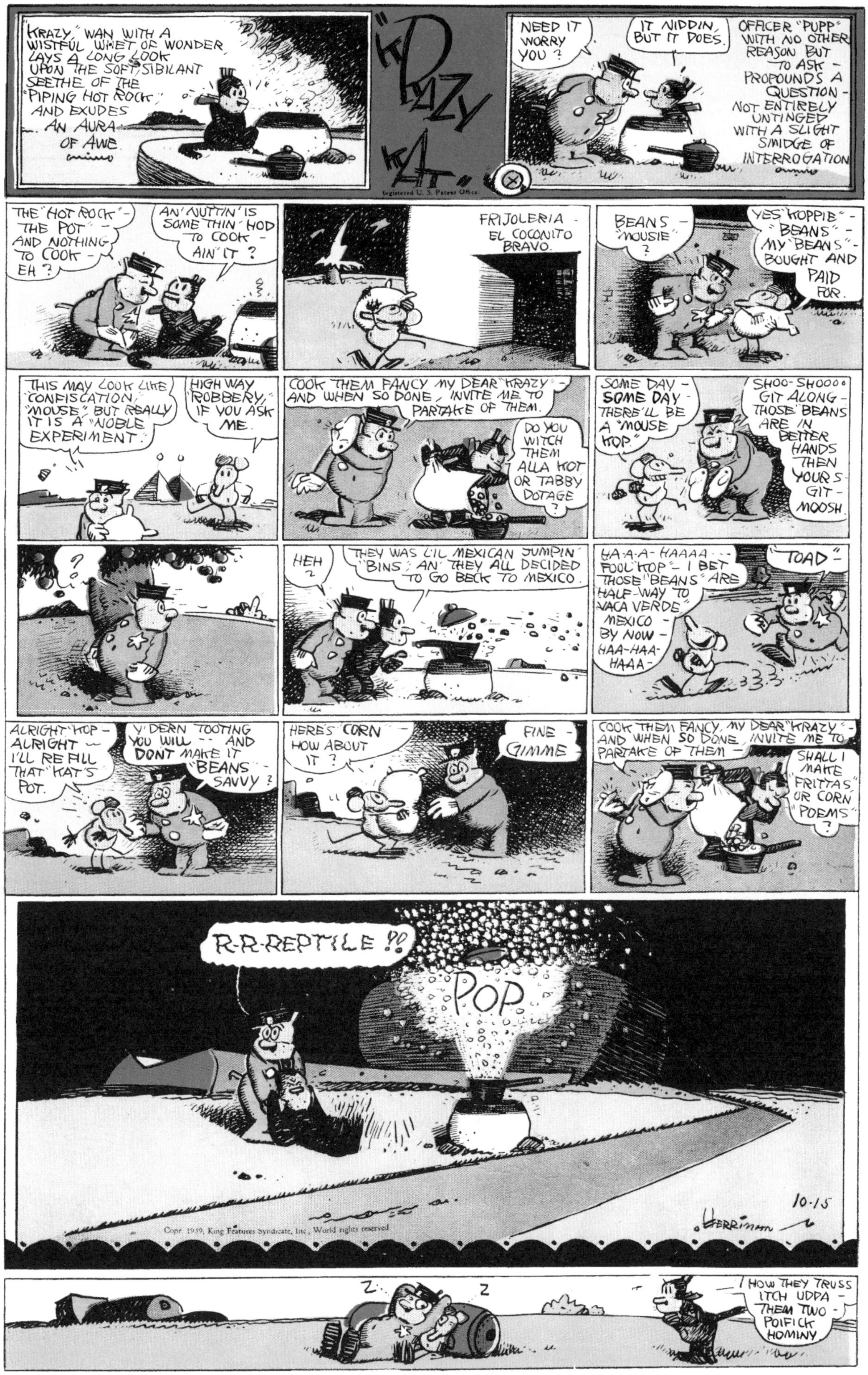
"KRAZY" KAT
Registered U. S. Patent Office.
"KRAZY" WAN WITH A WISTFUL WHET OF WONDER LAYS A LONG LOOK UPON THE SOFT, SIBILANT SEETHE OF THE "PIPING HOT ROCK" AND EXUDES AN AURA OF AWE
NEED IT WORRY YOU ?
IT NIDDIN, BUT IT DOES.
OFFICER "PUPP" WITH NO OTHER REASON BUT TO ASK - PROPOUNDS A QUESTION - NOT ENTIRELY UNTINGED WITH A SLIGHT SMIDGE OF INTERROGATION
THE "HOT ROCK" - THE POT - AND NOTHING TO COOK - EH ?
AN' NUTTIN' IS SOME THIN' HOD TO COOK - AIN' IT ?
FRIJOLERIA - EL COCONITO BRAVO.
BEANS - "MOUSIE" ?
YES "KOPPIE" - "BEANS" - MY "BEANS" - BOUGHT AND PAID FOR.
THIS MAY LOOK LIKE "CONFISCATION," "MOUSE," BUT REALLY IT IS A "NOBLE EXPERIMENT."
HIGH WAY "ROBBERY," IF YOU ASK ME.
COOK THEM FANCY MY DEAR "KRAZY" - AND WHEN SO DONE, INVITE ME TO PARTAKE OF THEM.
DO YOU WITCH THEM ALLA KOT OR TABBY DOTAGE ?
SOME DAY - SOME DAY - THERE'LL BE A "MOUSE KOP."
SHOO-SHOOOO GIT ALONG - THOSE "BEANS" ARE IN BETTER HANDS THEN YOUR'S GIT - MOOSH.
?
HEH ?
THEY WAS L'IL MEXICAN JUMPIN' "BINS," AN' THEY ALL DECIDED TO GO BECK TO MEXICO.
HA-A-A-HAAAA - FOOL "KOP" - I BET THOSE "BEANS" ARE HALF-WAY TO "VACA VERDE," MEXICO - BY NOW - HAA-HAA-HAAA -
"TOAD" -
ALRIGHT "KOP" - ALRIGHT - I'LL RE FILL THAT "KAT'S" POT.
Y' DERN TOOTING YOU WILL - - AND DONT MAKE IT "BEANS" - SAVVY ?
HERE'S "CORN" - HOW ABOUT IT ?
FINE - GIMME -
COOK THEM FANCY, MY DEAR "KRAZY" - AND WHEN SO DONE, INVITE ME TO PARTAKE OF THEM -
SHALL I MAKE "FRITTAS" OR CORN "POEMS" ?
R-R-REPTILE !?!
POP
10-15
Herriman
Copr. 1939, King Features Syndicate, Inc., World rights reserved
Z
Z
HOW THEY TRUSS ITCH UDDA - THEM TWO - POIFICK HOMINY

October 15th, 1939.

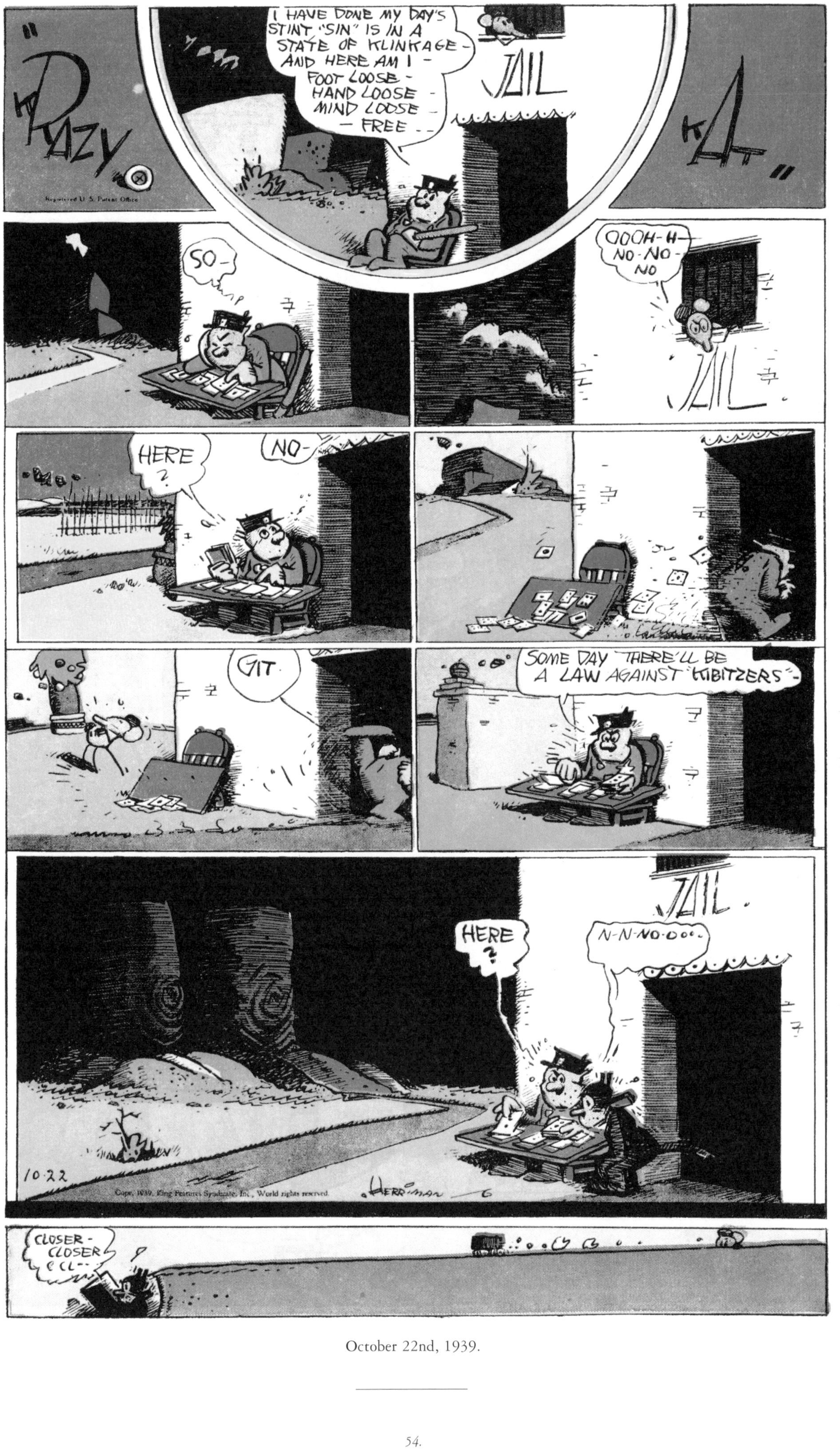
"KRAZY KAT"
Registered U. S. Patent Office
I HAVE DONE MY DAY'S STINT, "SIN" IS IN A STATE OF KLINKAGE - AND HERE AM I - FOOT LOOSE - HAND LOOSE - MIND LOOSE - FREE - -
JAIL
SO -
OOOH-H- NO-NO-NO
JAIL
HERE ?
NO -
GIT
SOME DAY THERE'LL BE A LAW AGAINST KIBITZERS -
JAIL
HERE ?
N-N-NO-O...
10-22
Copr. 1939, King Features Syndicate, Inc., World rights reserved.
HERRIMAN
CLOSER - CLOSER - C CL - -

October 22nd, 1939.

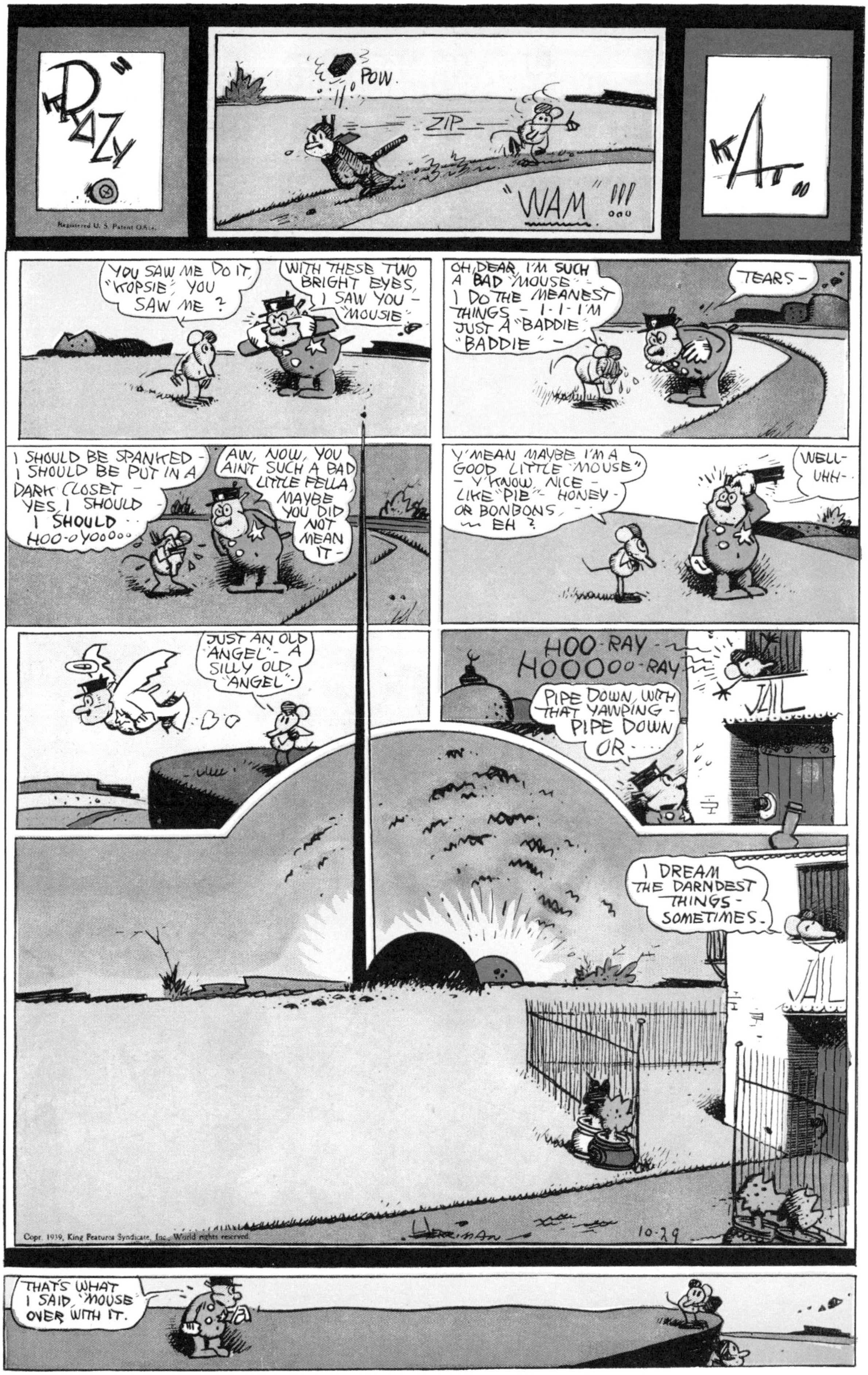
KRAZY
KAT
Registered U. S. Patent Office.
POW
ZIP
"WAM"!!!
YOU SAW ME DO IT, "KOPSIE" YOU SAW ME ?
WITH THESE TWO BRIGHT EYES, I SAW YOU - "MOUSIE"
OH DEAR, I'M SUCH A BAD "MOUSE" - I DO THE MEANEST THINGS - I-I-I'M JUST A "BADDIE" "BADDIE" -
TEARS -
I SHOULD BE SPANKED - I SHOULD BE PUT IN A DARK CLOSET - YES, I SHOULD - I SHOULD HOO-O YOOOOO
AW, NOW, YOU AINT SUCH A BAD LITTLE FELLA, MAYBE YOU DID NOT MEAN IT -
Y'MEAN MAYBE I'M A GOOD LITTLE "MOUSE" - Y'KNOW, NICE - LIKE "PIE" - HONEY - OR BONBONS - EH ?
WELL - UHH -
JUST AN OLD "ANGEL" - A SILLY OLD "ANGEL"
HOO-RAY - HOOOOO-RAY
JAIL
PIPE DOWN, WITH THAT YAWPING - PIPE DOWN OR
I DREAM THE DARNDEST THINGS - SOMETIMES -
JAIL
Copr. 1939, King Features Syndicate, Inc., World rights reserved.
HERRIMAN
10-29
THAT'S WHAT I SAID, "MOUSE" OVER WITH IT.

October 29th, 1939.

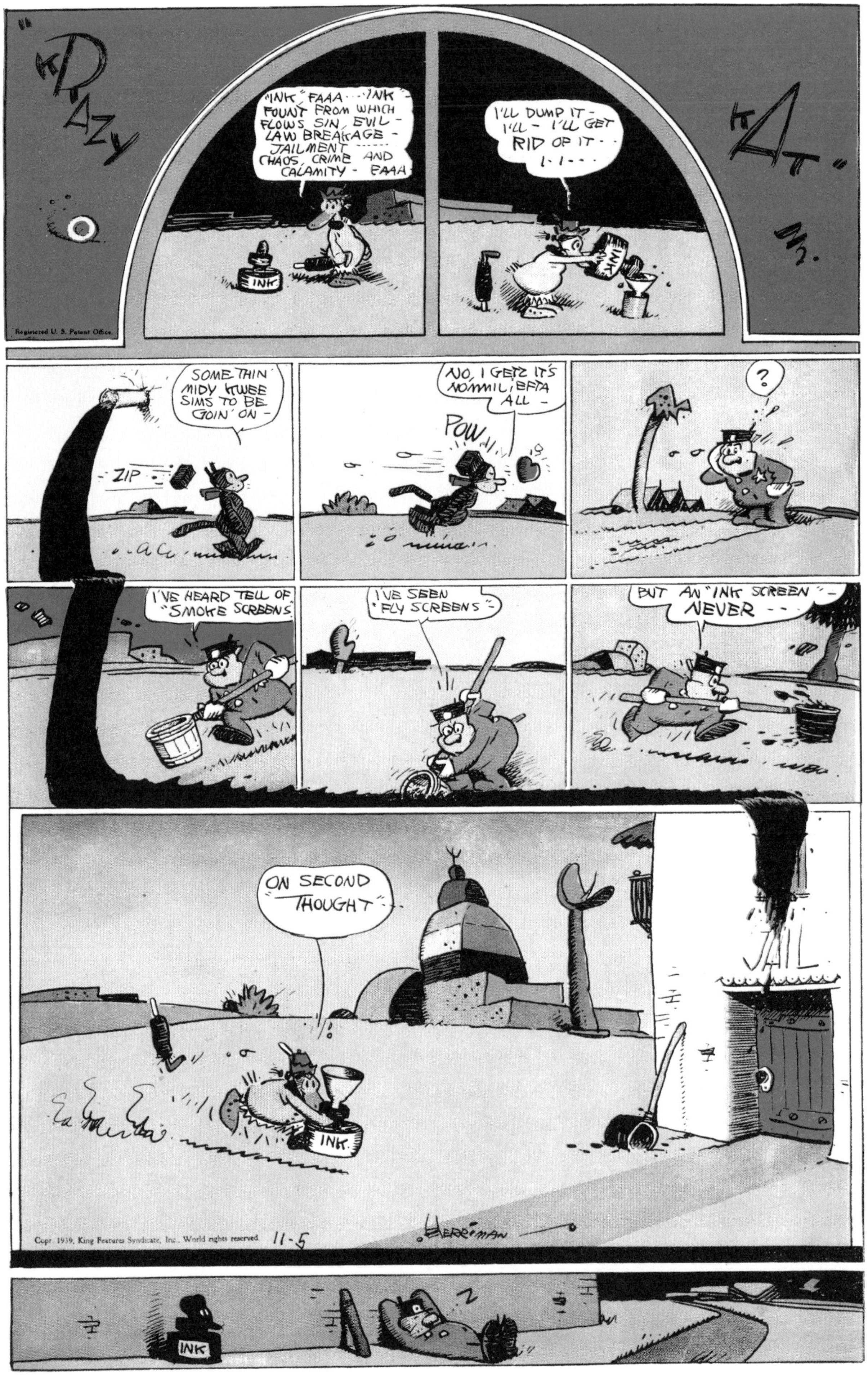
"KRAZY KAT"
Registered U. S. Patent Office.
"INK," FAAA - - INK - FOUNT FROM WHICH FLOWS SIN, EVIL - LAW BREAKAGE - JAILMENT ----- CHAOS, CRIME AND CALAMITY - FAAA
I'LL DUMP IT - I'LL - I'LL GET RID OF IT - - I - I - - -
SOME-THIN' MIDY KWEE SIMS TO BE GOIN' ON -
ZIP
NO, I GETZ IT'S NOMMIL, EFTA ALL -
POW
?
I'VE HEARD TELL OF "SMOKE SCREENS"
I'VE SEEN "FLY SCREENS"
BUT AN "INK SCREEN" - - NEVER - - -
ON SECOND THOUGHT
INK
Copr. 1939, King Features Syndicate, Inc., World rights reserved. 11-5
HERRIMAN
INK
Z

November 5th, 1939.

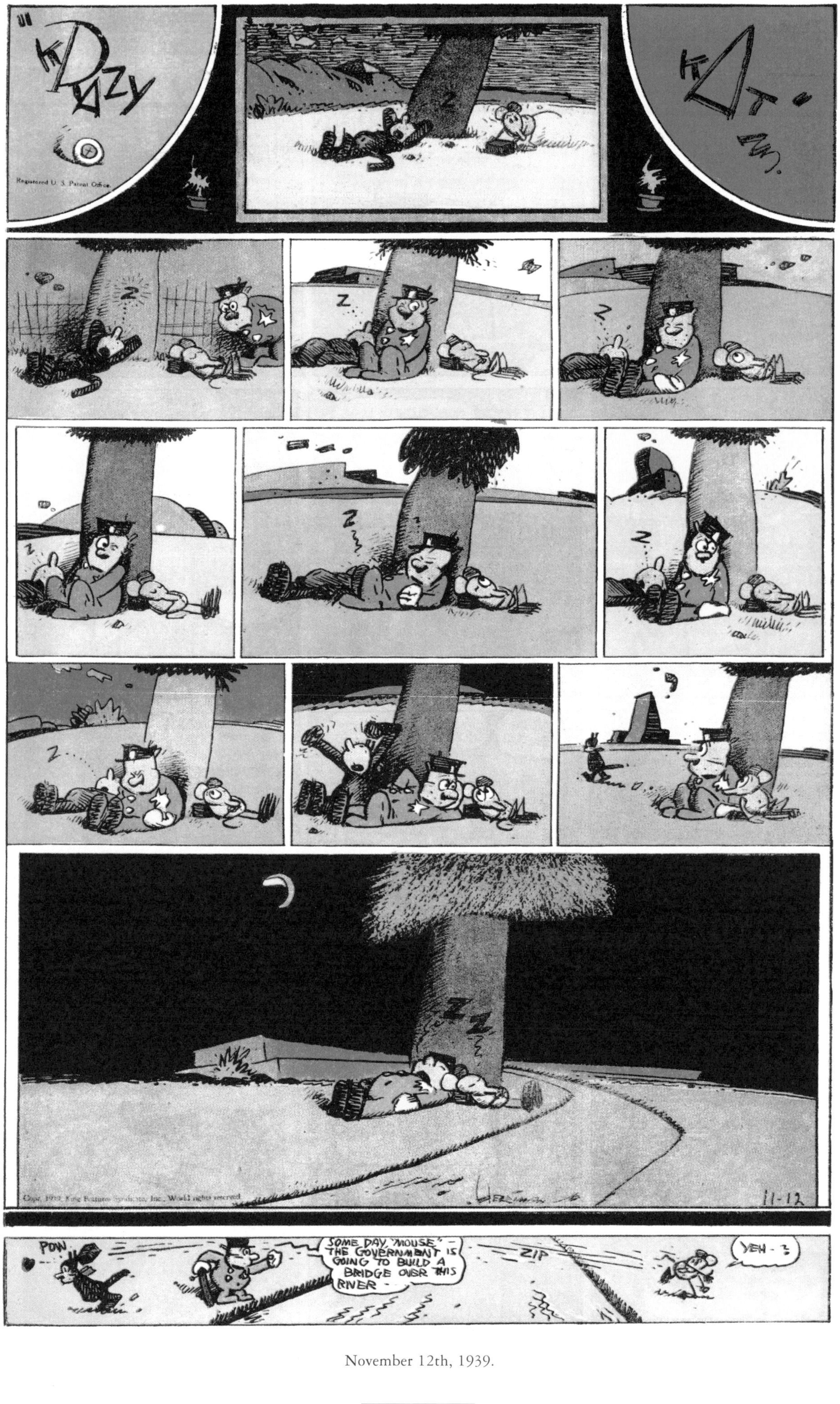
Krazy Kat
Registered U. S. Patent Office
Z
Z
Z
Z
Z
Z
Z
Z
Copr. 1939, King Features Syndicate, Inc., World rights reserved.
Herriman
11-12
POW
SOME DAY, "MOUSE" - THE GOVERNMENT IS GOING TO BUILD A BRIDGE OVER THIS RIVER -
ZIP
YEH - ?

November 12th, 1939.

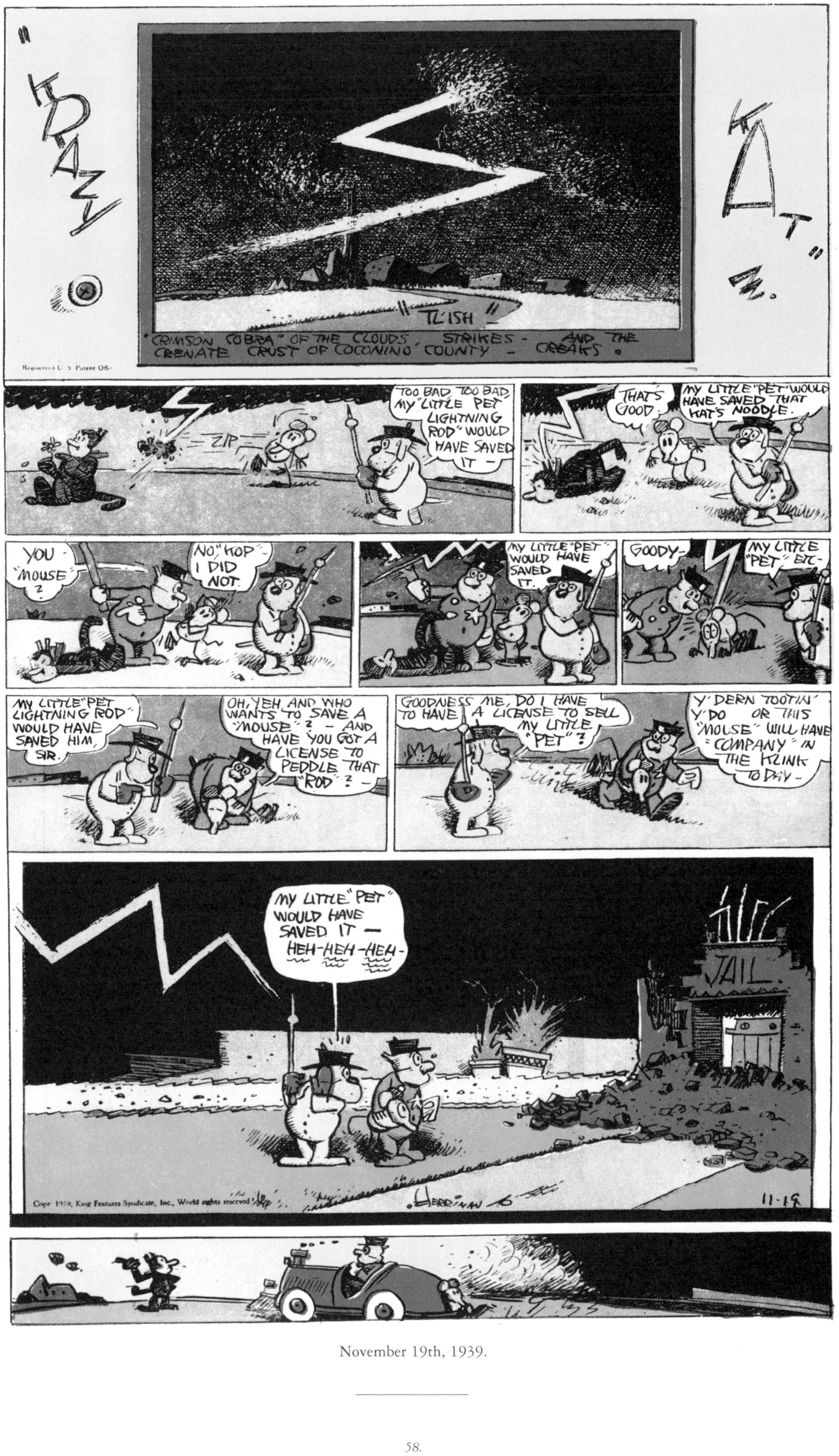
"KRAZY KAT"
"TL'ISH"
"CRIMSON COBRA" OF THE CLOUDS STRIKES - AND THE CRENATE CRUST OF COCONINO COUNTY - CREAKS.
ZIP
TOO BAD TOO BAD, MY "LITTLE PET LIGHTNING ROD" WOULD HAVE SAVED IT -
THAT'S GOOD.
MY LITTLE "PET" WOULD HAVE SAVED THAT KAT'S NOODLE.
YOU - "MOUSE"?
NO, "KOP" - I DID NOT.
MY LITTLE "PET" WOULD HAVE SAVED IT.
GOODY-
MY LITTLE "PET" ETC-
MY LITTLE "PET LIGHTNING ROD" WOULD HAVE SAVED HIM, SIR.
OH, YEH, AND WHO WANTS TO SAVE A "MOUSE"? - AND HAVE YOU GOT A LICENSE TO PEDDLE THAT "ROD"? -
GOODNESS ME, DO I HAVE TO HAVE A LICENSE TO SELL MY LITTLE "PET"?
Y'DERN TOOTIN' Y'DO OR THIS "MOUSE" WILL HAVE "COMPANY" IN THE KLINK TO DAY -
MY LITTLE "PET" WOULD HAVE SAVED IT — HEH-HEH-HEH-
JAIL
Copr 1939, King Features Syndicate, Inc., World rights reserved
HERRIMAN
11-19

November 19th, 1939.

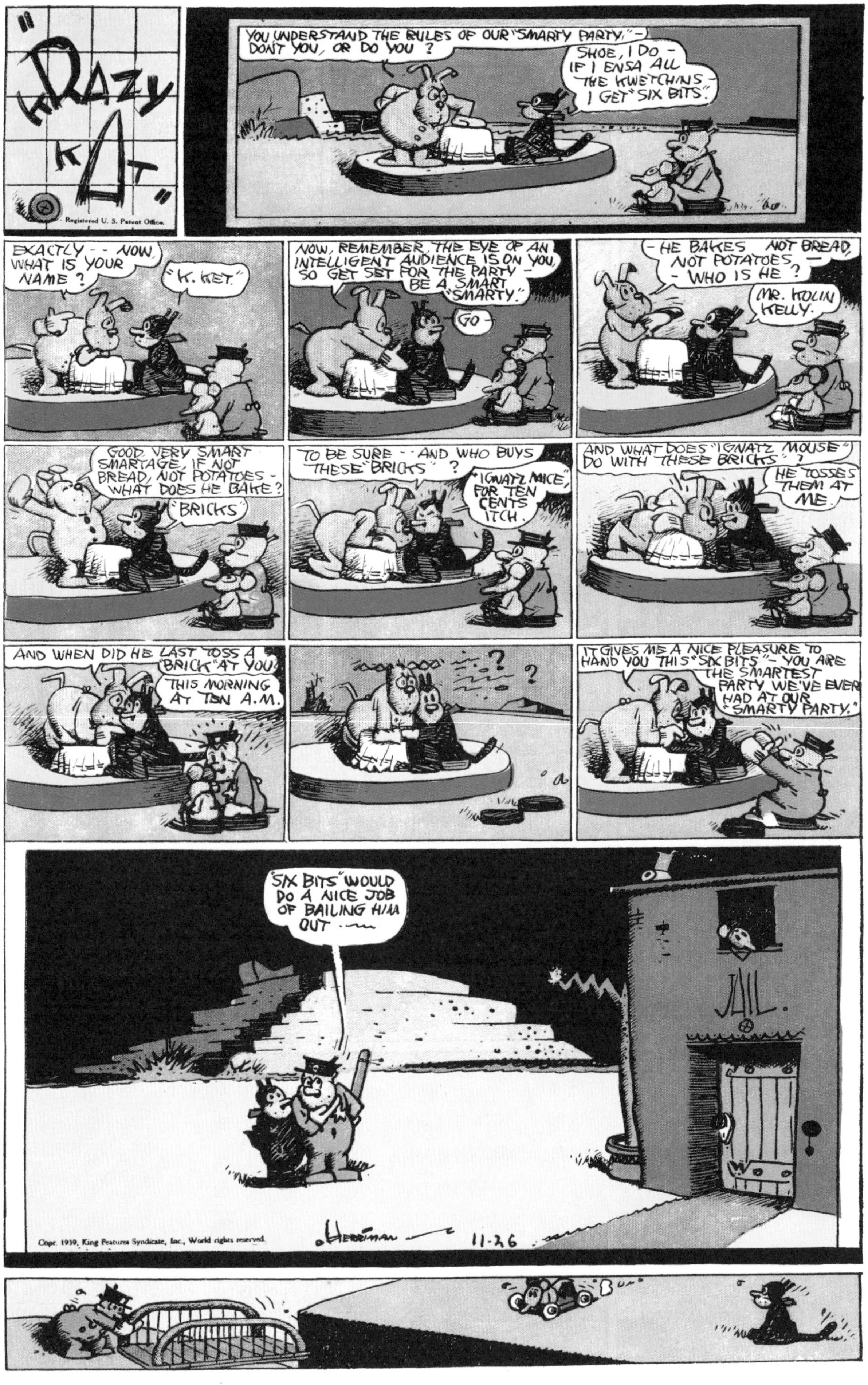
"KRAZY KAT"
Registered U. S. Patent Office.
YOU UNDERSTAND THE RULES OF OUR "SMARTY PARTY," — DON'T YOU, OR DO YOU ?
SHOE, I DO — IF I ENSA ALL THE KWETCHINS — I GET "SIX BITS".
EXACTLY — — NOW, WHAT IS YOUR NAME ?
"K. KET."
NOW, REMEMBER, THE EYE OF AN INTELLIGENT AUDIENCE IS ON YOU, SO GET SET FOR THE PARTY — BE A SMART "SMARTY."
GO —
— HE BAKES NOT BREAD, NOT POTATOES, — — WHO IS HE ?
MR. KOLIN KELLY.
GOOD, VERY SMART SMARTAGE, IF NOT BREAD, NOT POTATOES — WHAT DOES HE BAKE ?
"BRICKS"
TO BE SURE — — AND WHO BUYS THESE "BRICKS" ?
"IGNATZ MICE," FOR TEN CENTS ITCH.
AND WHAT DOES "IGNATZ MOUSE" DO WITH THESE BRICKS ?
HE TOSSES THEM AT ME.
AND WHEN DID HE LAST TOSS A "BRICK" AT YOU ?
THIS MORNING AT TEN A.M.
? ?
IT GIVES ME A NICE PLEASURE TO HAND YOU THIS "SIX BITS" — YOU ARE THE SMARTEST PARTY WE'VE EVER HAD AT OUR "SMARTY PARTY."
"SIX BITS" WOULD DO A NICE JOB OF BAILING HIM OUT —
JAIL.
Copr. 1939, King Features Syndicate, Inc., World rights reserved.
Herriman
11-26

November 26th, 1939.

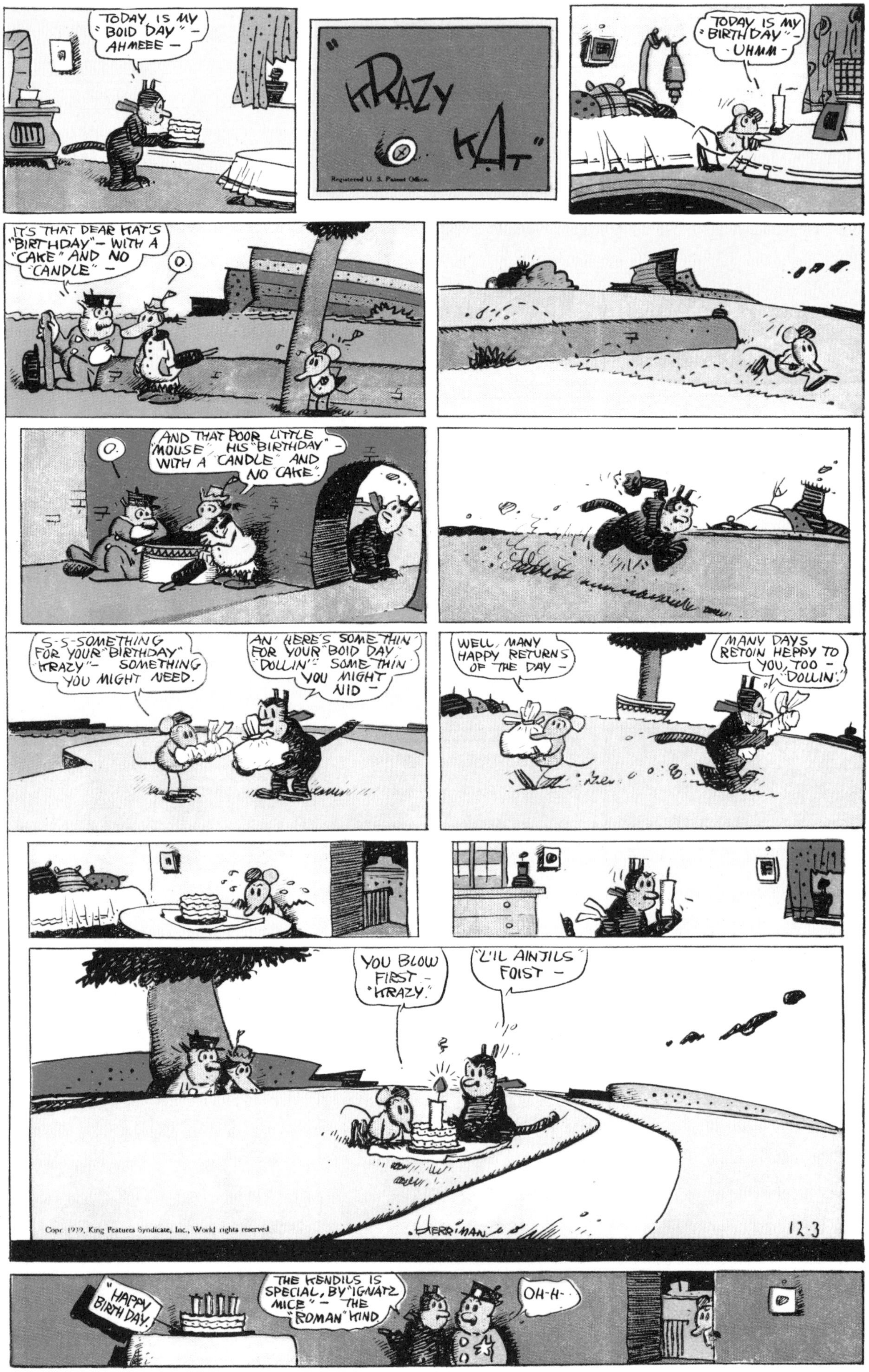
TODAY IS MY BOID DAY" — AHMEEE —
"KRAZY KAT"
Registered U. S. Patent Office.
"TODAY IS MY BIRTHDAY" — UHMM —
IT'S THAT DEAR KAT'S "BIRTHDAY" — WITH A "CAKE" AND NO "CANDLE" —
O.
O.
AND THAT POOR LITTLE "MOUSE" HIS "BIRTHDAY" — WITH A "CANDLE" AND NO "CAKE".
S-S-SOMETHING FOR YOUR "BIRTHDAY" "KRAZY" — SOMETHING YOU MIGHT NEED.
AN' HERE'S SOME THIN FOR YOUR "BOID DAY" "DOLLIN'" — SOME THIN YOU MIGHT NID —
WELL, MANY HAPPY RETURNS OF THE DAY —
MANY DAYS RETOIN HEPPY TO YOU, TOO — "DOLLIN'."
YOU BLOW FIRST — "KRAZY."
"L'IL AINJILS" FOIST —
Copr. 1939, King Features Syndicate, Inc., World rights reserved
HERRIMAN
12-3
"HAPPY BIRTHDAY."
THE KENDILS IS SPECIAL, BY "IGNATZ MICE" — THE "ROMAN" KIND
OH-H-

December 3rd, 1939.

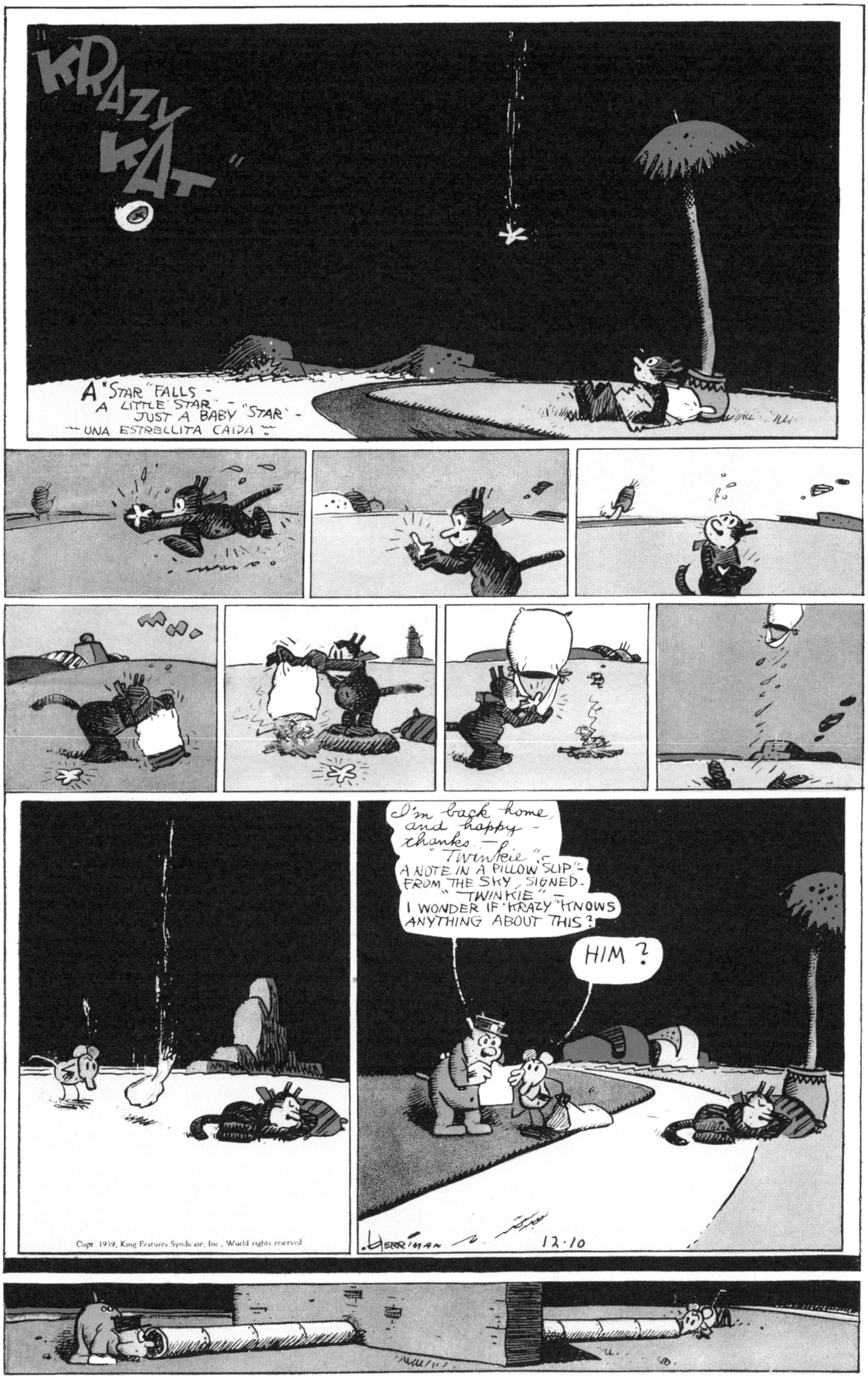
KRAZY KAT
A "STAR" FALLS -
A LITTLE 'STAR' -
JUST A BABY "STAR" -
UNA ESTRELLITA CAIDA
I'm back home, and happy - thanks - "Twinkie".
A NOTE IN A PILLOW 'SLIP' - FROM THE SKY, SIGNED - "TWINKIE" - I WONDER IF 'KRAZY' KNOWS ANYTHING ABOUT THIS?
HIM?
Copr 1939, King Features Syndicate, Inc., World rights reserved
HERRIMAN
12-10

December 10th, 1939.

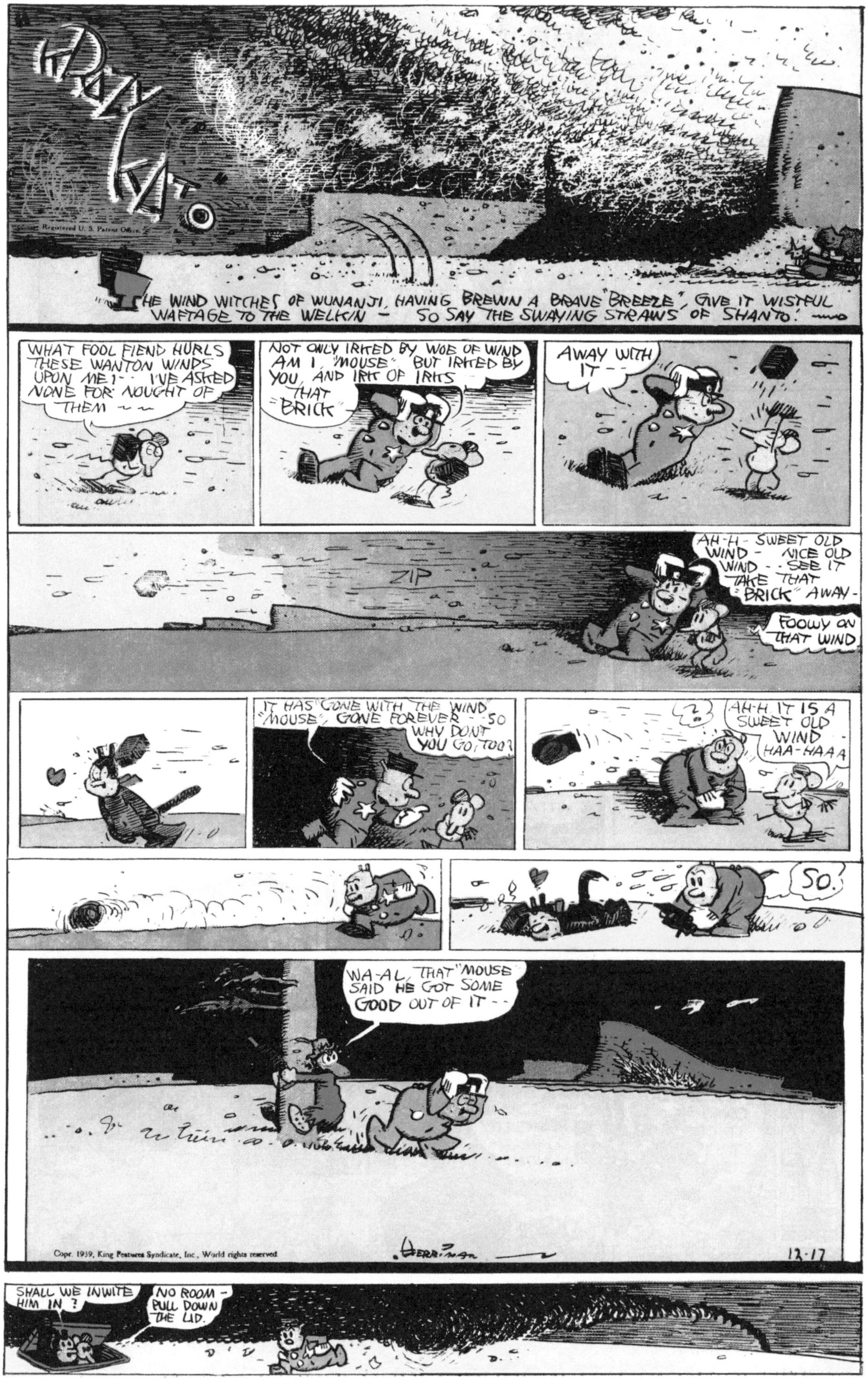
Krazy Kat
Registered U.S. Patent Office.
"The wind witches of Wunanji, having brewn a brave "breeze", give it wistful waftage to the welkin - so say the swaying strains of Shanto."
What fool fiend hurls these wanton winds upon me!- I've asked none for nought of them ~~
Not only irked by woe of wind am I, "Mouse" but irked by you, and irk of irks - that - brick -
Away with it - -
Zip
Ah-h - sweet old wind - nice old wind - - see it take that "brick" away -
Foowy on that wind
It has "gone with the wind" "mouse", gone forever - so why dont you go, too?
?
Ah-h it is a sweet old wind haa-haaa
So.
Wa-al, that "mouse" said he got some good out of it - -
Copr. 1939, King Features Syndicate, Inc., World rights reserved.
Herriman
12-17
Shall we inwite him in?
No room - pull down the lid.

December 17th, 1939.

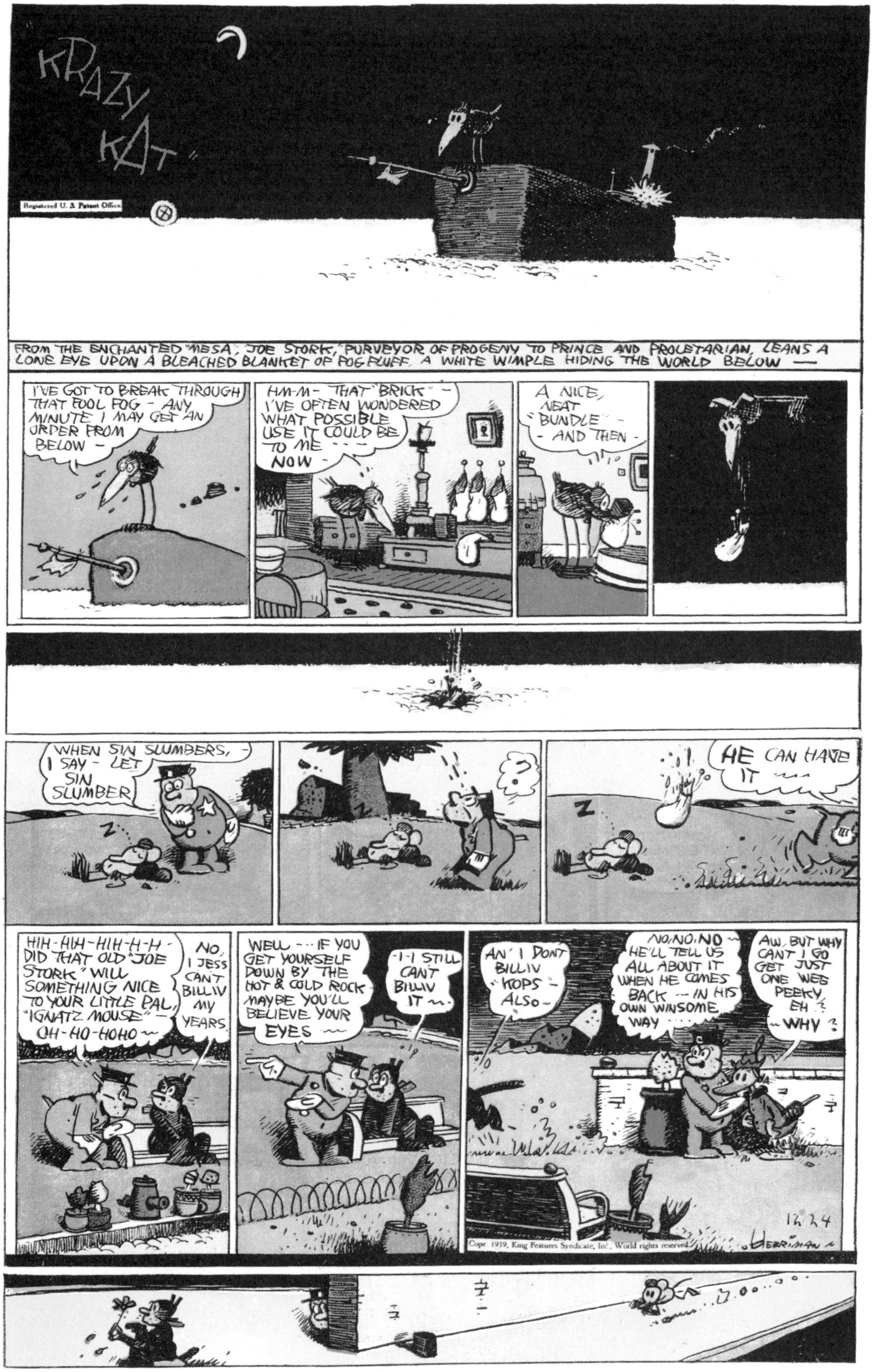
KRAZY KAT
Registered U. S. Patent Office
FROM THE ENCHANTED "MESA", "JOE STORK," PURVEYOR OF PROGENY TO PRINCE AND PROLETARIAN, LEANS A LONE EYE UPON A BLEACHED BLANKET OF FOG FLUFF. A WHITE WIMPLE HIDING THE WORLD BELOW —
I'VE GOT TO BREAK THROUGH THAT FOOL FOG - ANY MINUTE I MAY GET AN ORDER FROM BELOW -
HM-M - THAT "BRICK" - I'VE OFTEN WONDERED WHAT POSSIBLE USE IT COULD BE TO ME - - - NOW -
A NICE, NEAT "BUNDLE" - - AND THEN -
WHEN SIN SLUMBERS, - I SAY - LET SIN SLUMBER
HE CAN HAVE IT
HIH - HIH - HIH - H - H - DID THAT OLD "JOE STORK" WILL SOMETHING NICE TO YOUR LITTLE PAL, "IGNATZ MOUSE" - OH - HO - HOHO
NO, I JESS CAN'T BILLIV MY YEARS.
WELL - - - IF YOU GET YOURSELF DOWN BY THE HOT & COLD ROCK - MAYBE YOU'LL BELIEVE YOUR EYES
- I - I STILL CAN'T BILLIV IT
AN' I DONT BILLIV "KOPS" - ALSO
NO, NO, NO - HE'LL TELL US ALL ABOUT IT WHEN HE COMES BACK - - IN HIS OWN WINSOME WAY . . . .
AW, BUT WHY CANT I GO GET JUST ONE WEE PEEKY, EH ? - WHY ?
12.24
Copr. 1939, King Features Syndicate, Inc., World rights reserved.
HERRIMAN

December 24th, 1939.

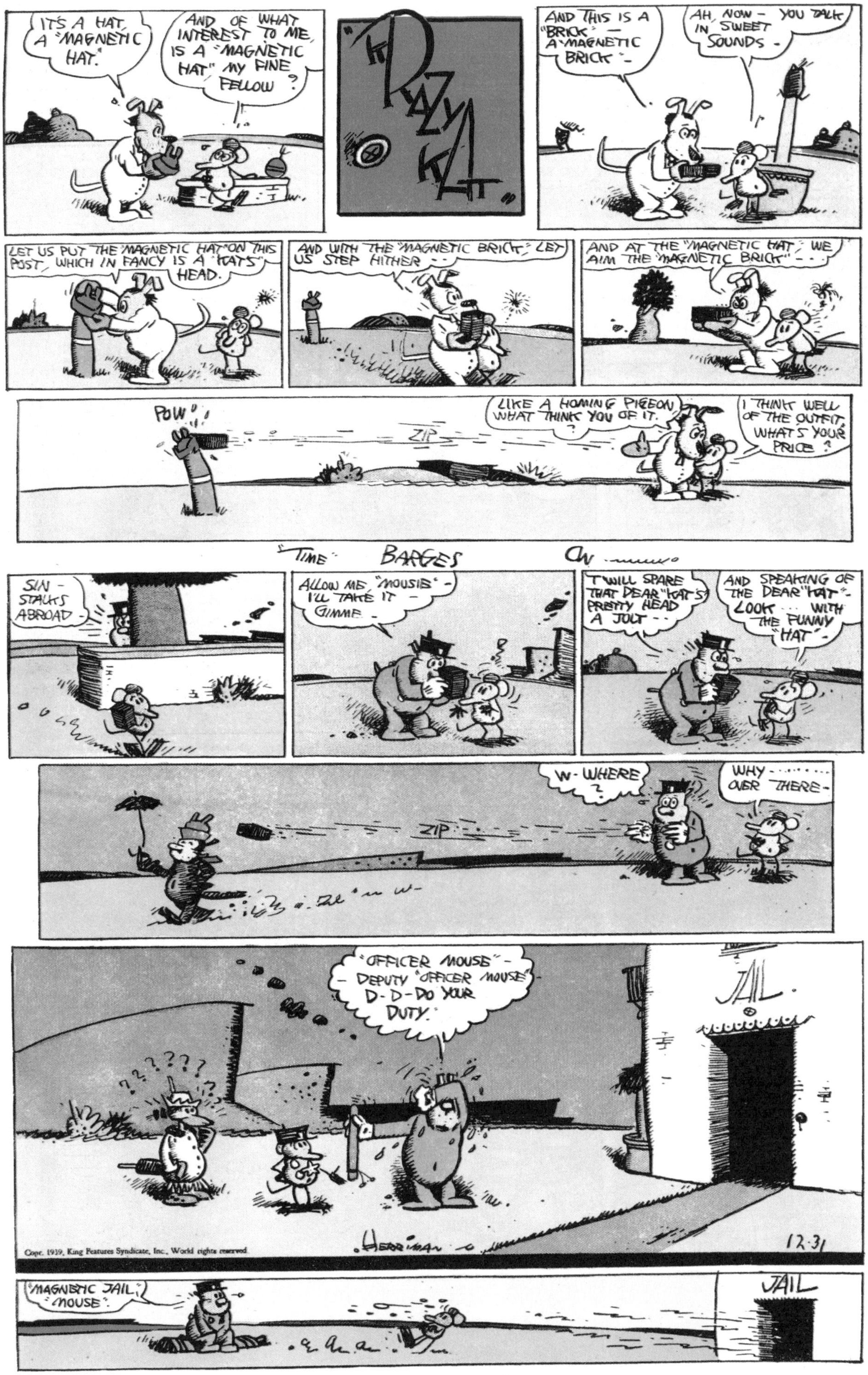

IT'S A HAT, A "MAGNETIC HAT."
AND OF WHAT INTEREST TO ME, IS A "MAGNETIC HAT" MY FINE FELLOW ?
"KRAZY KAT"
AND THIS IS A "BRICK" — A MAGNETIC BRICK —
AH, NOW — YOU TALK IN SWEET SOUNDS —
LET US PUT THE "MAGNETIC HAT" ON THIS POST, WHICH IN FANCY IS A "KATS" HEAD.
AND WITH THE "MAGNETIC BRICK" LET US STEP HITHER — —
AND AT THE "MAGNETIC HAT" WE AIM THE "MAGNETIC BRICK" — —
POW !!
ZIP
LIKE A HOMING PIGEON WHAT THINK YOU OF IT ?
I THINK WELL OF THE OUTFIT, WHAT'S YOUR PRICE ?
"TIME" BARGES ON
SIN — STALKS ABROAD —
ALLOW ME, "MOUSIE" — I'LL TAKE IT — GIMME —
T'WILL SPARE THAT DEAR "KAT'S" PRETTY HEAD A JOLT — —
AND SPEAKING OF THE DEAR "KAT" — LOOK … WITH THE FUNNY "HAT" —
W-WHERE ?
WHY — OVER THERE —
ZIP
"OFFICER MOUSE" — DEPUTY "OFFICER MOUSE" D-D-DO YOUR DUTY.
JAIL
HERRIMAN
12-31
"MAGNETIC JAIL" "MOUSE".
JAIL

December 31st, 1939.

1940.

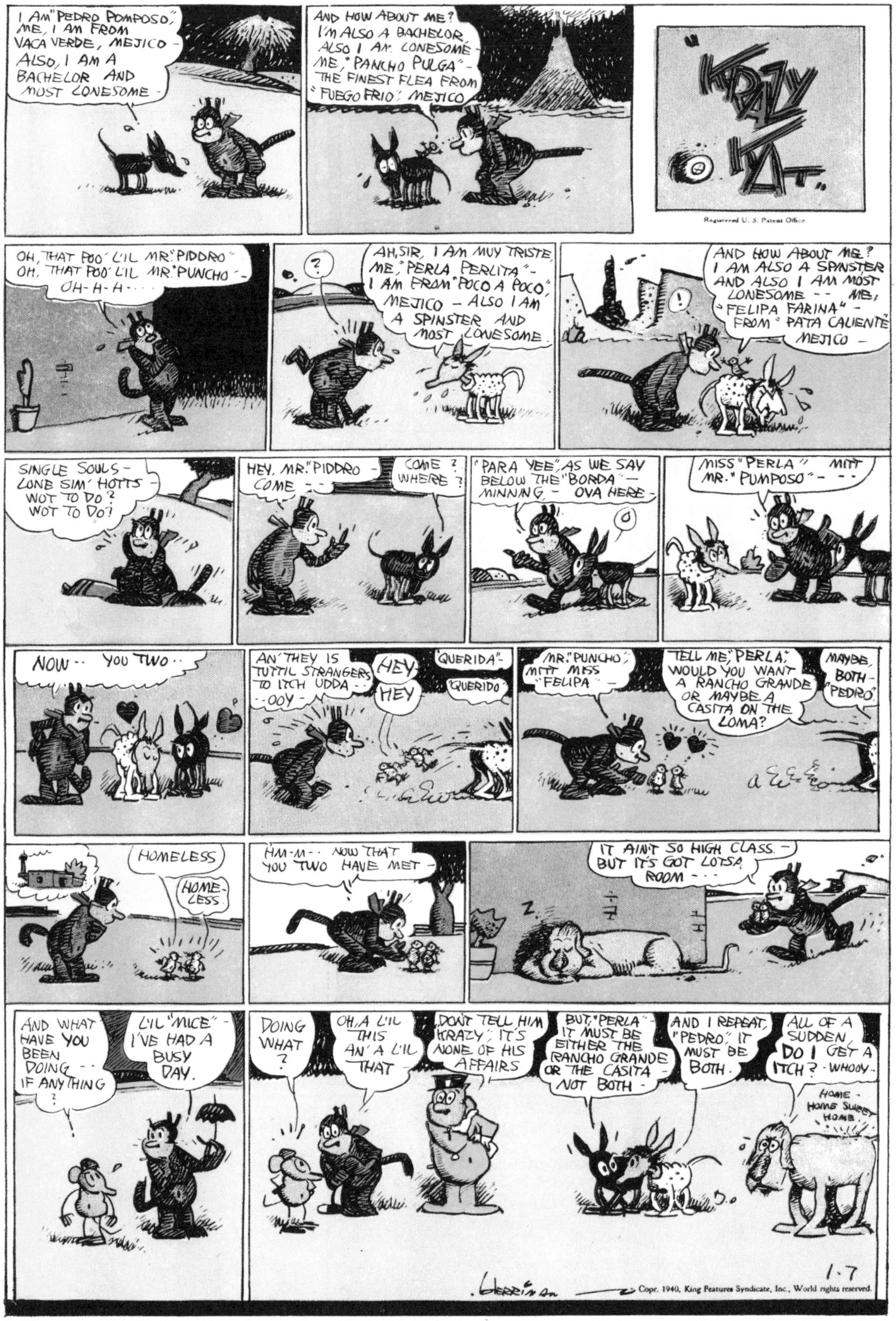

I AM "PEDRO POMPOSO", ME, I AM FROM VACA VERDE, MEJICO - ALSO, I AM A BACHELOR AND MOST LONESOME -
AND HOW ABOUT ME? I'M ALSO A BACHELOR, ALSO I AM CONESOME - ME, "PANCHO PULGA" - THE FINEST FLEA FROM "FUEGO FRIO", MEJICO
"KRAZY KAT"
Registered U. S. Patent Office
OH, THAT POO' L'IL MR. "PIDDRO" OH, THAT POO' L'IL MR. "PUNCHO" - OH-H-H
?
AH, SIR, I AM MUY TRISTE ME, "PERLA PERLITA" - I AM FROM "POCO A POCO", MEJICO - ALSO I AM A SPINSTER AND MOST LONESOME
!
AND HOW ABOUT ME? I AM ALSO A SPINSTER AND ALSO I AM MOST LONESOME -- ME, "FELIPA FARINA" - FROM "PATA CALIENTE" MEJICO -
SINGLE SOULS - LONE SIM' HOTTS - WOT TO DO? WOT TO DO?
HEY, MR. "PIDDRO" - COME - - -
COME? WHERE?
"PARA YEE", AS WE SAY BELOW THE "BORDA" - MINNING, - OVA HERE -
MISS "PERLA" MITT MR. "PUMPOSO" - - -
NOW -- YOU TWO --
AN' THEY IS TUTTIL STRANGERS TO ITCH UDDA - - OOY -
HEY HEY
"QUERIDA"
"QUERIDO"
MR. "PUNCHO", MITT MISS "FELIPA" -
TELL ME, "PERLA", WOULD YOU WANT A RANCHO GRANDE OR MAYBE A CASITA ON THE LOMA?
MAYBE, BOTH - "PEDRO"
HOMELESS
HOME-LESS
HM-M -- NOW THAT YOU TWO HAVE MET -
IT AIN'T SO HIGH CLASS. - BUT IT'S GOT LOTSA ROOM - - -
AND WHAT HAVE YOU BEEN DOING -- IF ANYTHING?
L'IL "MICE" - I'VE HAD A BUSY DAY.
DOING WHAT?
OH, A L'IL THIS AN' A L'IL THAT -
DON'T TELL HIM KRAZY, IT'S NONE OF HIS AFFAIRS
BUT, "PERLA" IT MUST BE EITHER THE RANCHO GRANDE OR THE CASITA - NOT BOTH -
AND I REPEAT, "PEDRO", IT MUST BE BOTH.
ALL OF A SUDDEN, DO I GET A ITCH? - WHOOY -
HOME - HOME SWEET HOME
1-7
Herriman
Copr. 1940, King Features Syndicate, Inc., World rights reserved.

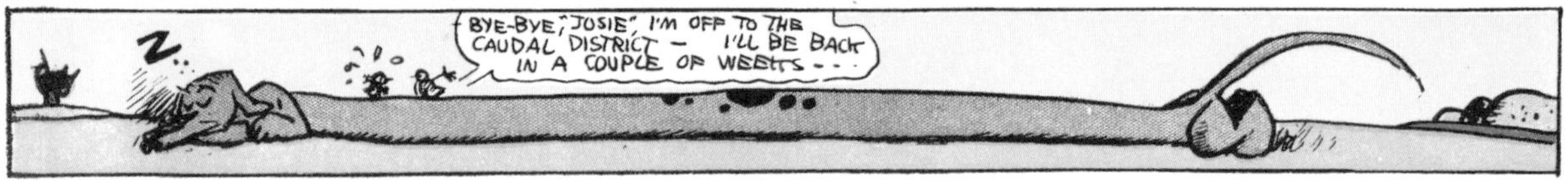

BYE-BYE, "JOSIE", I'M OFF TO THE CAUDAL DISTRICT - I'LL BE BACK IN A COUPLE OF WEEKS - - -

January 7th, 1940.

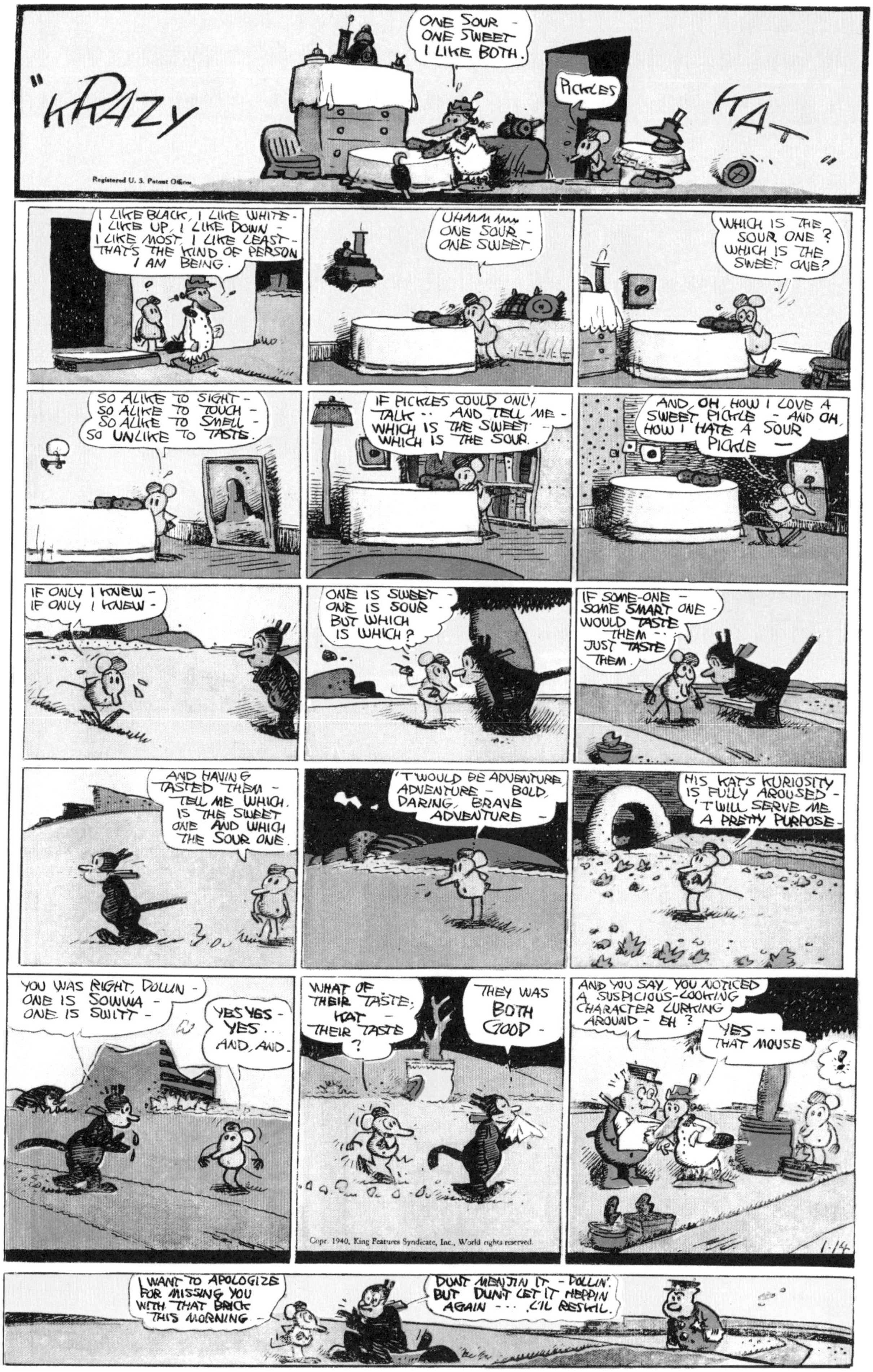
"KRAZY KAT"
Registered U. S. Patent Office
ONE SOUR - ONE SWEET I LIKE BOTH.
PICKLES
I LIKE BLACK, I LIKE WHITE - I LIKE UP, I LIKE DOWN - I LIKE MOST, I LIKE LEAST - THAT'S THE KIND OF PERSON I AM BEING.
UHMM MM - ONE SOUR - ONE SWEET.
WHICH IS THE SOUR ONE? WHICH IS THE SWEET ONE?
SO ALIKE TO SIGHT - SO ALIKE TO TOUCH - SO ALIKE TO SMELL - SO UNLIKE TO TASTE.
IF PICKLES COULD ONLY TALK -- AND TELL ME - WHICH IS THE SWEET WHICH IS THE SOUR.
AND, OH, HOW I LOVE A SWEET PICKLE - AND OH, HOW I HATE A SOUR PICKLE -
IF ONLY I KNEW - IF ONLY I KNEW -
ONE IS SWEET - ONE IS SOUR - BUT WHICH IS WHICH?
IF SOME-ONE - SOME SMART ONE WOULD TASTE THEM -- JUST TASTE THEM.
AND HAVING TASTED THEM - TELL ME WHICH IS THE SWEET ONE AND WHICH THE SOUR ONE
'TWOULD BE ADVENTURE - ADVENTURE - BOLD, DARING, BRAVE ADVENTURE -
HIS KAT'S KURIOSITY IS FULLY AROUSED - 'TWILL SERVE ME A PRETTY PURPOSE -
YOU WAS RIGHT, DOLLIN - ONE IS SOWWA - ONE IS SWITT -
YES YES - YES... AND, AND -
WHAT OF THEIR TASTE, KAT - THEIR TASTE?
THEY WAS BOTH GOOD -
AND YOU SAY, YOU NOTICED A SUSPICIOUS-LOOKING CHARACTER LURKING AROUND - EH?
YES - - THAT MOUSE
!
Copr. 1940, King Features Syndicate, Inc., World rights reserved.
1-14
I WANT TO APOLOGIZE FOR MISSING YOU WITH THAT BRICK THIS MORNING -
DUNT MENJIN IT - DOLLIN'. BUT DUNT LET IT HEPPIN AGAIN --- LIL RESKIL.

January 14th, 1940.

KRAZY KAT
Registered U. S. Patent Office.
FOR TONIGHT - - I YEMMA WINDOW - IN A RODDIDGE - BY A SEA -
?
"PAUSE MOUSE" PAUSE !!!
YOUR PRESENCE HERE IS QUITE UNDESIRABLE, MY FINE, FESTIVE FELLOW - QUITE
SEE YOU YON ROAD ?
HIT IT - PRONTO
AND GOOD-BYE -
AND IT COULD BE - FOR EVER - -
YES - FOR - EVER -
UH-HMM
F-FOR A LONG LONG TIME - ANY WAY -
YEH-H - -
HE MUST BE AT A SAFE DISTANCE BY N-N-NOW
AND I USED TO THINK THAT "CIRCULAR ROADS" NEVER TOOK YOU ANY PLACE -
Z
HERRIMAN
Copr. 1940, King Features Syndicate, Inc., World rights reserved. 1-21

WERE HORSES NATIVE TO AMERICA?
(ANSWER OPPOSITE)
CURTISS Butterfinger 5¢
CANDY IS DELICIOUS FOOD - ENJOY SOME EVERY DAY
IS RICH IN PURE DEXTROSE THE SUGAR YOUR BODY USES DIRECTLY FOR ENERGY
ANSWER: NO...Brought here by Spanish explorers

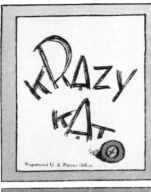

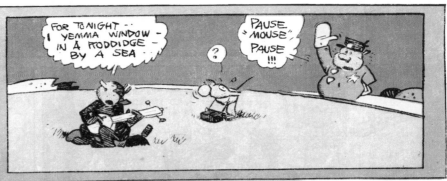

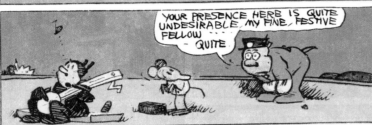

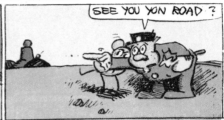

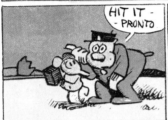

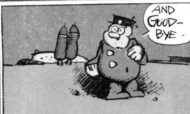

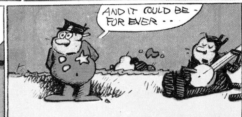

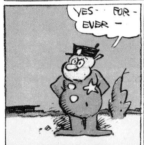

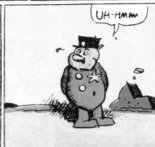

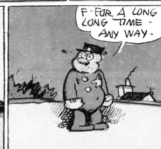

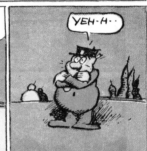

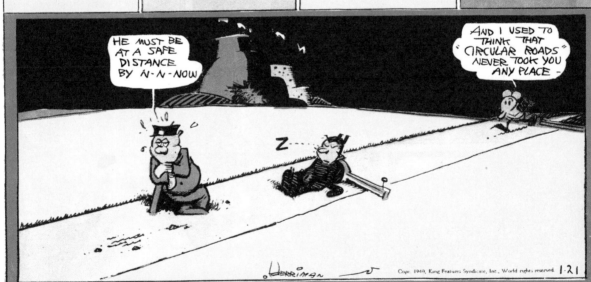

January 21st, 1940.

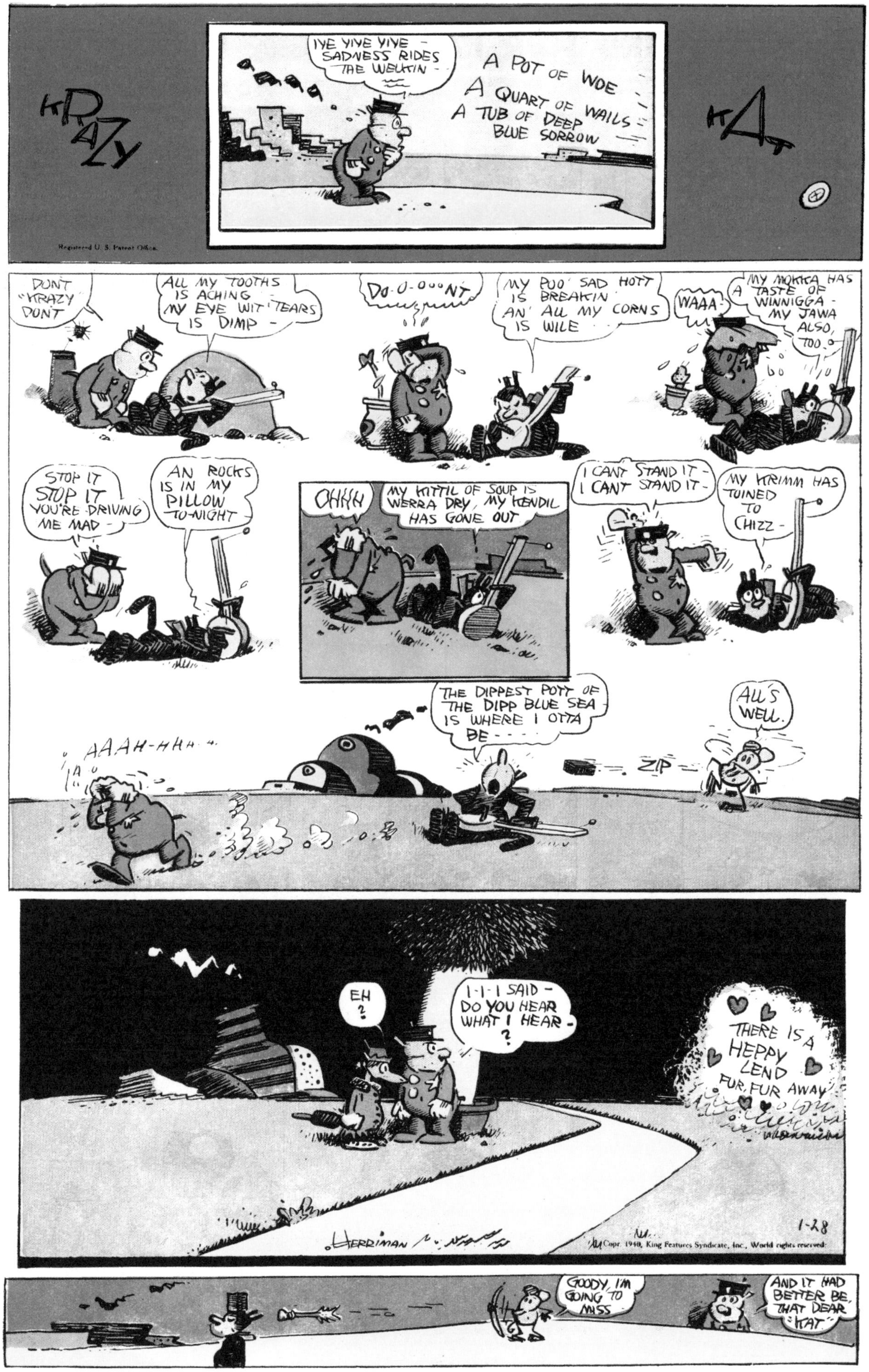
KRAZY KAT
IYE YIYE YIYE - SADNESS RIDES THE WELKIN -
A POT OF WOE A QUART OF WAILS A TUB OF DEEP BLUE SORROW
Registered U.S. Patent Office.
DONT "KRAZY" DONT
ALL MY TOOTHS IS ACHING MY EYE WIT TEARS IS DIMP -
DO-O-OOONT
MY POO' SAD HOTT IS BREAKIN AN' ALL MY CORNS IS WILE -
WAAA
MY MOKKA HAS A TASTE OF WINNIGGA - MY JAWA ALSO, TOO.
STOP IT STOP IT YOU'RE DRIVING ME MAD -
AN ROCKS IS IN MY PILLOW TO-NIGHT
OHHH
MY KITTIL OF SOUP IS WERRA DRY, MY KENDIL HAS GONE OUT
I CAN'T STAND IT - I CANT STAND IT -
MY KRIMM HAS TUINED TO CHIZZ -
AAAH-HHA
THE DIPPEST POTT OF THE DIPP BLUE SEA IS WHERE I OTTA BE - - -
ZIP
ALL'S WELL.
EH ?
I-I-I SAID - DO YOU HEAR WHAT I HEAR - ?
THERE IS A HEPPY LEND FUR, FUR AWAY
HERRIMAN
1-28
Copr. 1940, King Features Syndicate, Inc., World rights reserved.
GOODY, I'M GOING TO MISS
AND IT HAD BETTER BE, THAT DEAR KAT.

January 28th, 1940.

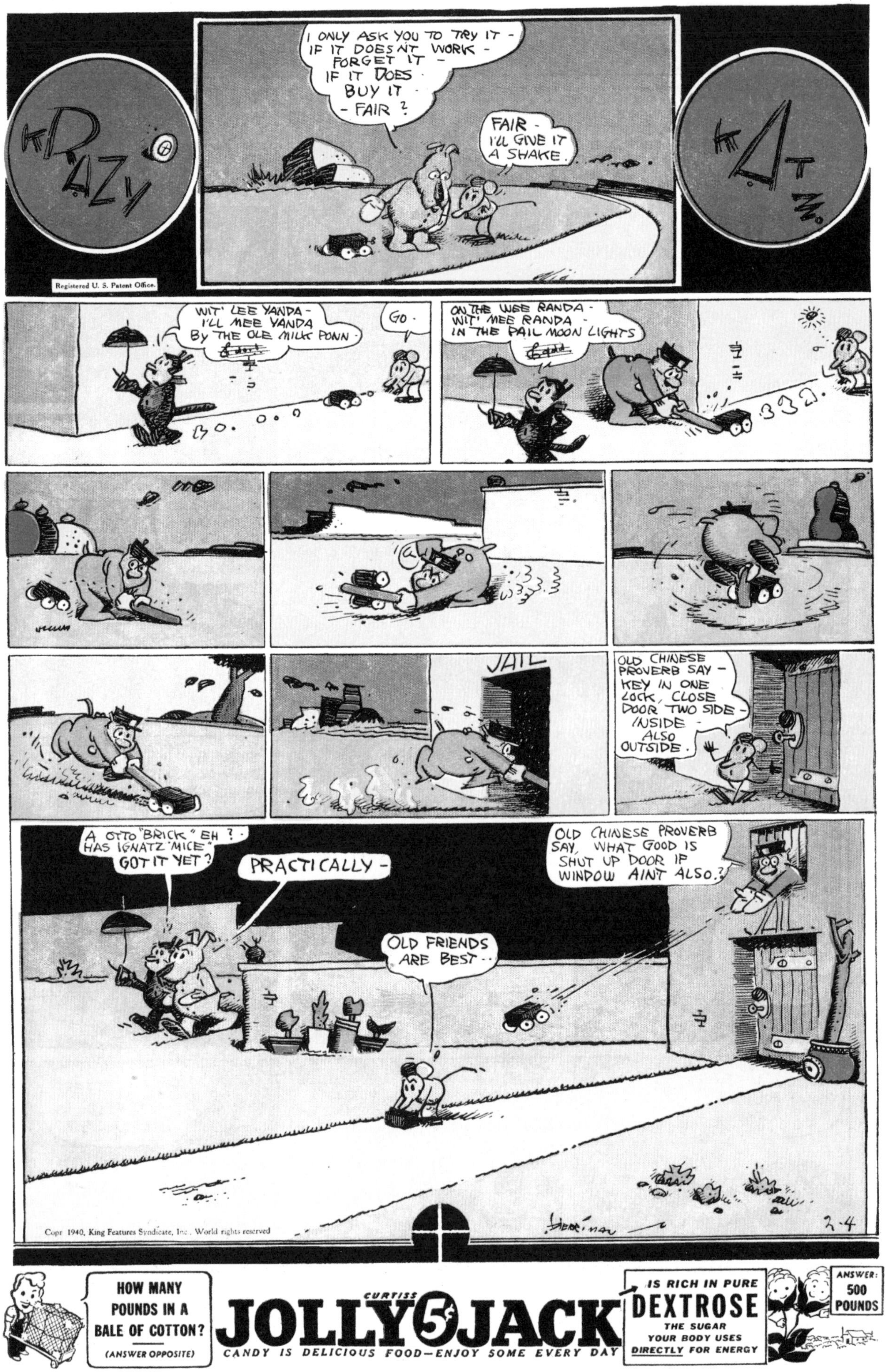

KRAZY
KAT
I ONLY ASK YOU TO TRY IT - IF IT DOES'NT WORK - FORGET IT - IF IT DOES BUY IT - FAIR ?
FAIR - I'LL GIVE IT A SHAKE.
Registered U. S. Patent Office.
WIT' LEE YANDA - I'LL MEE YANDA BY THE OLE MILK PONN -
GO -
ON THE WEE RANDA - WIT' MEE RANDA - IN THE PAIL MOON LIGHTS
JAIL
OLD CHINESE PROVERB SAY - KEY IN ONE LOCK, CLOSE DOOR TWO SIDE - INSIDE - ALSO OUTSIDE.
A OTTO "BRICK" EH ? - HAS IGNATZ "MICE" GOT IT YET ?
PRACTICALLY -
OLD CHINESE PROVERB SAY, WHAT GOOD IS SHUT UP DOOR IF WINDOW AINT ALSO. ?
OLD FRIENDS ARE BEST - -
Copr 1940, King Features Syndicate, Inc., World rights reserved
Herriman
2-4
HOW MANY POUNDS IN A BALE OF COTTON? (ANSWER OPPOSITE)
CURTISS JOLLY 5¢ JACK
CANDY IS DELICIOUS FOOD—ENJOY SOME EVERY DAY
IS RICH IN PURE DEXTROSE THE SUGAR YOUR BODY USES DIRECTLY FOR ENERGY
ANSWER: 500 POUNDS

February 4th, 1940.

KRAZY
KAT
"A HORNET APARTMENT HOUSE"
Registered U. S. Patent Office.
TREACHEROUS INSECTS - FAH-H · · NEXT TO MICE - I DISLIKE THEM EXCEEDINGLY · · FAH-H · · ·
AH · IT SEEMS THE CONSTABULARY OF COCONINO COUNTY IS UNDERGOING A MOMENT OF FEAR - WINGED TERROR - STING SCARE - HEH-HEH-HEH -
WHAT ARE YOU SNOOPING AROUND HERE FOR - HEH ? - - YOU SKULKING RASCAL -
COULD I HELP IT IF I SAW A HORNETS' NEST ? AND, I MIGHT ADD, A BRAVE KOP - - - AND - -
AND WHAT, POLTROON, AND WHAT ?
AND, COULD I HELP IT IF I HAPPENED TO NOTICE THAT THE BRAVE KOP QUIVERED A BIT, QUAKED A BIT, QUAILED A BIT ?
INSIPID OAF - HE SAW TOO MUCH - - - AND YET I CAN'T ARREST HIM FOR THAT -
I'LL FOLLOW HIM - - IF HE SO MUCH AS LOOKS AT A BRICK I'LL JAIL HIM - ON SUSPICION - - I'M STILL AHEAD OF HIM -
SOME DAY - - THERE'LL BE A LAW ABOUT HORNETS - - A DRASTIC LAW -
ZIP
Copr. 1940, King Features Syndicate, Inc., World rights reserved.
2-11
HERRIMAN
HEH-HEH-HEH - - WHAT QUAINT THINGS ONE CAN DO WITH SNOW -

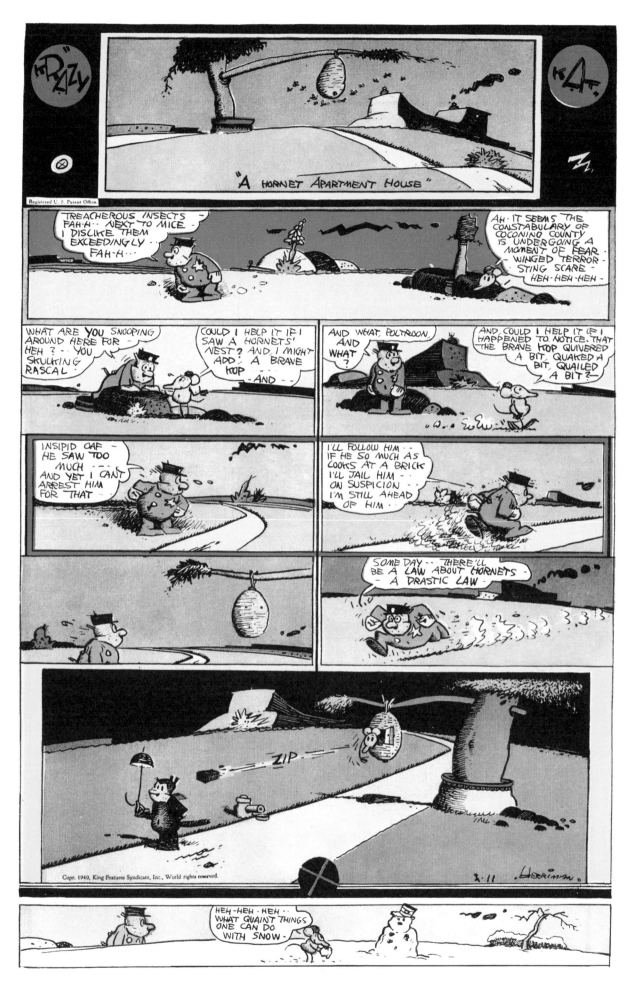

February 11th, 1940.

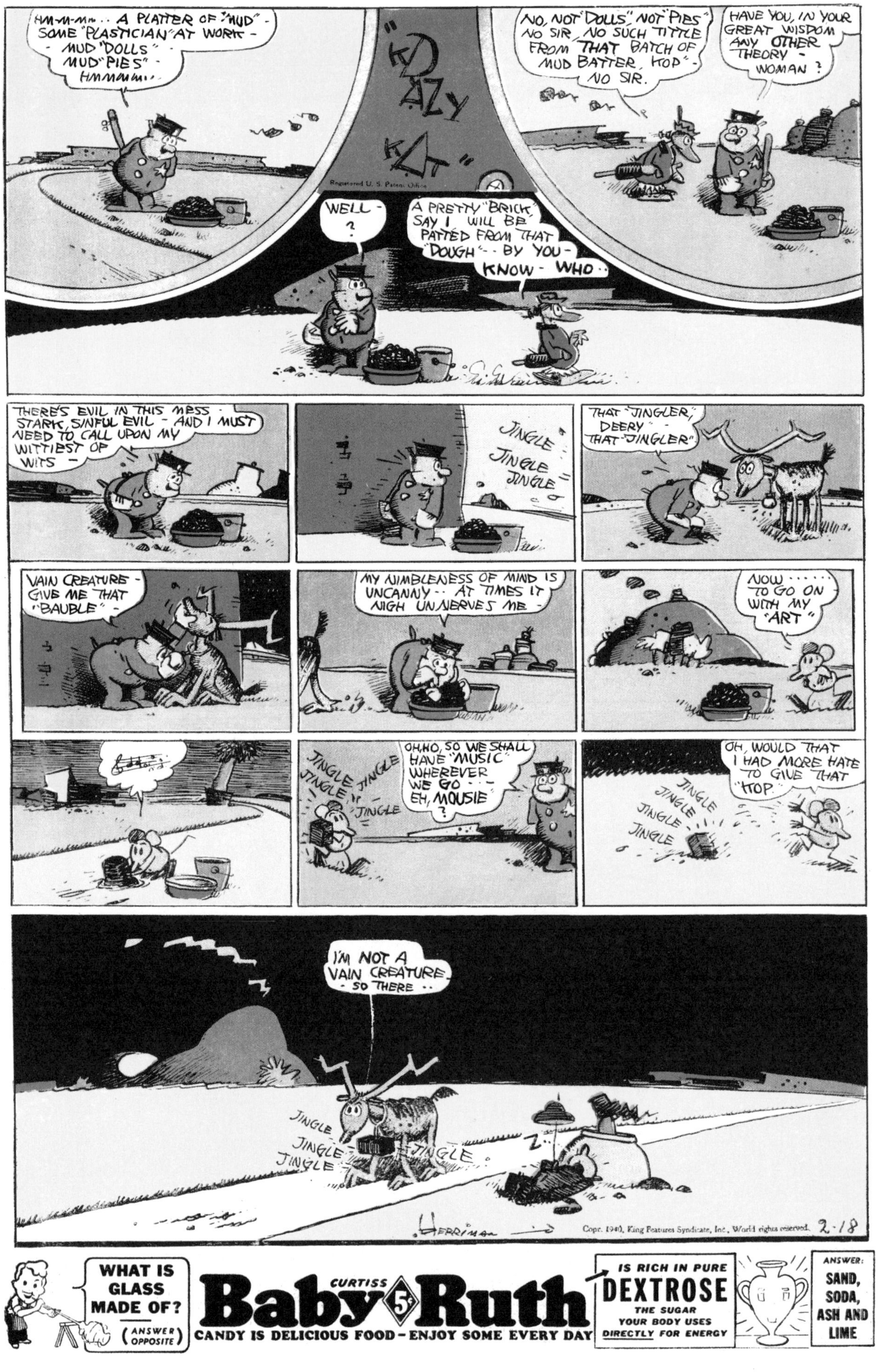

HM-M-M.. A PLATTER OF "MUD" - SOME "PLASTICIAN" AT WORK - - MUD "DOLLS" - MUD "PIES" - HMMMM..
"KRAZY KAT"
Registered U. S. Patent Office
NO, NOT "DOLLS", NOT "PIES" NO SIR, NO SUCH TITTLE FROM THAT BATCH OF MUD BATTER, KOP - NO SIR.
HAVE YOU, IN YOUR GREAT WISDOM ANY OTHER THEORY - WOMAN ?
WELL - ?
A PRETTY "BRICK", SAY I, WILL BE PATTED FROM THAT "DOUGH" - BY YOU-KNOW-WHO..
THERE'S EVIL IN THIS MESS - STARK, SINFUL EVIL - AND I MUST NEED TO CALL UPON MY WITTIEST OF WITS -
JINGLE JINGLE JINGLE
THAT "JINGLER", DEERY - THAT "JINGLER"
VAIN CREATURE - GIVE ME THAT "BAUBLE" -
MY NIMBLENESS OF MIND IS UNCANNY - AT TIMES IT NIGH UNNERVES ME -
NOW ..... TO GO ON WITH MY "ART"
JINGLE JINGLE JINGLE JINGLE
OH, HO, SO WE SHALL HAVE "MUSIC" WHEREVER WE GO - - EH, MOUSIE ?
OH, WOULD THAT I HAD MORE HATE TO GIVE THAT "KOP"
JINGLE JINGLE JINGLE JINGLE
I'M NOT A VAIN CREATURE - SO THERE -
JINGLE JINGLE JINGLE JINGLE
Z
HERRIMAN
Copr. 1940, King Features Syndicate, Inc., World rights reserved.
2-18
WHAT IS GLASS MADE OF?
(ANSWER OPPOSITE)
CURTISS Baby 5¢ Ruth
CANDY IS DELICIOUS FOOD - ENJOY SOME EVERY DAY
IS RICH IN PURE DEXTROSE
THE SUGAR YOUR BODY USES DIRECTLY FOR ENERGY
ANSWER: SAND, SODA, ASH AND LIME

February 18th, 1940.

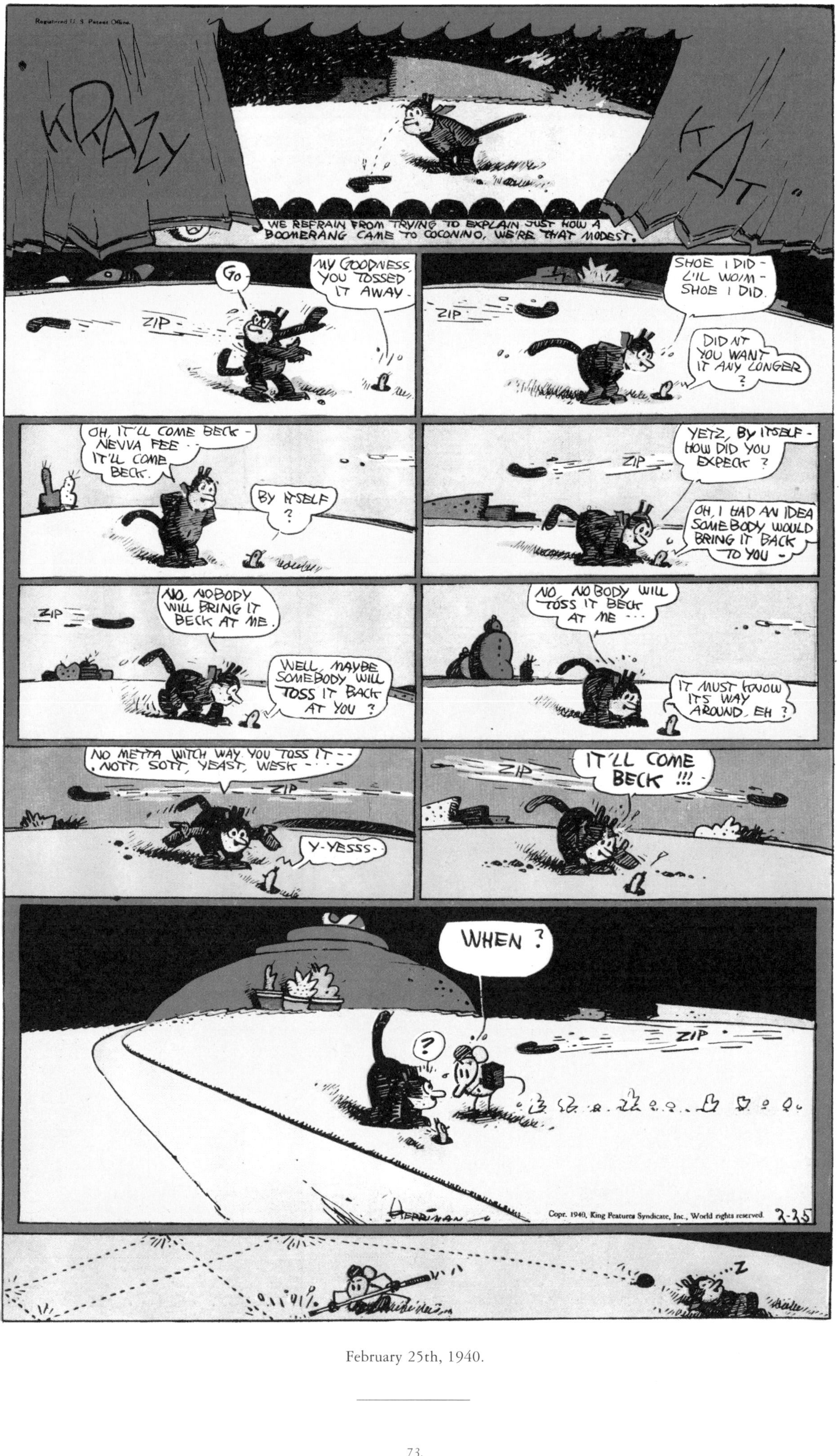
Registered U. S. Patent Office.
KRAZY
KAT
WE REFRAIN FROM TRYING TO EXPLAIN JUST HOW A BOOMERANG CAME TO COCONINO, WE'RE THAT MODEST.
GO-
ZIP
MY GOODNESS YOU TOSSED IT AWAY.
ZIP
SHOE I DID - L'IL WOIM - SHOE I DID.
DIDN'T YOU WANT IT ANY LONGER ?
OH, IT'LL COME BECK - NEVVA FEE - IT'LL COME BECK.
BY ITSELF ?
ZIP
YETZ, BY ITSELF - HOW DID YOU EXPECK ?
OH, I HAD AN IDEA SOMEBODY WOULD BRING IT BACK TO YOU -
ZIP
NO, NOBODY WILL BRING IT BECK AT ME.
WELL, MAYBE SOMEBODY WILL TOSS IT BACK AT YOU ?
NO, NOBODY WILL TOSS IT BECK AT ME ---
IT MUST KNOW ITS WAY AROUND, EH ?
NO METTA WITCH WAY YOU TOSS IT - NOTT, SOTT, YEAST, WESK -
ZIP
Y-YESSS -
ZIP
IT'LL COME BECK !!!
WHEN ?
?
ZIP
HERRIMAN
Copr. 1940, King Features Syndicate, Inc., World rights reserved.
2-25
Z

February 25th, 1940.

"KRAZY KAT"
WOULD A LITTLE TEENY WEENY LUMP OF MUD LIKE THIS HURT A "KAT'S" HEAD "KOP"?
N-NO-OOOO I THINK NOT--
Registered U. S. Patent Office.
GOOD, I HAVE HERE A DISH OF "MUD", WHICH REPRESENTS AN OLEAGINOUS AMPLITUDE OF "PELLETS" -
YES- YES- YES.
AND I'M JUST WONDERING IF IT WOULD MATTER MUCH TO YOU IF I PELTED THEM AT THAT DEAR "KAT" "KRAZY" -
SUCH MODEST PILLS - SO WEE, SO TINY - THEY WOULD BOUNCE WITH A PRETTY PATTER ON THAT SWEET "KAT'S" PATE GO RIGHT AHEAD.
A TOSS -- EVEN BIT BY BIT, SUCH AS THIS - WERE BETTER, INDEED, THAN NO TOSS AT ALL.
ERE YOU HAVE TOSSED THEM ALL, MOUSE, YOUR ARM WILL HAVE SWUNG ITSELF LAME - MUCH ADOING, NOTHING DONE - SAY I
YES, MY GOOD RIGHT WING WILL, NO DOUBT, UNDERGO A GREAT FATIGUE -- YET, WHAT ELSE TO DO? WHAT ELSE?
ONE "LUMP" ONE "TOSS" - IF YOU KNOW WHAT I MEAN -
IF YOU MEAN -- "CONCENTRATION" -
AND IT MIGHT EVEN BE PATTED INTO THE GENERAL SHAPE OF A "BRICK".
YETZ, MRS. KWEKK WEKK, ONE "TOSS" AS UJIL. WY?
AH-H--- MY ADVICE WAS NOT IN VAIN.
JAIL.
Copr. 1940, King Features Syndicate, Inc., World rights reserved.
3-3
PACKAGE FOR "IGNATZ MOUSE" PACKAGE FOR MR. "IGNATZ MOUSE"

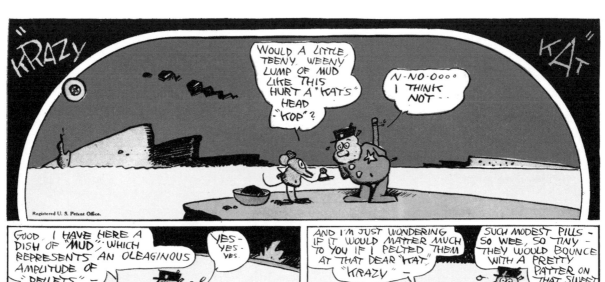

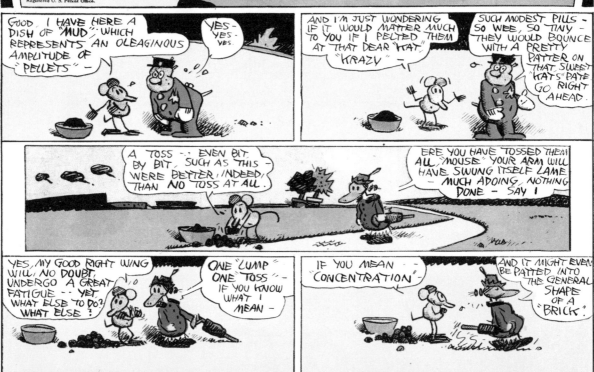

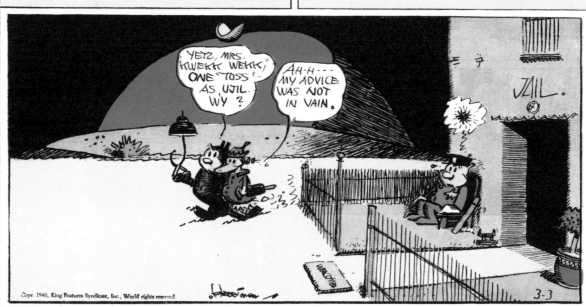

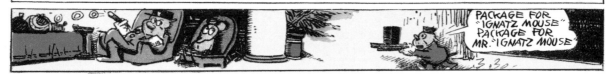

March 3rd, 1940.

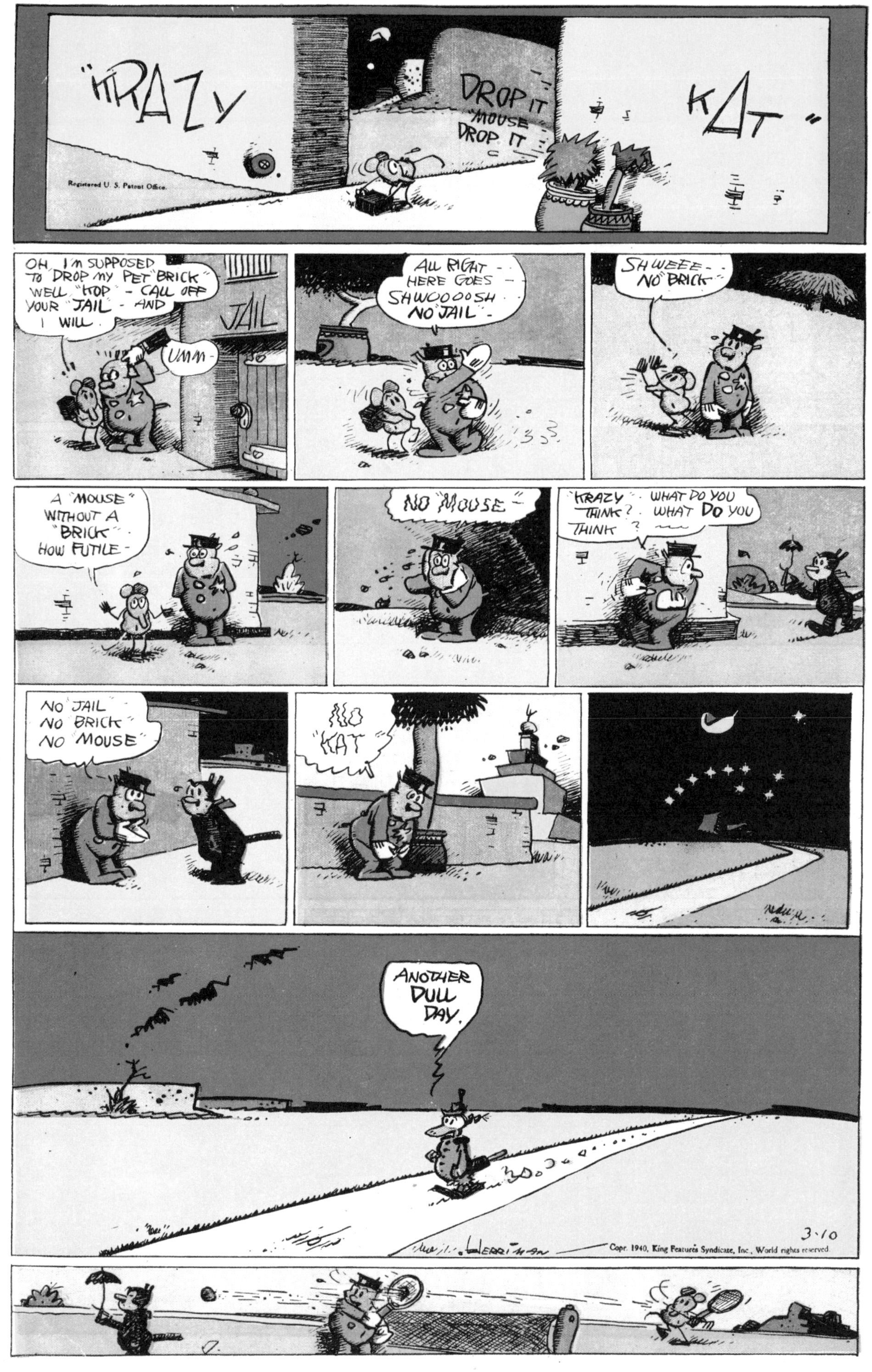
"KRAZY KAT"
DROP IT "MOUSE" DROP IT
Registered U. S. Patent Office.
OH, I'M SUPPOSED TO DROP MY PET BRICK WELL "STOP" - CALL OFF YOUR "JAIL" - AND I WILL.
JAIL
UMM-
ALL RIGHT - HERE GOES - SHWOOOOSH - NO JAIL -
SHWEEE - NO BRICK -
A "MOUSE" WITHOUT A "BRICK" HOW FUTILE -
NO "MOUSE"
"KRAZY" THINK? WHAT DO YOU THINK? WHAT DO YOU
NO JAIL - NO BRICK - NO MOUSE
NO KAT
ANOTHER DULL DAY.
3-10
HERRIMAN
Copr. 1940, King Features Syndicate, Inc., World rights reserved.

March 10th, 1940.

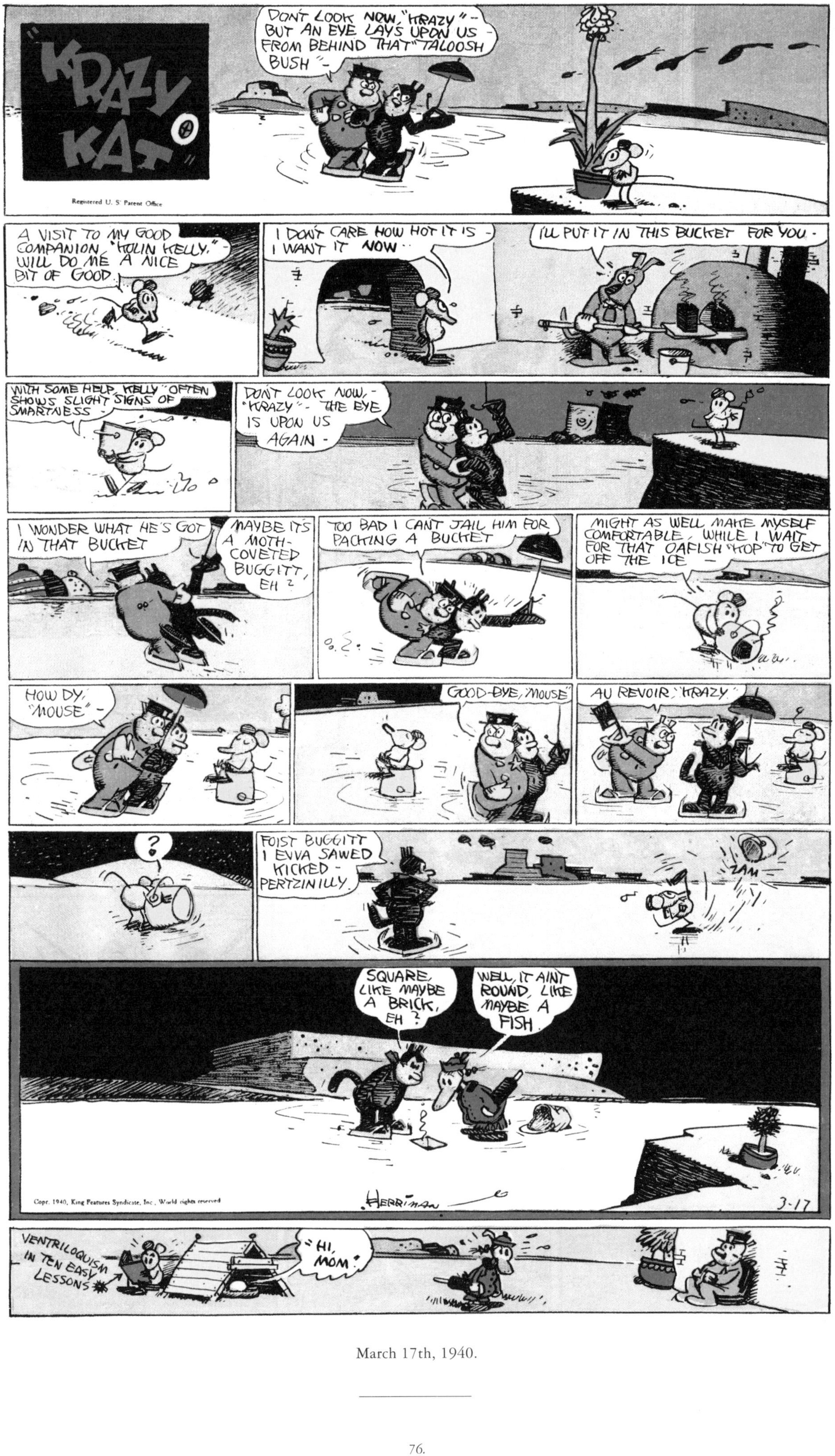
Krazy Kat
Registered U. S. Patent Office
DON'T LOOK NOW, "KRAZY" - BUT AN EYE LAYS UPON US - FROM BEHIND THAT "TALOOSH BUSH" -
A VISIT TO MY GOOD COMPANION, "KOLIN KELLY," WILL DO ME A NICE BIT OF GOOD.
I DON'T CARE HOW HOT IT IS - I WANT IT NOW -
I'LL PUT IT IN THIS BUCKET FOR YOU -
WITH SOME HELP, "KELLY" OFTEN SHOWS SLIGHT SIGNS OF SMARTNESS -
DON'T LOOK NOW, - "KRAZY" - THE EYE IS UPON US AGAIN -
I WONDER WHAT HE'S GOT IN THAT BUCKET
MAYBE IT'S A MOTH-COVETED BUGGITT, EH?
TOO BAD I CAN'T JAIL HIM FOR PACKING A BUCKET
MIGHT AS WELL MAKE MYSELF COMFORTABLE, WHILE I WAIT FOR THAT OAFISH "KOP" TO GET OFF THE ICE -
HOW DY, "MOUSE" -
GOOD-BYE, "MOUSE"
AU REVOIR, "KRAZY"
?
FOIST BUGGITT I EVVA SAWED KICKED - PERTZINILLY
ZAM
SQUARE, LIKE MAYBE A BRICK, EH?
WELL, IT AIN'T ROUND, LIKE MAYBE A FISH.
Copr. 1940, King Features Syndicate, Inc., World rights reserved
HERRIMAN
3-17
VENTRILOQUISM IN TEN EASY LESSONS
"HI, MOM!"

March 17th, 1940.

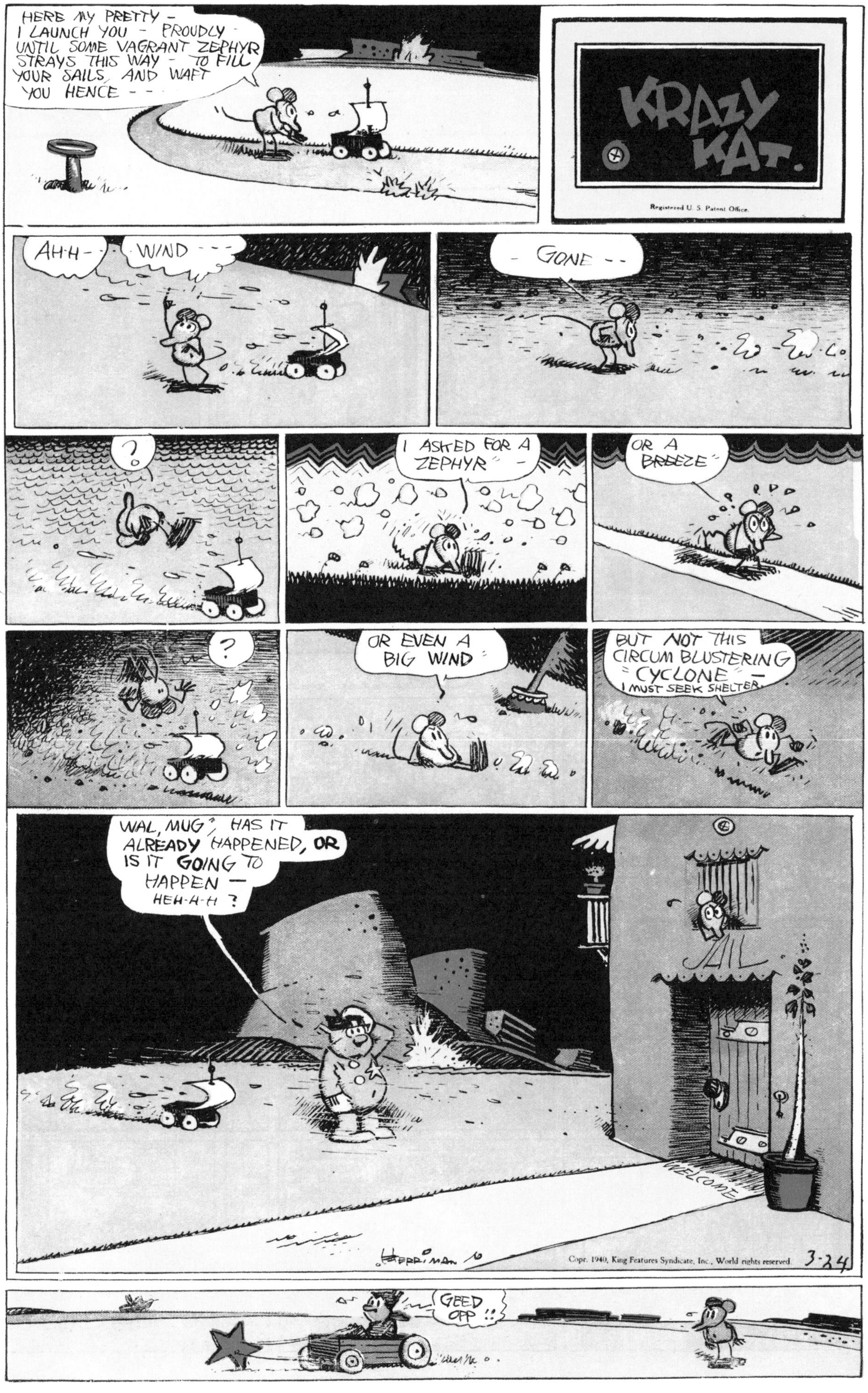
HERE MY PRETTY - I LAUNCH YOU - PROUDLY UNTIL SOME VAGRANT ZEPHYR STRAYS THIS WAY - TO FILL YOUR SAILS, AND WAFT YOU HENCE - - -
KRAZY KAT.
Registered U. S. Patent Office.
AH-H - -
WIND - - -
- GONE - -
?
I ASKED FOR A ZEPHYR -
OR A BREEZE
?
OR EVEN A BIG WIND
BUT NOT THIS CIRCUM BLUSTERING "CYCLONE" - I MUST SEEK SHELTER.
WAL, MUG, HAS IT ALREADY HAPPENED, OR IS IT GOING TO HAPPEN - HEH-A-H ?
WELCOME
HERRIMAN
Copr. 1940, King Features Syndicate, Inc., World rights reserved.
3-24
GEED OPP !!

March 24th, 1940.

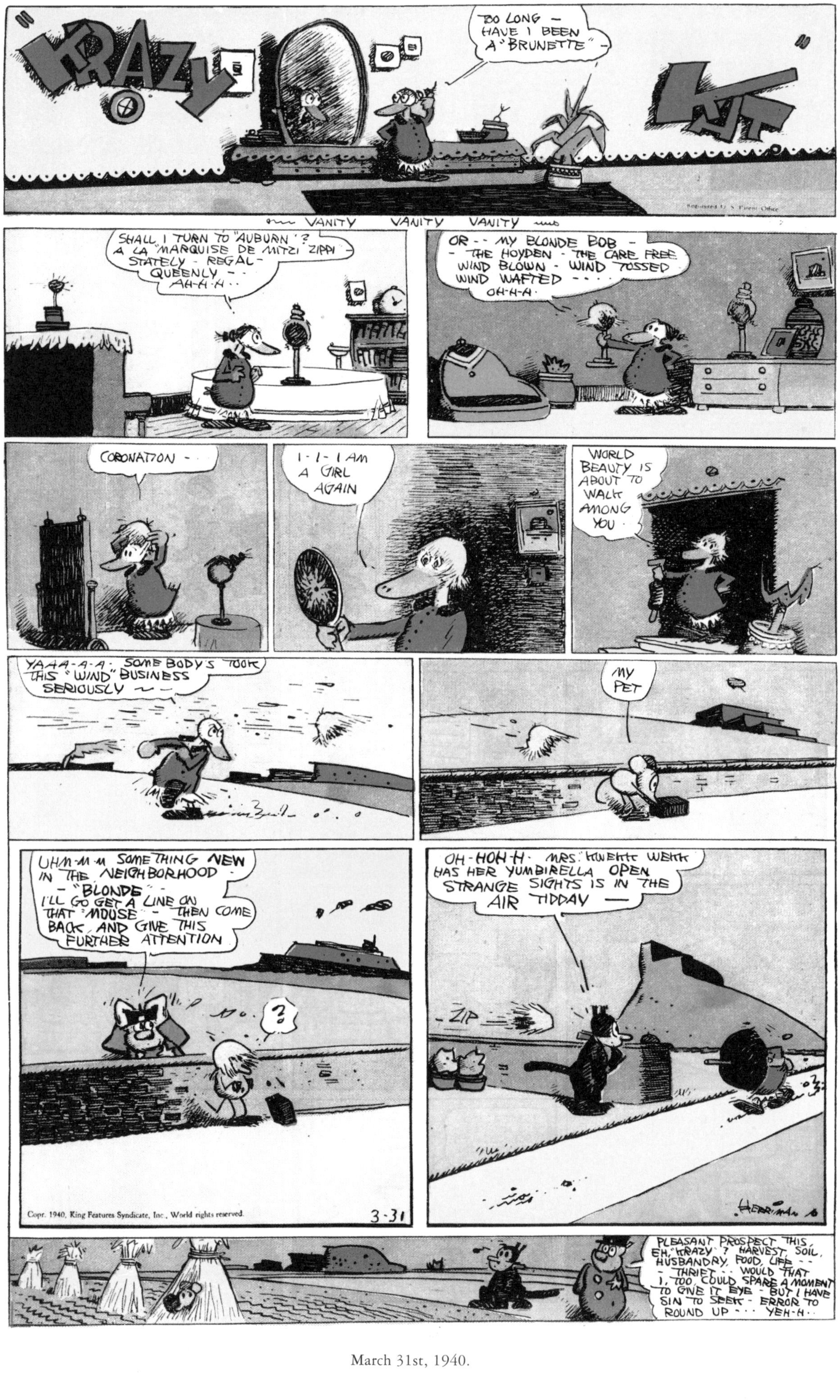
"KRAZY KAT"
TOO LONG - HAVE I BEEN A "BRUNETTE" -
Registered U. S. Patent Office
VANITY VANITY VANITY
SHALL I TURN TO "AUBURN" ? A LA "MARQUISE DE MITZI ZIPPI" - STATELY - REGAL - QUEENLY - - AH-H-H - -
OR - - MY BLONDE BOB - - THE HOYDEN - THE CARE FREE WIND BLOWN - WIND TOSSED WIND WAFTED - - - OH-H-H -
CORONATION - -
I - I - I AM A GIRL AGAIN
WORLD BEAUTY IS ABOUT TO WALK AMONG YOU -
YAAA-A-A - SOME BODY'S TOOK THIS "WIND" BUSINESS SERIOUSLY ~ ~
MY PET
UHM-M-M SOMETHING NEW IN THE NEIGHBORHOOD - - "BLONDE" - I'LL GO GET A LINE ON THAT MOUSE - THEN COME BACK AND GIVE THIS FURTHER ATTENTION
?
Copr. 1940, King Features Syndicate, Inc., World rights reserved.
3-31
OH-HOH-H - MRS. "KWEKK WEKK" HAS HER YUMBIRELLA OPEN STRANGE SIGHTS IS IN THE AIR TIDDAY —
ZIP
HERRIMAN
PLEASANT PROSPECT THIS, EH, "KRAZY" ? HARVEST, SOIL, HUSBANDRY, FOOD, LIFE - - - THRIFT - - WOULD THAT I, TOO, COULD SPARE A MOMENT TO GIVE IT EYE - BUT I HAVE SIN TO SEEK - ERROR TO ROUND UP - - - YEH-H - -

March 31st, 1940.

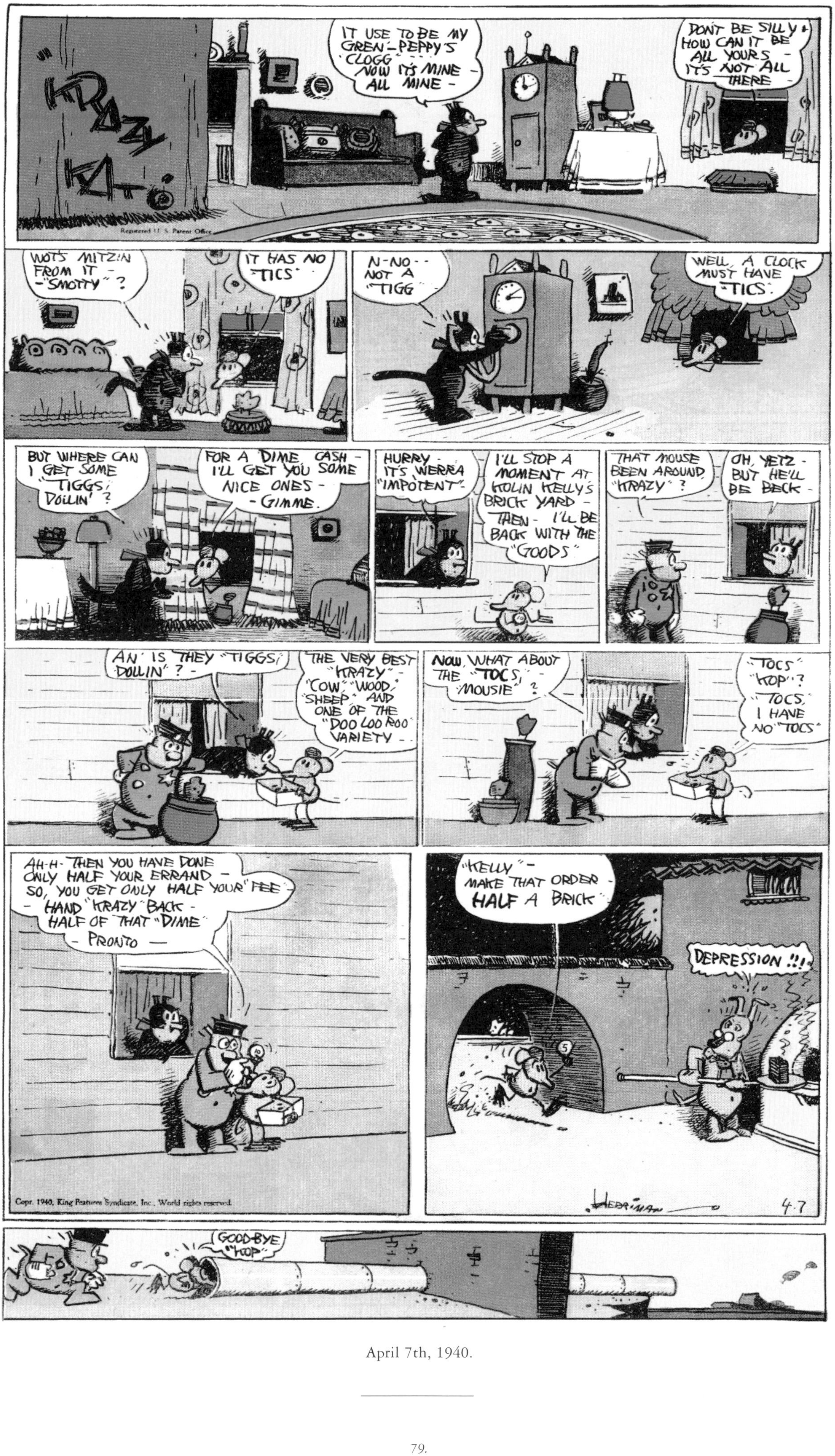
Krazy Kat
Registered U.S. Patent Office
IT USE TO BE MY GREN-PEPPY'S "CLOGG" - NOW IT'S MINE - ALL MINE -
DON'T BE SILLY - HOW CAN IT BE ALL YOURS - IT'S NOT ALL THERE
WOT'S MITZ'IN FROM IT - "SMOTTY"?
IT HAS NO "TICS"
N-NO - NOT A "TIGG"
WELL, A CLOCK MUST HAVE "TICS".
BUT WHERE CAN I GET SOME "TIGGS," DOLLIN'?
FOR A "DIME" CASH - I'LL GET YOU SOME NICE ONES - GIMME.
HURRY - IT'S WERRA "IMPOTENT" -
I'LL STOP A MOMENT AT KOLIN KELLY'S BRICK YARD - THEN - I'LL BE BACK WITH THE "GOODS"
THAT MOUSE BEEN AROUND "KRAZY"?
OH, YETZ - BUT HE'LL BE BECK -
AN IS "THEY" "TIGGS," DOLLIN'? -
THE VERY BEST "KRAZY" - "COW," "WOOD," "SHEEP" AND ONE OF THE "DOO LOO ROO" VARIETY -
NOW, WHAT ABOUT THE "TOCS," "MOUSIE"?
"TOCS" "KOP"? "TOCS," I HAVE NO "TOCS"
AH-H- THEN YOU HAVE DONE ONLY HALF YOUR ERRAND - SO, YOU GET ONLY HALF YOUR "FEE" - HAND "KRAZY" BACK HALF OF THAT "DIME" - PRONTO -
"KELLY" - MAKE THAT ORDER HALF A BRICK
DEPRESSION !!!
Copr. 1940, King Features Syndicate, Inc., World rights reserved.
HERRIMAN
4-7
GOOD-BYE "KOP"

April 7th, 1940.

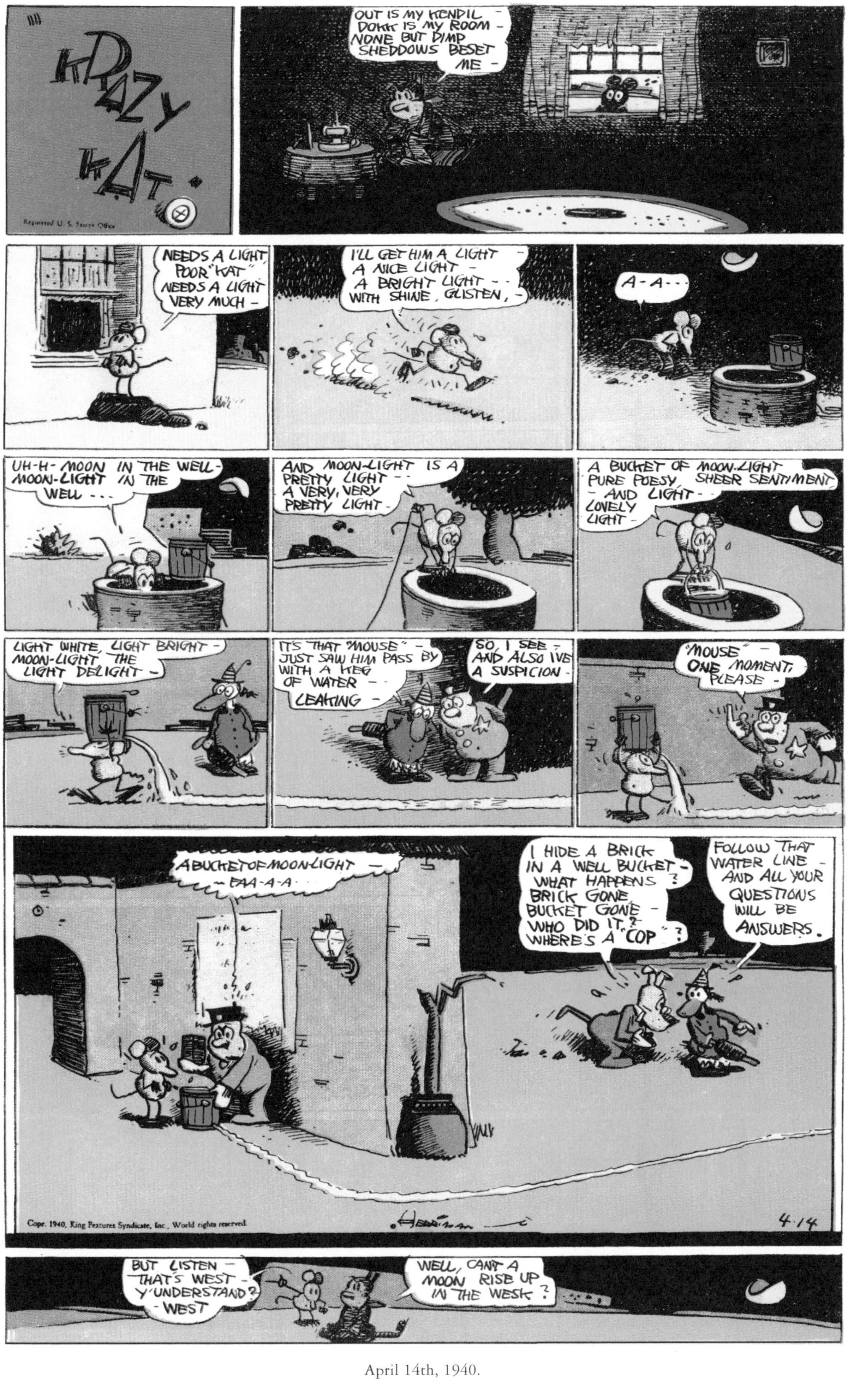
KRAZY KAT
Registered U. S. Patent Office
OUT IS MY KENDIL - DOHK IS MY ROOM - NONE BUT DIMP SHEDDOWS BESET ME -
NEEDS A LIGHT POOR "KAT" NEEDS A LIGHT VERY MUCH -
I'LL GET HIM A LIGHT - A NICE LIGHT - A BRIGHT LIGHT - - WITH SHINE, GLISTEN, -
A - A - - -
UH-H- MOON IN THE WELL- MOON-LIGHT IN THE WELL - - -
AND MOON-LIGHT IS A PRETTY LIGHT - - A VERY, VERY PRETTY LIGHT -
A BUCKET OF MOON-LIGHT PURE POESY, SHEER SENTIMENT, - AND LIGHT - LOVELY LIGHT -
LIGHT WHITE, LIGHT BRIGHT - MOON-LIGHT, THE LIGHT DELIGHT -
IT'S THAT "MOUSE" - JUST SAW HIM PASS BY WITH A KEG OF WATER - - LEAKING -
SO, I SEE - AND ALSO I'VE A SUSPICION -
"MOUSE" - ONE MOMENT, PLEASE -
A BUCKET OF MOON-LIGHT - FAA-A-A
I HIDE A BRICK IN A WELL BUCKET - WHAT HAPPENS ? BRICK GONE BUCKET GONE - WHO DID IT ? WHERE'S A "COP" ?
FOLLOW THAT WATER LINE - AND ALL YOUR QUESTIONS WILL BE ANSWERS.
Copr. 1940, King Features Syndicate, Inc., World rights reserved.
Herriman
4-14
BUT LISTEN - THAT'S WEST - Y'UNDERSTAND? - WEST
WELL, CAN'T A MOON RISE UP IN THE WEST ?

April 14th, 1940.

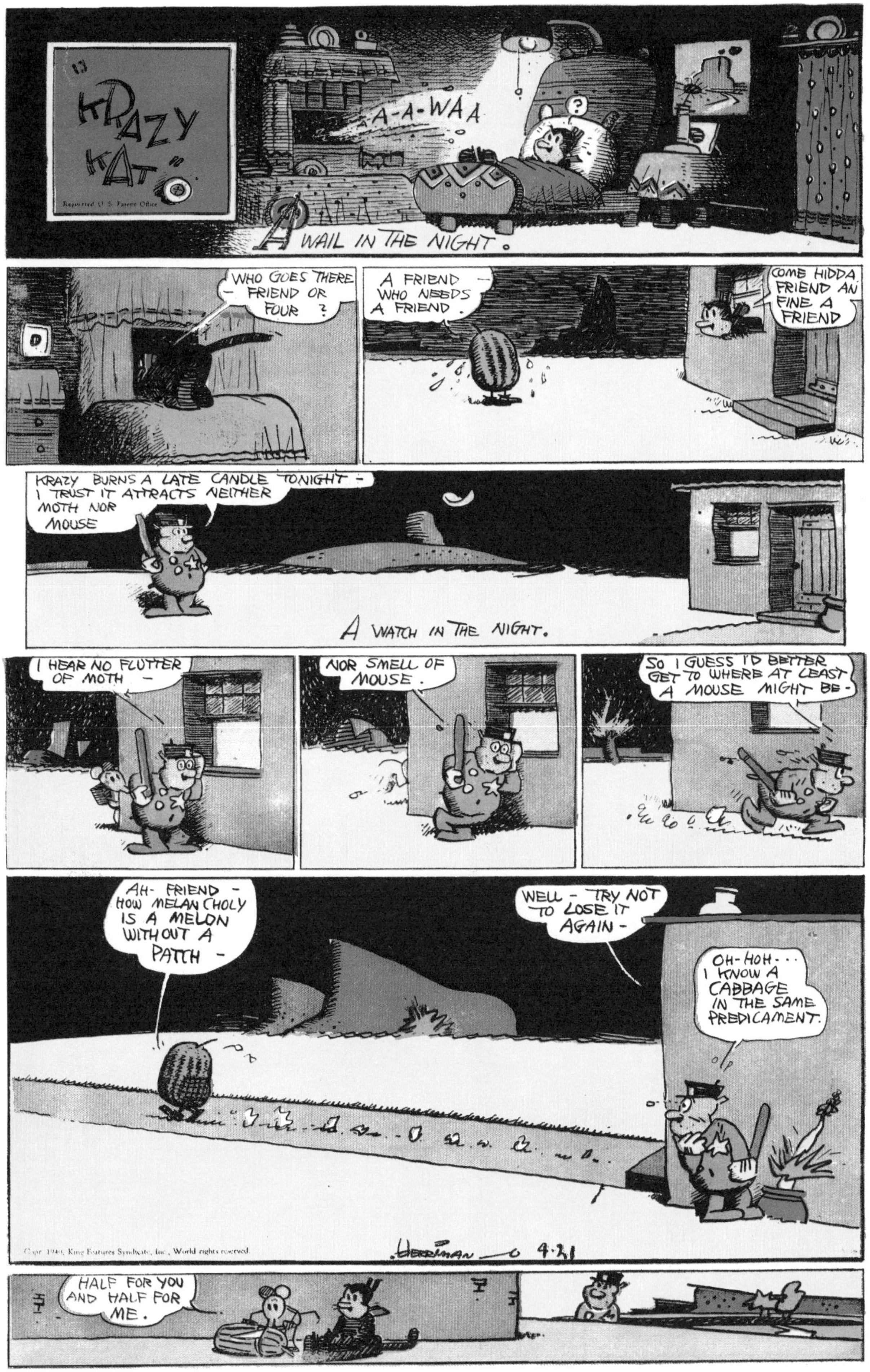
KRAZY KAT
Registered U.S. Patent Office
A-A-WAA
?
A WAIL IN THE NIGHT.
WHO GOES THERE – FRIEND OR FOUR ?
A FRIEND – WHO NEEDS A FRIEND.
COME HIDDA FRIEND AN FINE A FRIEND
KRAZY BURNS A LATE CANDLE TONIGHT – I TRUST IT ATTRACTS NEITHER MOTH NOR MOUSE
A WATCH IN THE NIGHT.
I HEAR NO FLUTTER OF MOTH –
NOR SMELL OF MOUSE.
SO I GUESS I'D BETTER GET TO WHERE AT LEAST A MOUSE MIGHT BE –
AH- FRIEND – HOW MELAN CHOLY IS A MELON WITHOUT A PATCH –
WELL – TRY NOT TO LOSE IT AGAIN –
OH- HOH- · · I KNOW A CABBAGE IN THE SAME PREDICAMENT.
Copr. 1940, King Features Syndicate, Inc., World rights reserved.
HERRIMAN 4·21
HALF FOR YOU AND HALF FOR ME.

April 21st, 1940.

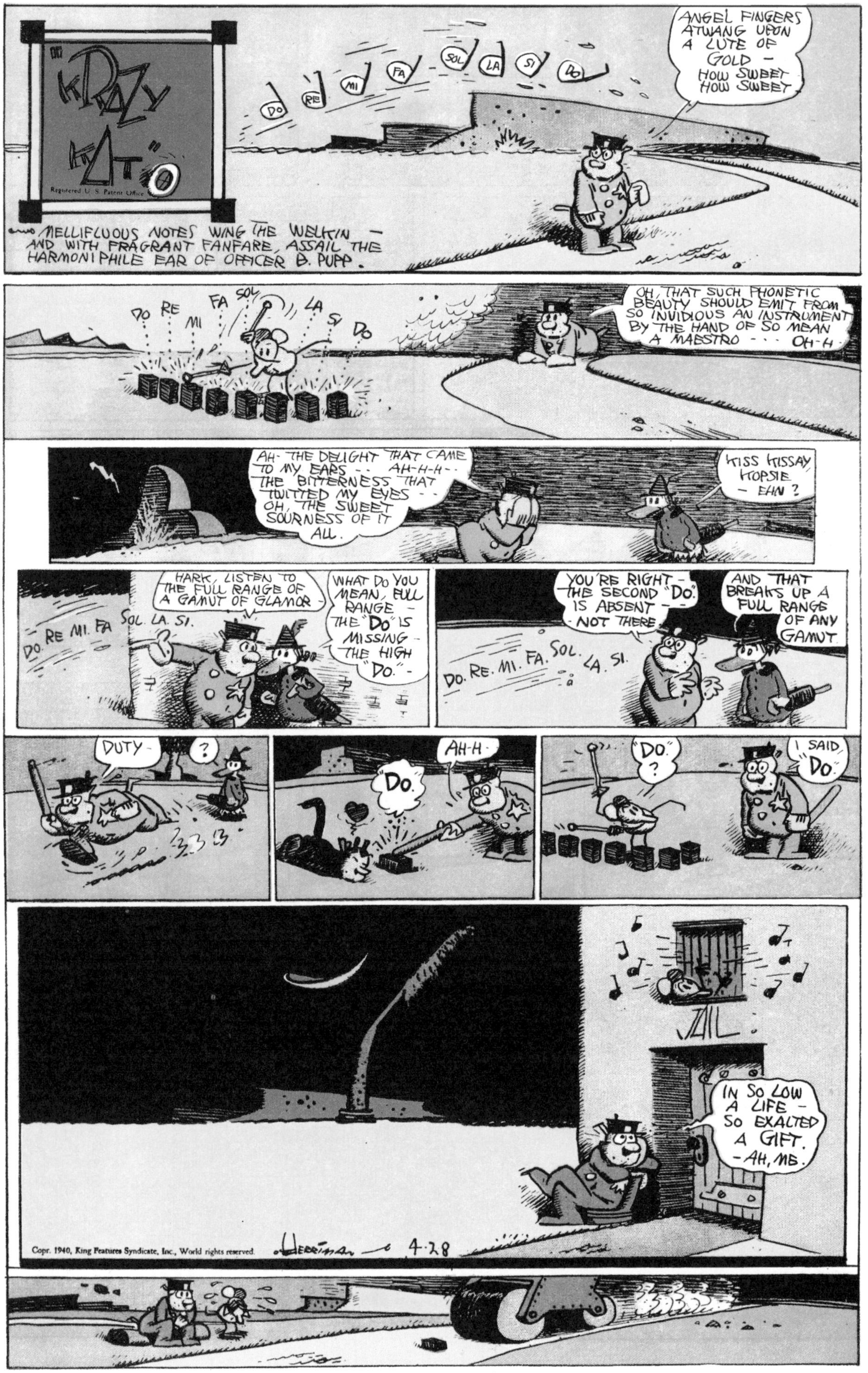
Krazy Kat
Registered U.S. Patent Office
MELLIFLUOUS NOTES WING THE WELKIN — AND WITH FRAGRANT FANFARE, ASSAIL THE HARMONIPHILE EAR OF OFFICER B. PUPP.
DO RE MI FA SOL LA SI DO
ANGEL FINGERS ATWANG UPON A LUTE OF GOLD — HOW SWEET HOW SWEET
DO RE MI FA SOL LA SI DO
OH, THAT SUCH PHONETIC BEAUTY SHOULD EMIT FROM SO INVIDIOUS AN INSTRUMENT BY THE HAND OF SO MEAN A MAESTRO - - - OH-H
AH- THE DELIGHT THAT CAME TO MY EARS -- AH-H-H- THE BITTERNESS THAT TWITTED MY EYES -- OH, THE SWEET SOURNESS OF IT ALL.
KISS KISSAY KOPSIE — EHH ?
HARK, LISTEN TO THE FULL RANGE OF A GAMUT OF GLAMOR
DO. RE MI. FA SOL. LA. SI.
WHAT DO YOU MEAN, FULL RANGE — THE "DO" IS MISSING — THE HIGH "DO."
YOU'RE RIGHT — THE SECOND "DO." IS ABSENT — — NOT THERE
AND THAT BREAKS UP A FULL RANGE OF ANY GAMUT
DO. RE. MI. FA. SOL. LA. SI.
DUTY
?
"DO."
AH-H
"DO." ?
I SAID "DO."
JAIL
IN SO LOW A LIFE — SO EXALTED A GIFT. — AH, ME.
Copr. 1940, King Features Syndicate, Inc., World rights reserved.
Herriman 4-28

April 28th, 1940.

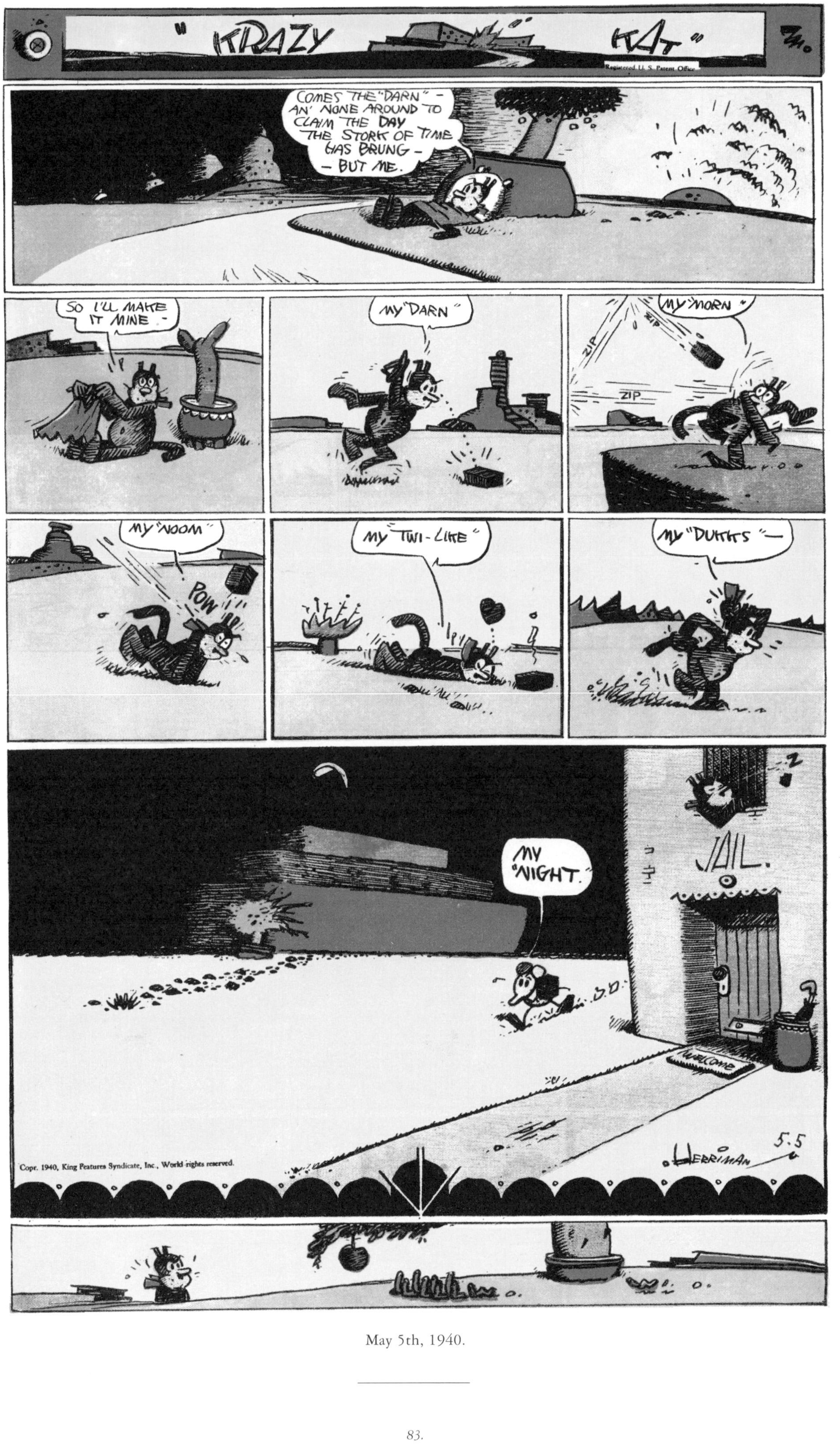
"KRAZY KAT"
Registered U.S. Patent Office
COMES THE "DARN" – AN' NONE AROUND TO CLAIM THE DAY THE STORK OF TIME HAS BRUNG – – BUT ME.
SO I'LL MAKE IT MINE –
MY "DARN"
MY "MORN"
ZIP
ZIP
ZIP
MY "NOOM"
POW
MY "TWI-LIKE"
MY "DUKKS" —
MY "NIGHT."
JAIL.
WELCOME
Copr. 1940, King Features Syndicate, Inc., World rights reserved.
HERRIMAN
5.5

May 5th, 1940.

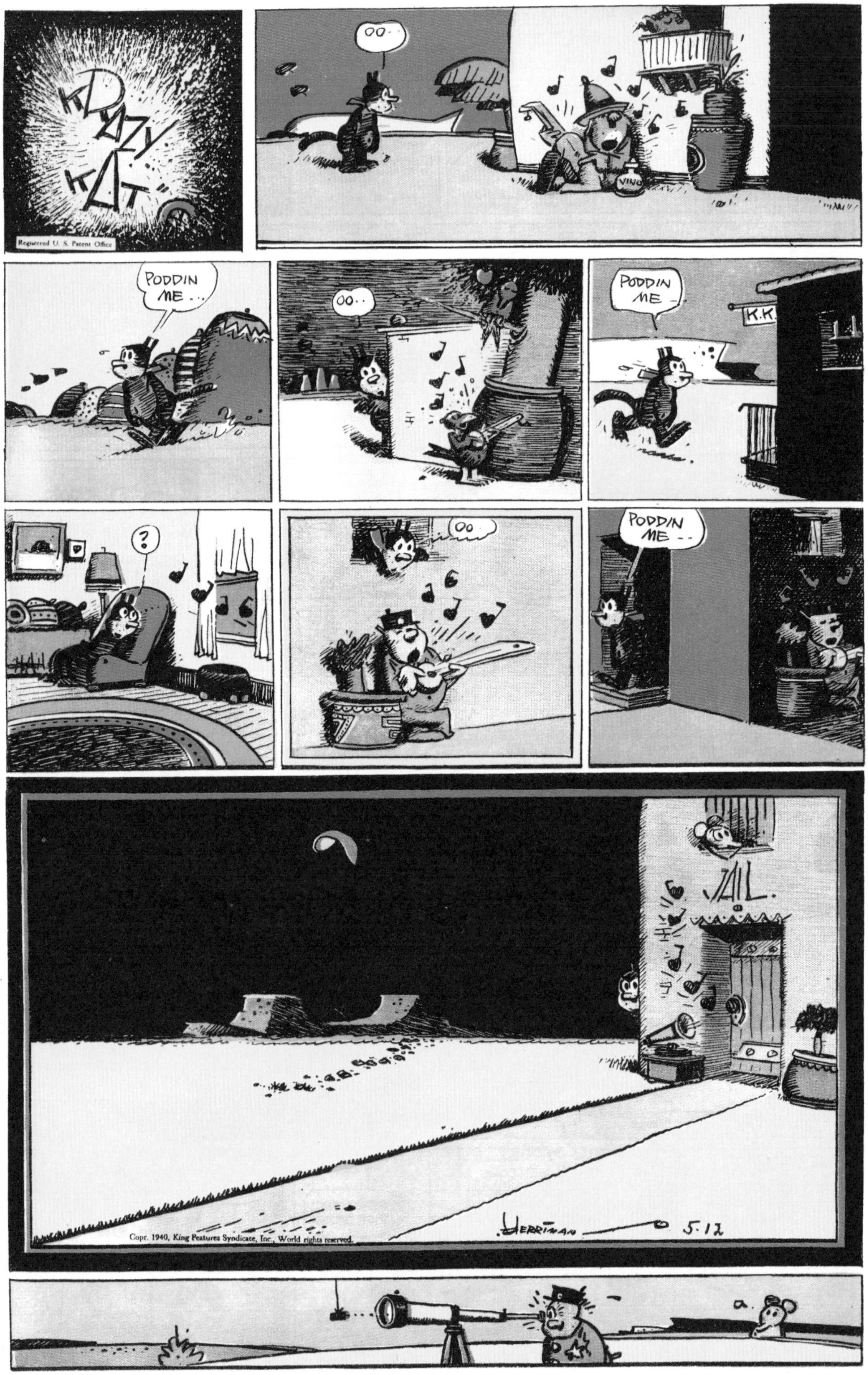
KRAZY KAT
Registered U. S. Patent Office
OO..
VINO
PODDIN ME...
OO..
PODDIN ME
K.K.
?
OO
PODDIN ME--
JAIL
Copr. 1940, King Features Syndicate, Inc., World rights reserved.
HERRIMAN 5.12

May 12th, 1940.

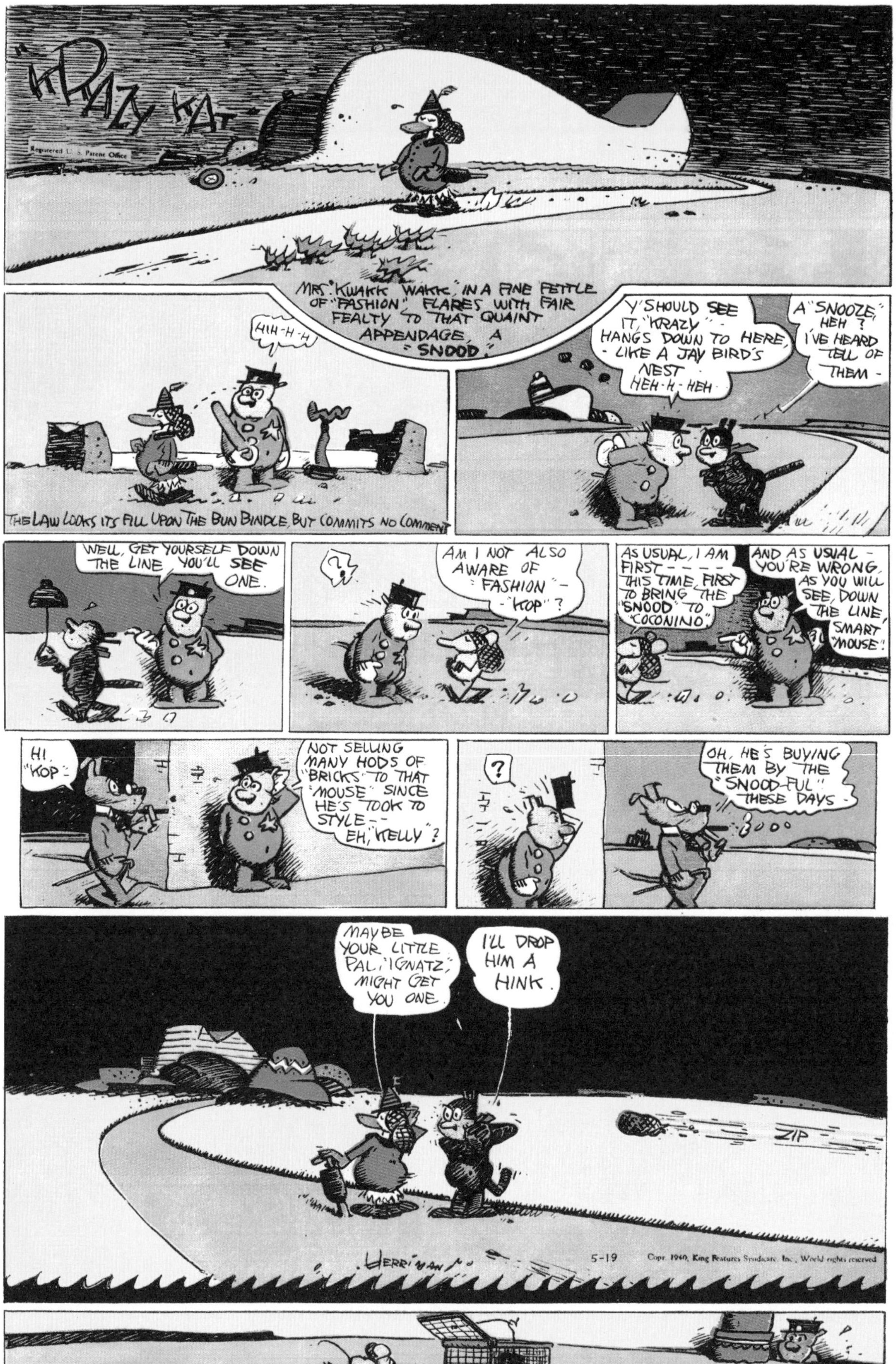
"Krazy Kat"
Registered U. S. Patent Office
MRS. "KWAKK WAKK," IN A FINE FETTLE OF "FASHION," FLARES WITH FAIR FEALTY TO THAT QUAINT APPENDAGE, A "SNOOD."
HIH-H-H
THE LAW LOOKS ITS FILL UPON THE BUN BINDLE, BUT COMMITS NO COMMENT
Y'SHOULD SEE IT, "KRAZY" -- HANGS DOWN TO HERE, - LIKE A JAY BIRD'S NEST HEH-H-HEH
A "SNOOZE," HEH ? I'VE HEARD TELL OF THEM -
WELL, GET YOURSELF DOWN THE LINE, YOU'LL SEE ONE.
AM I NOT ALSO AWARE OF "FASHION" - - "KOP" ?
AS USUAL, I AM FIRST - - - - THIS TIME, FIRST TO BRING THE "SNOOD" TO "COCONINO"
AND AS USUAL - YOU'RE WRONG, AS YOU WILL SEE, DOWN THE LINE, SMART "MOUSE."
HI, "KOP"
NOT SELLING MANY HODS OF "BRICKS" TO THAT "MOUSE" SINCE HE'S TOOK TO STYLE - - EH, "KELLY" ?
?
OH, HE'S BUYING THEM BY THE "SNOOD-FUL" THESE DAYS -
MAYBE YOUR LITTLE PAL, "IGNATZ," MIGHT GET YOU ONE.
I'LL DROP HIM A HINK.
ZIP
HERRIMAN
5-19
Copr. 1940, King Features Syndicate, Inc., World rights reserved

May 19th, 1940.

"KRAZY KAT"
Registered U. S. Patent Office
Z..
"SOPOR"
"...WE LOOKED IT UP IN THE DICTIONARY AND IT MEANS "SLEEP."
Z
"NIGHT."
JAIL.
Z
"SOPOR."
IT STILL MEANS "SLEEP."
Copr. 1940, King Features Syndicate, Inc., World rights reserved.
5.26 Herriman
DO YOU S-SEE IT?
D-D-DO YOU?

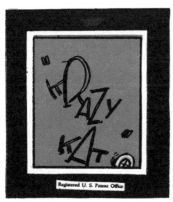

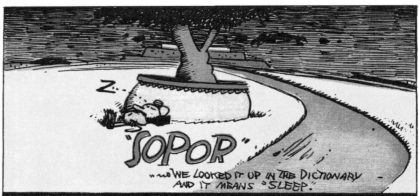

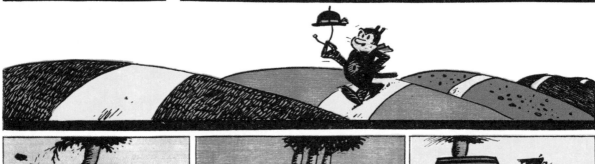

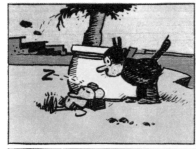

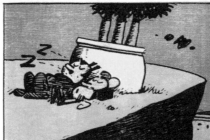

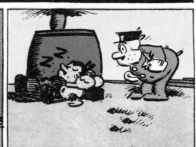

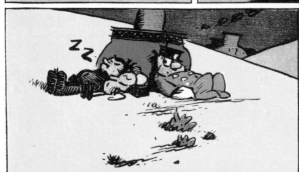

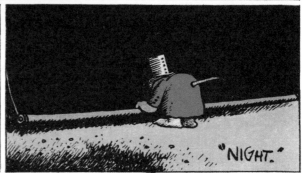

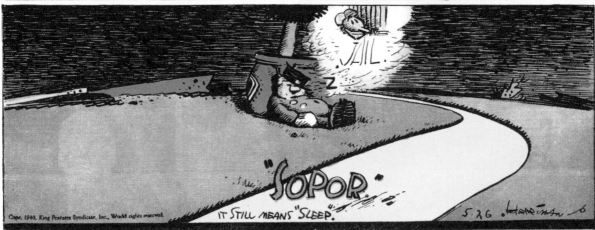

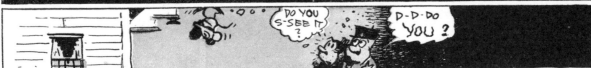

May 26th, 1940.

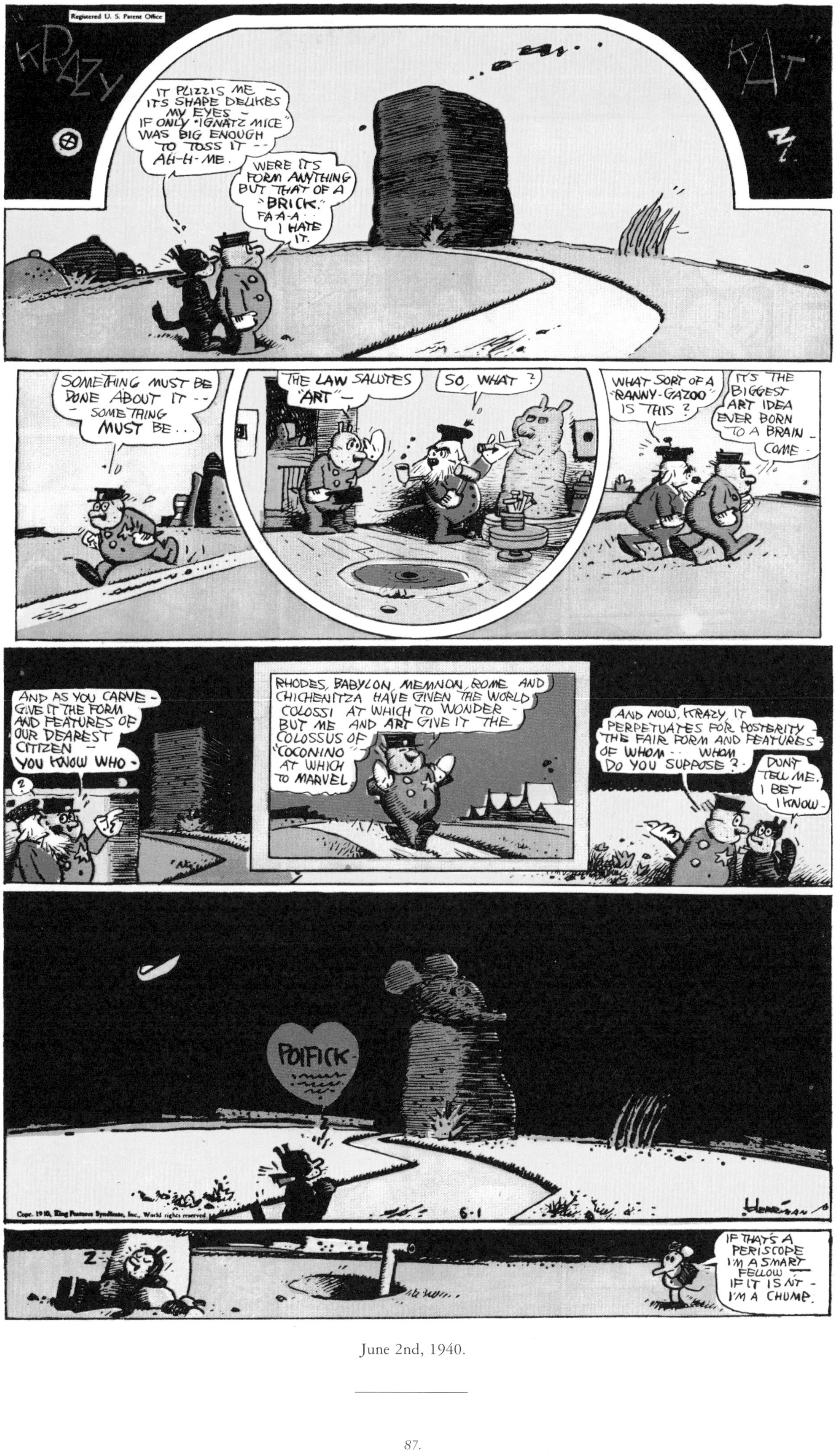
Registered U. S. Patent Office
"KRAZY KAT"
IT PUZZIS ME — ITS SHAPE DELIKES MY EYES — IF ONLY "IGNATZ MICE" WAS BIG ENOUGH TO TOSS IT AH-H-ME.
WERE ITS FORM ANYTHING BUT THAT OF A "BRICK" FA-A-A I HATE IT.
SOMETHING MUST BE DONE ABOUT IT -- SOMETHING MUST BE..
THE LAW SALUTES "ART" —
SO, WHAT ?
WHAT SORT OF A "RANNY-GAZOO" IS THIS ?
IT'S THE BIGGEST ART IDEA EVER BORN TO A BRAIN - COME -
AND AS YOU CARVE - GIVE IT THE FORM AND FEATURES OF OUR DEAREST CITIZEN - YOU KNOW WHO -
?
RHODES, BABYLON, MEMNON, ROME AND CHICHENITZA HAVE GIVEN THE WORLD COLOSSI AT WHICH TO WONDER - BUT ME AND ART GIVE IT THE COLOSSUS OF "COCONINO" AT WHICH TO MARVEL
AND NOW, KRAZY, IT PERPETUATES FOR POSTERITY - THE FAIR FORM AND FEATURES OF WHOM -- WHOM DO YOU SUPPOSE ?
DON'T TELL ME. I BET I KNOW -
POIFICK
Copr. 1940, King Features Syndicate, Inc., World rights reserved.
6-1
Herriman
Z
IF THAT'S A PERISCOPE I'M A SMART FELLOW — IF IT IS N'T — I'M A CHUMP.

June 2nd, 1940.

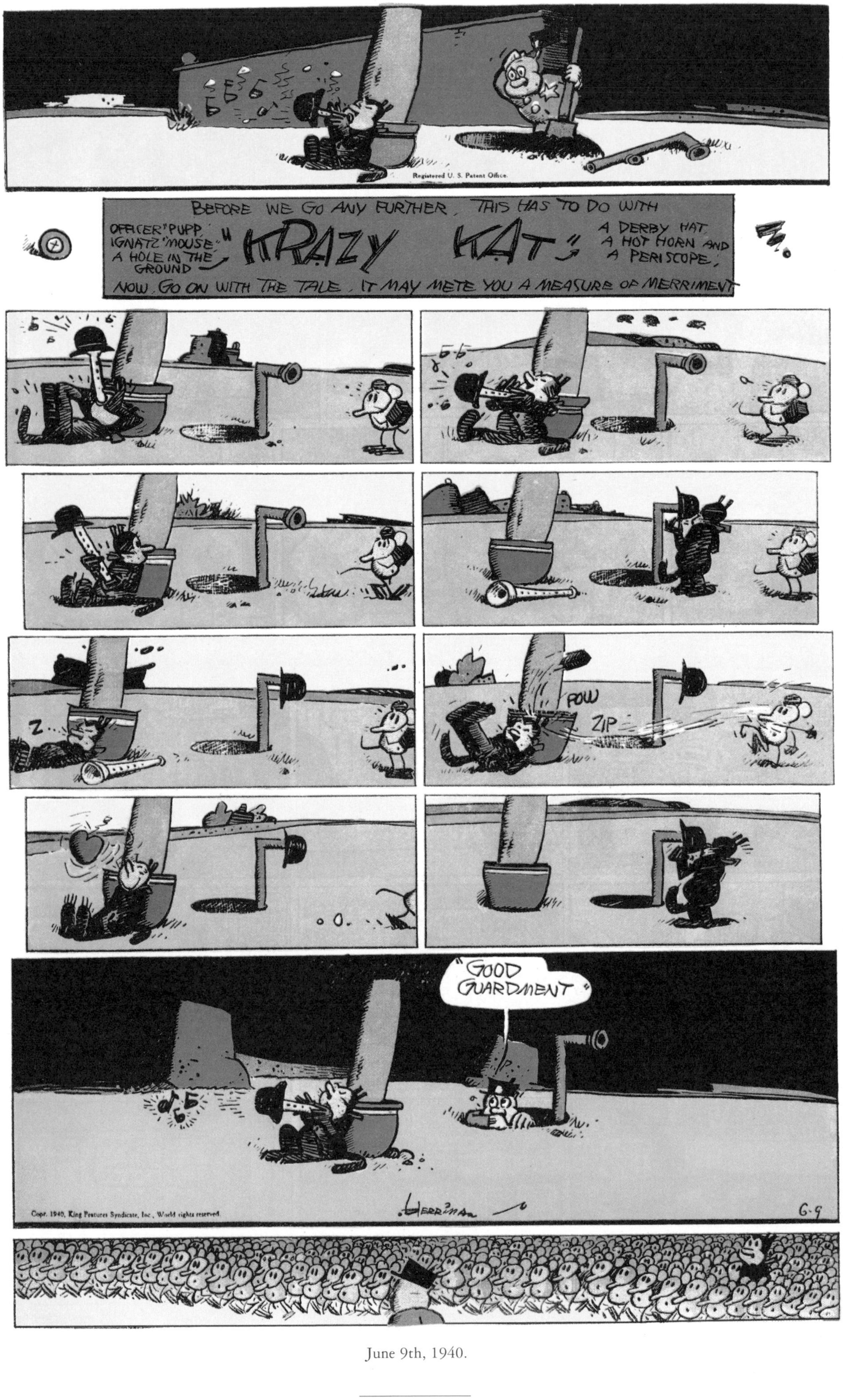
Registered U. S. Patent Office.
BEFORE WE GO ANY FURTHER, THIS HAS TO DO WITH
OFFICER "PUPP, IGNATZ "MOUSE" A HOLE IN THE GROUND
"KRAZY KAT"
A DERBY HAT A HOT HORN AND A PERISCOPE,
NOW GO ON WITH THE TALE, IT MAY METE YOU A MEASURE OF MERRIMENT
Z...
POW
ZIP
"GOOD GUARDMENT"
Copr. 1940, King Features Syndicate, Inc., World rights reserved.
Herriman
G-9

June 9th, 1940.

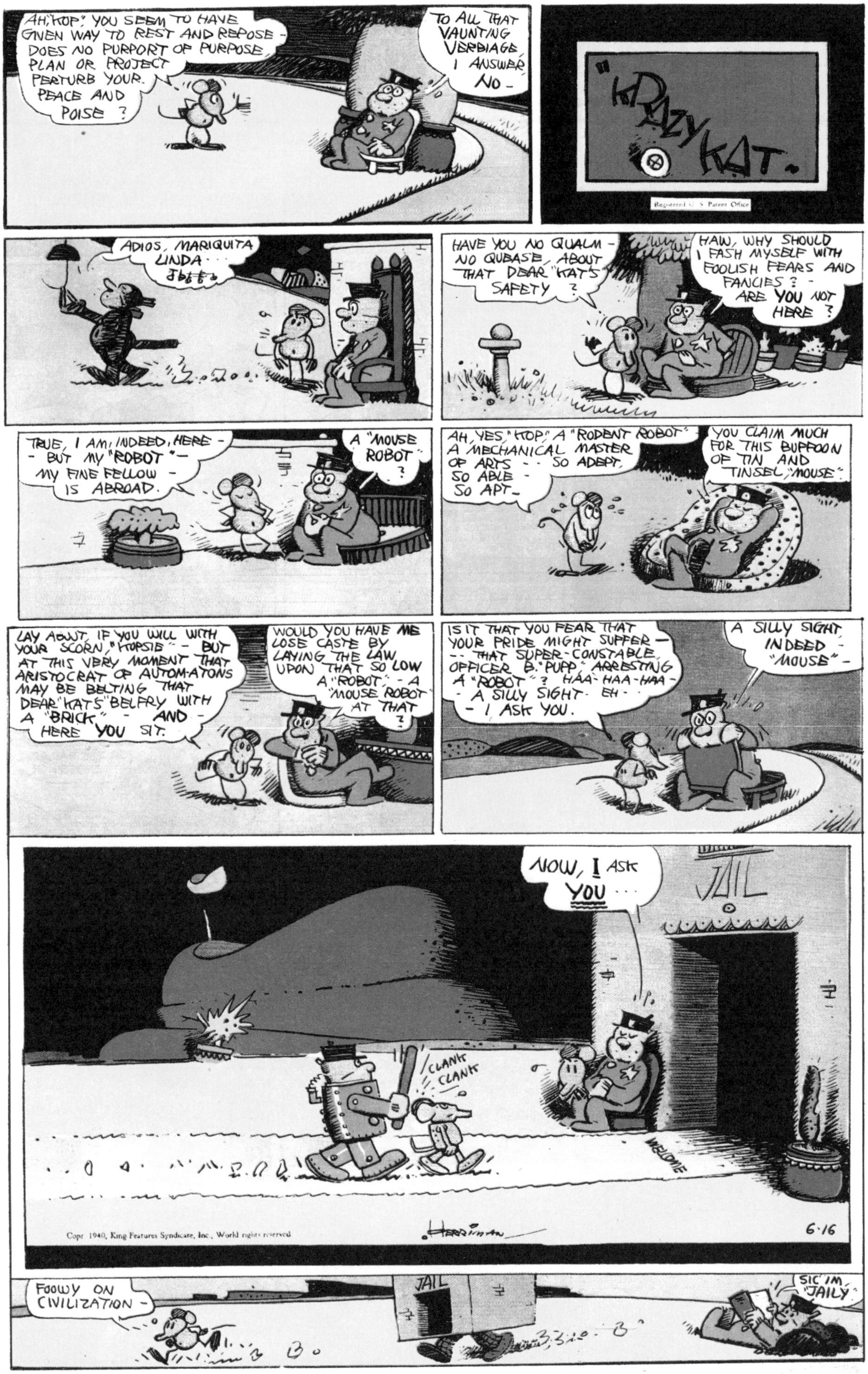
AH, "KOP," YOU SEEM TO HAVE GIVEN WAY TO REST AND REPOSE - DOES NO PURPORT OF PURPOSE, PLAN OR PROJECT PERTURB YOUR PEACE AND POISE ?
TO ALL THAT VAUNTING VERBIAGE, I ANSWER, NO -
"KRAZY KAT."
Registered U. S. Patent Office
ADIOS, MARIQUITA LINDA
HAVE YOU NO QUALM - NO QUBASE, ABOUT THAT DEAR "KAT'S" SAFETY ?
HAW, WHY SHOULD I FASH MYSELF WITH FOOLISH FEARS AND FANCIES ? - ARE YOU NOT HERE ?
TRUE, I AM, INDEED, HERE - - BUT MY "ROBOT" - MY FINE FELLOW - IS ABROAD.
A "MOUSE ROBOT" ?
AH, YES, "KOP," A "RODENT ROBOT" A MECHANICAL MASTER OF ARTS - SO ADEPT, SO ABLE - SO APT -
YOU CLAIM MUCH FOR THIS BUFFOON OF TIN AND TINSEL, "MOUSE."
LAY ABOUT, IF YOU WILL WITH YOUR SCORN, "TOPSIE" - BUT AT THIS VERY MOMENT THAT ARISTOCRAT OF AUTOMATONS MAY BE BELTING THAT DEAR "KAT'S" BELFRY WITH A "BRICK," - AND - HERE YOU SIT.
WOULD YOU HAVE ME LOSE CASTE BY LAYING THE LAW UPON THAT SO LOW A "ROBOT," - A "MOUSE ROBOT" AT THAT ?
IS IT THAT YOU FEAR THAT YOUR PRIDE MIGHT SUFFER - - THAT SUPER-CONSTABLE, OFFICER B. "PUPP," ARRESTING A "ROBOT" ? HAA-HAA-HAA - A SILLY SIGHT - EH - - I ASK YOU.
A SILLY SIGHT INDEED "MOUSE" -
NOW, I ASK YOU . . .
JAIL
CLANK CLANK
WELCOME
Copr 1940, King Features Syndicate, Inc., World rights reserved.
Herriman
6·16
FOOWY ON CIVILIZATION -
JAIL
SIC 'IM "JAILY."

June 16th, 1940.

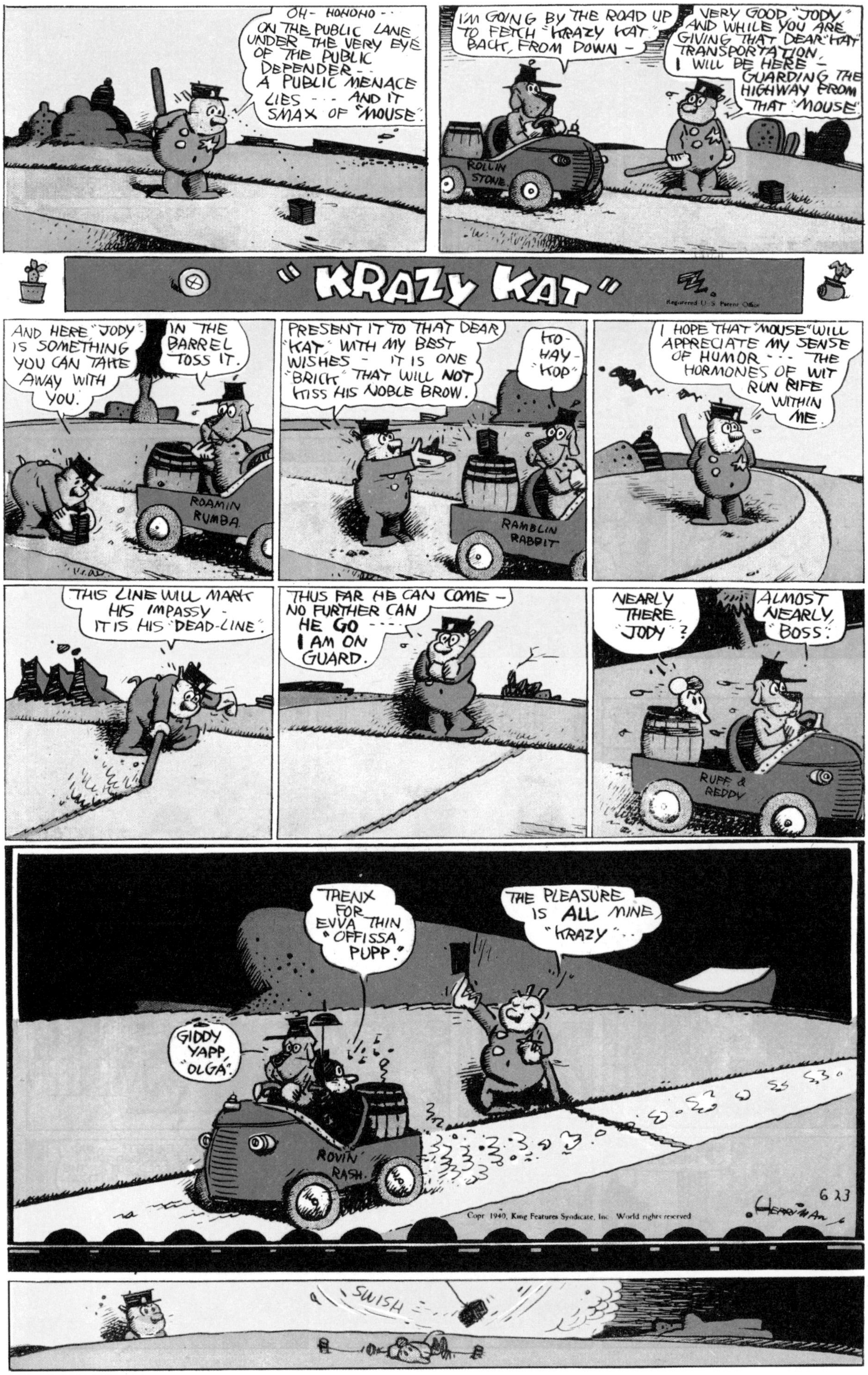
OH- HOHOHO - - ON THE PUBLIC LANE UNDER THE VERY EYE OF THE PUBLIC DEPENDER - A PUBLIC MENACE LIES - - - AND IT SMAX OF "MOUSE".
I'M GOING BY THE ROAD UP TO FETCH "KRAZY KAT" BACK, FROM DOWN -
VERY GOOD "JODY" AND WHILE YOU ARE GIVING THAT DEAR "KAT" TRANSPORTATION, I WILL BE HERE GUARDING THE HIGHWAY FROM THAT "MOUSE".
ROLLIN STONE
"KRAZY KAT"
Registered U.S. Patent Office
AND HERE "JODY" IS SOMETHING YOU CAN TAKE AWAY WITH YOU.
IN THE BARREL TOSS IT.
ROAMIN RUMBA
PRESENT IT TO THAT DEAR "KAT" WITH MY BEST WISHES - IT IS ONE "BRICK" THAT WILL NOT KISS HIS NOBLE BROW.
HO-HAY-KOP"
RAMBLIN RABBIT
I HOPE THAT "MOUSE" WILL APPRECIATE MY SENSE OF HUMOR - - - THE HORMONES OF WIT RUN RIFE WITHIN ME.
THIS LINE WILL MARK HIS IMPASSY - IT IS HIS "DEAD-LINE".
THUS FAR HE CAN COME - NO FURTHER CAN HE GO - - - I AM ON GUARD.
NEARLY THERE "JODY"?
ALMOST NEARLY "BOSS".
RUFF & REDDY
THENX FOR EVVA THIN, "OFFISSA PUPP".
THE PLEASURE IS ALL MINE "KRAZY" - -
GIDDY YAPP, "OLGA".
ROVIN RASH.
6 23
Copr 1940, King Features Syndicate, Inc. World rights reserved
HERRIMAN
SWISH

June 23rd, 1940.

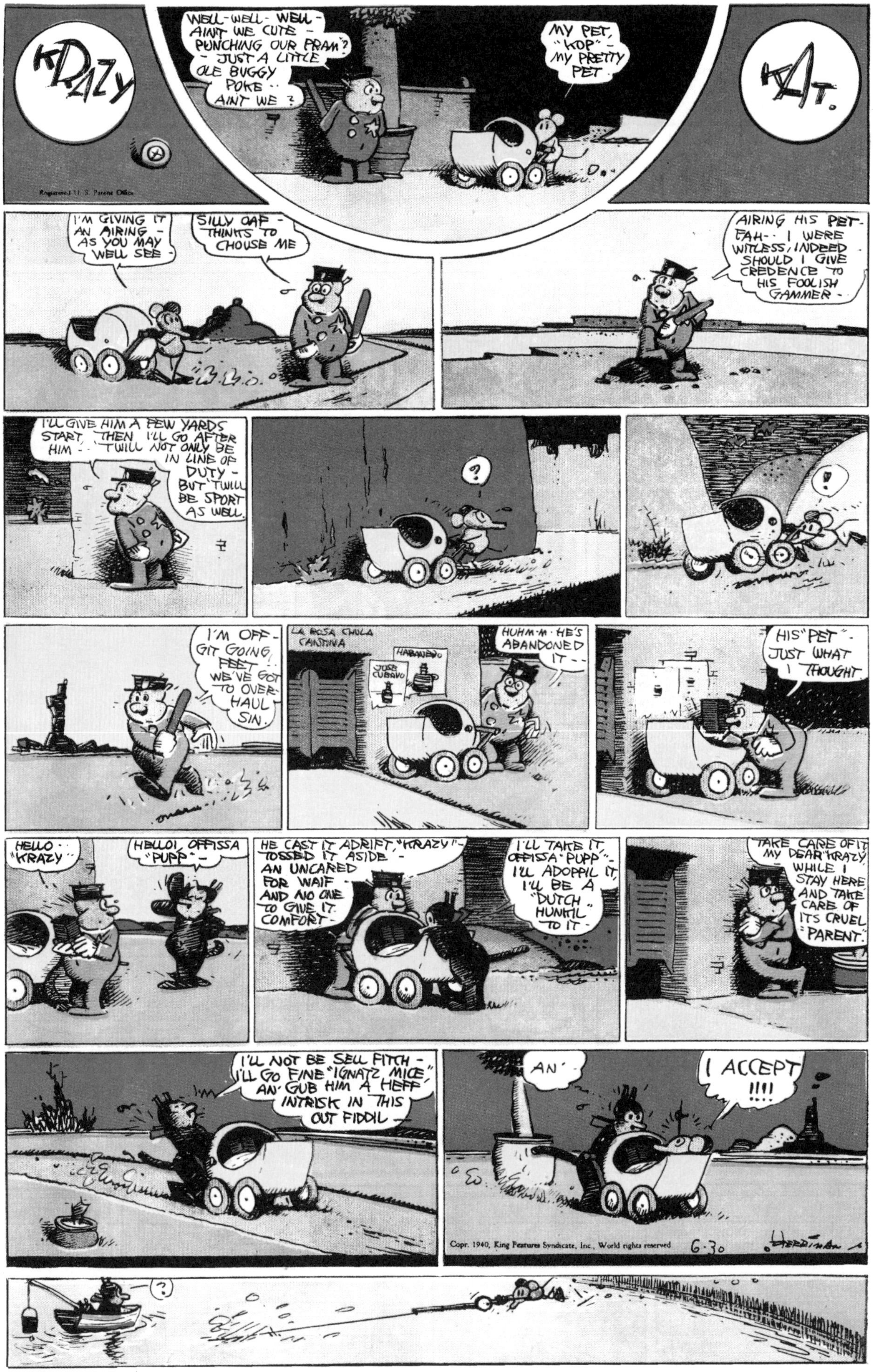
KRAZY
KAT.
Registered U. S. Patent Office
WELL-WELL-WELL - AINT WE CUTE - PUNCHING OUR PRAM? - JUST A LITTLE OLE BUGGY POKE - AINT WE ?
MY PET, "KOP" - MY PRETTY PET.
I'M GIVING IT AN AIRING - AS YOU MAY WELL SEE -
SILLY OAF - THINKS TO CHOUSE ME
AIRING HIS PET - FAH - I WERE WITLESS, INDEED SHOULD I GIVE CREDENCE TO HIS FOOLISH GAMMER -
I'LL GIVE HIM A FEW YARDS START, THEN I'LL GO AFTER HIM - 'TWILL NOT ONLY BE IN LINE OF DUTY - BUT 'TWILL BE SPORT AS WELL.
?
!
I'M OFF - GIT GOING FEET - WE'VE GOT TO OVER-HAUL SIN.
LA ROSA CHULA CANTINA
HABANERO
JOSE CUBANO
HUHM-M HE'S ABANDONED IT - -
HIS "PET" - JUST WHAT I THOUGHT
HELLO - "KRAZY" -
HELLO!, OFFISSA "PUPP" -
HE CAST IT ADRIFT, "KRAZY" - TOSSED IT ASIDE - AN UNCARED FOR WAIF - AND NO ONE TO GIVE IT COMFORT -
I'LL TAKE IT, OFFISSA "PUPP" - I'LL ADOPPIL IT, I'LL BE A "DUTCH" HUNKIL TO IT -
TAKE CARE OF IT, MY DEAR "KRAZY", WHILE I STAY HERE AND TAKE CARE OF ITS CRUEL "PARENT".
I'LL NOT BE SELL FITCH - I'LL GO FINE "IGNATZ MICE", AN' GUB HIM A HEFF INTRISK IN THIS OUT FIDDIL -
AN'
I ACCEPT !!!!
Copr. 1940, King Features Syndicate, Inc., World rights reserved.
6-30
HERRIMAN
?

June 30th, 1940.

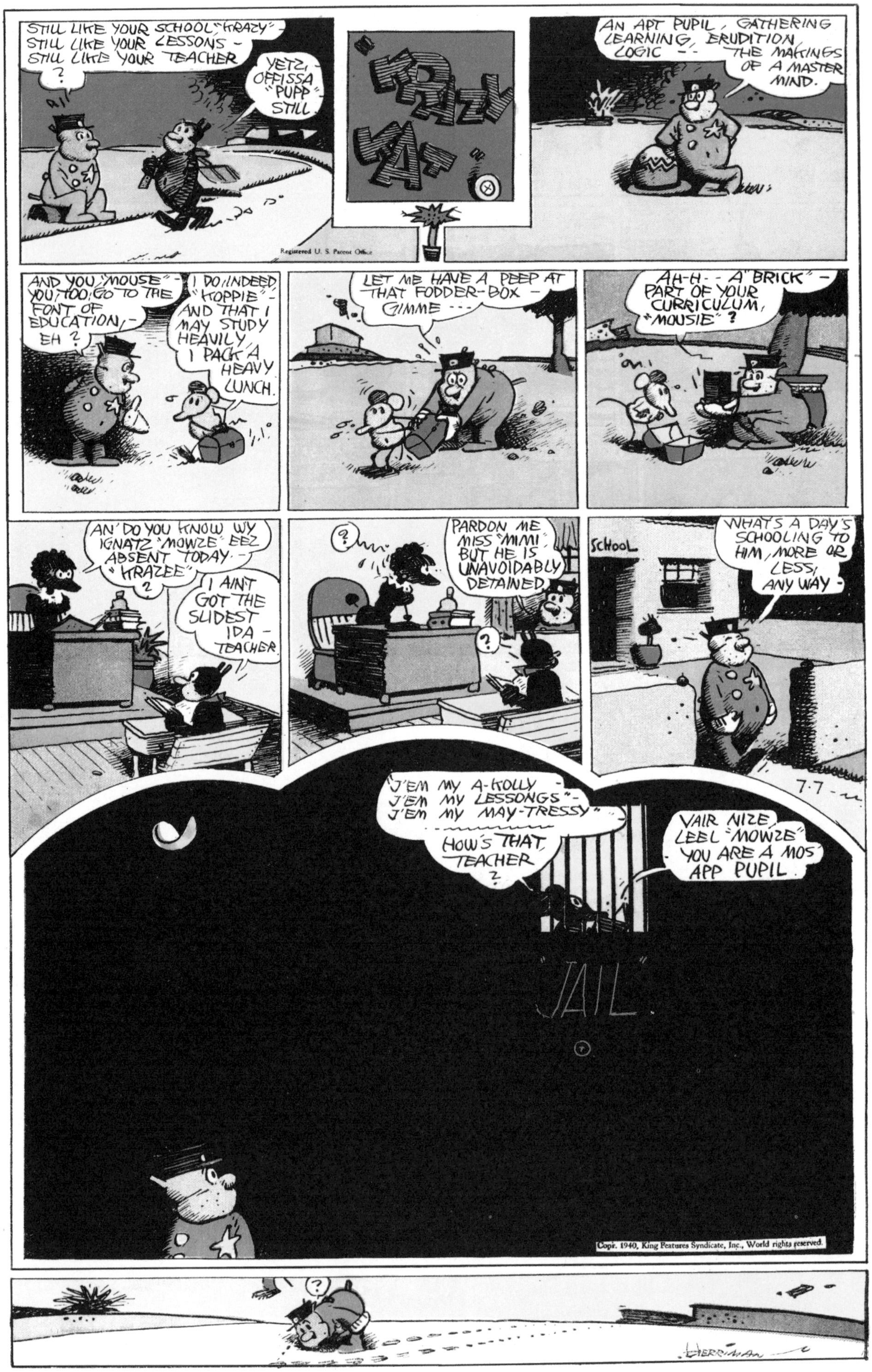
STILL LIKE YOUR SCHOOL, "KRAZY" - STILL LIKE YOUR LESSONS - STILL LIKE YOUR TEACHER ?
YETZ, OFFISSA "PUPP" - STILL
KRAZY KAT
Registered U. S. Patent Office
AN APT PUPIL, GATHERING LEARNING, ERUDITION, LOGIC -- THE MAKINGS OF A MASTER MIND.
AND YOU, "MOUSE" YOU, TOO, GO TO THE FONT OF EDUCATION, - EH ?
I DO, INDEED "KOPPIE" - AND THAT I MAY STUDY HEAVILY, I PACK A HEAVY LUNCH.
LET ME HAVE A PEEP AT THAT FODDER-BOX - GIMME ---
AH-H - A "BRICK" - PART OF YOUR CURRICULUM, "MOUSIE" ?
AN' DO YOU KNOW WY IGNATZ "MOWZE" EEZ ABSENT TODAY - "KRAZEE" ?
I AIN'T GOT THE SLIDEST IDA - TEACHER.
PARDON ME MISS "MIMI" BUT HE IS UNAVOIDABLY DETAINED.
SCHOOL
WHAT'S A DAY'S SCHOOLING TO HIM, MORE OR LESS, ANY WAY -
J'EM MY A-KOLLY - J'EM MY LESSONGS" - J'EM MY MAY-TRESSY" -
HOW'S THAT TEACHER ?
VAIR NIZE, LEEL "MOWZE" - YOU ARE A MOS' APP PUPIL.
JAIL
Copr. 1940, King Features Syndicate, Inc., World rights reserved.
HERRIMAN

July 7th, 1940.

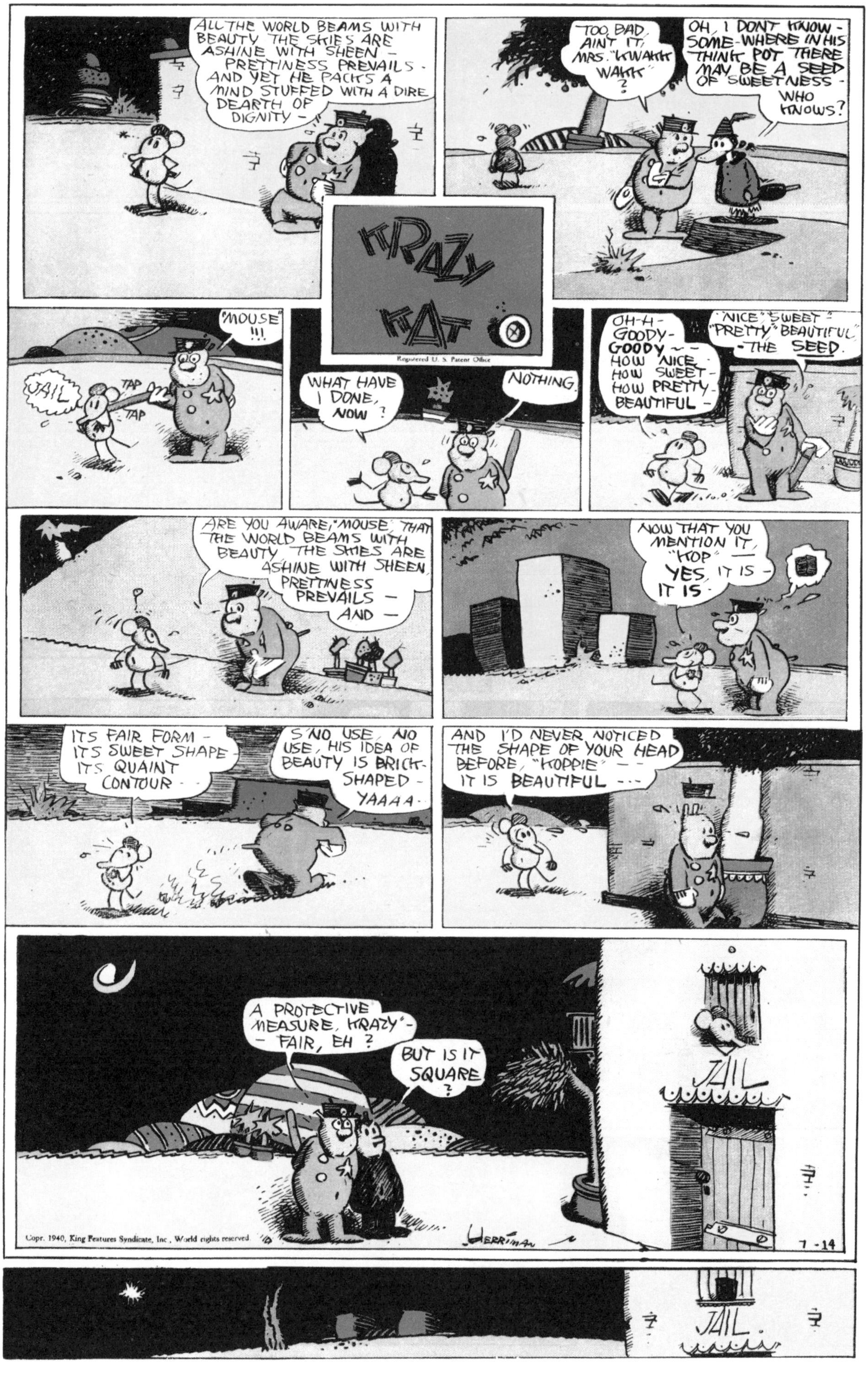
ALL THE WORLD BEAMS WITH BEAUTY THE SKIES ARE ASHINE WITH SHEEN - PRETTINESS PREVAILS - AND YET HE PACKS A MIND STUFFED WITH A DIRE DEARTH OF DIGNITY -
TOO BAD, AIN'T IT, MRS. "KWAKK WAKK" ?
OH, I DON'T KNOW - SOME-WHERE IN HIS THINK POT THERE MAY BE A SEED OF SWEETNESS - WHO KNOWS?
KRAZY KAT
Registered U. S. Patent Office
"MOUSE" !!!
JAIL
TAP
TAP
WHAT HAVE I DONE, NOW ?
NOTHING.
OH-H- GOODY- GOODY -- HOW NICE, HOW SWEET HOW PRETTY BEAUTIFUL -
"NICE" "SWEET" "PRETTY" "BEAUTIFUL" - THE SEED.
ARE YOU AWARE, "MOUSE" THAT THE WORLD BEAMS WITH BEAUTY THE SKIES ARE ASHINE WITH SHEEN, PRETTINESS PREVAILS - AND -
NOW THAT YOU MENTION IT, "KOP" — YES, IT IS - IT IS -
ITS FAIR FORM - ITS SWEET SHAPE - ITS QUAINT CONTOUR -
S'NO USE, NO USE, HIS IDEA OF BEAUTY IS BRICK-SHAPED - YAAAA -
AND I'D NEVER NOTICED THE SHAPE OF YOUR HEAD BEFORE, "KOPPIE" -- IT IS BEAUTIFUL ---
A PROTECTIVE MEASURE, KRAZY - FAIR, EH ?
BUT IS IT SQUARE ?
JAIL
Copr. 1940, King Features Syndicate, Inc., World rights reserved
HERRIMAN
7-14
JAIL

July 14th, 1940.

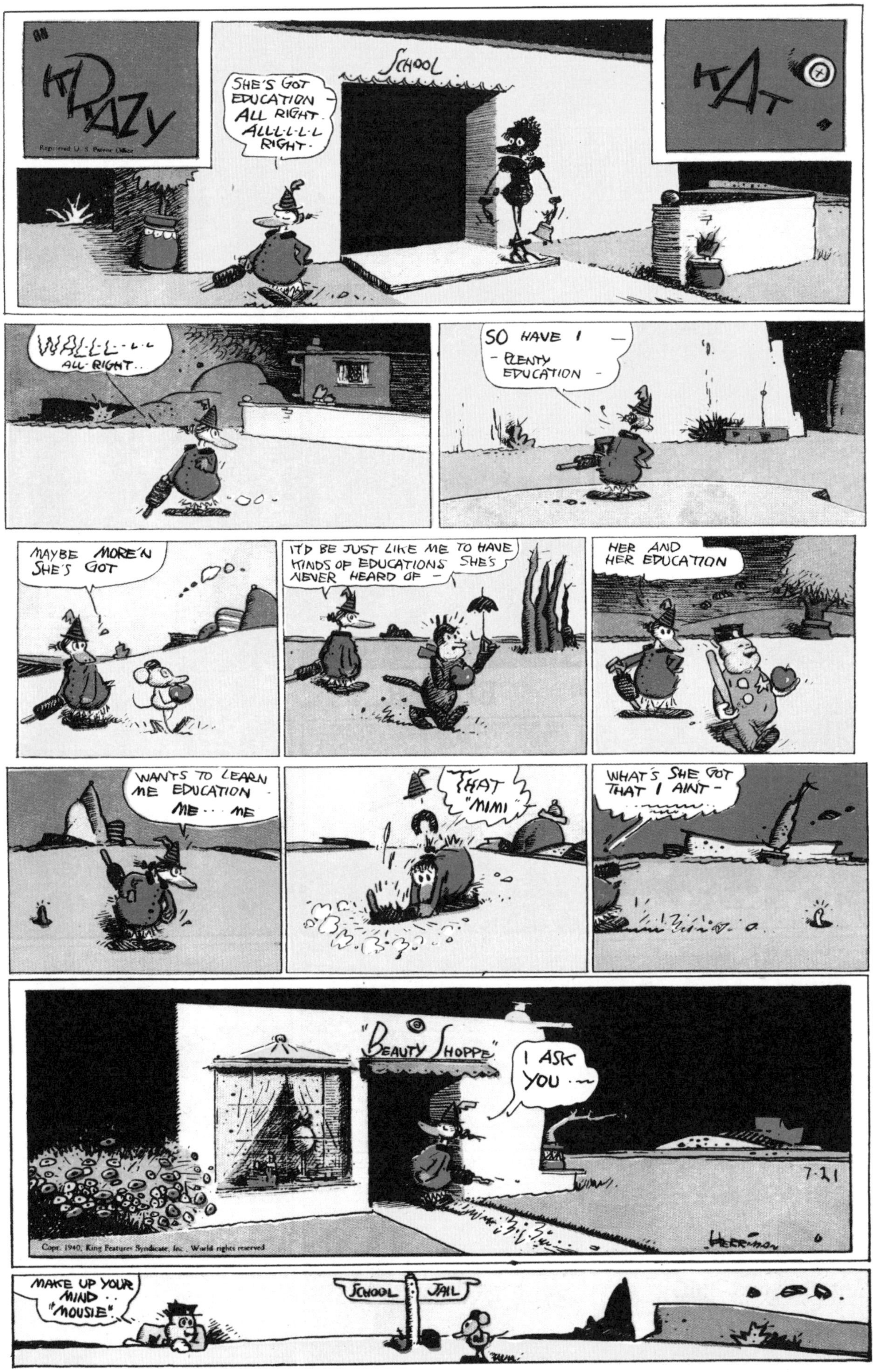
Krazy Kat
Registered U.S. Patent Office
School
SHE'S GOT EDUCATION - ALL RIGHT. ALLL-L-L-L RIGHT -
WALLL-L-L ALL-RIGHT..
SO HAVE I - - PLENTY EDUCATION -
MAYBE MORE'N SHE'S GOT
IT'D BE JUST LIKE ME TO HAVE KINDS OF EDUCATIONS SHE'S NEVER HEARD OF -
HER AND HER EDUCATION
WANTS TO LEARN ME EDUCATION - ME - - ME
THAT "MIMI"
WHAT'S SHE GOT THAT I AINT -
"BEAUTY SHOPPE"
I ASK YOU - -
7-21
Herriman
Copr. 1940, King Features Syndicate, Inc., World rights reserved
MAKE UP YOUR MIND - - "MOUSIE".
SCHOOL
JAIL

July 21st, 1940.

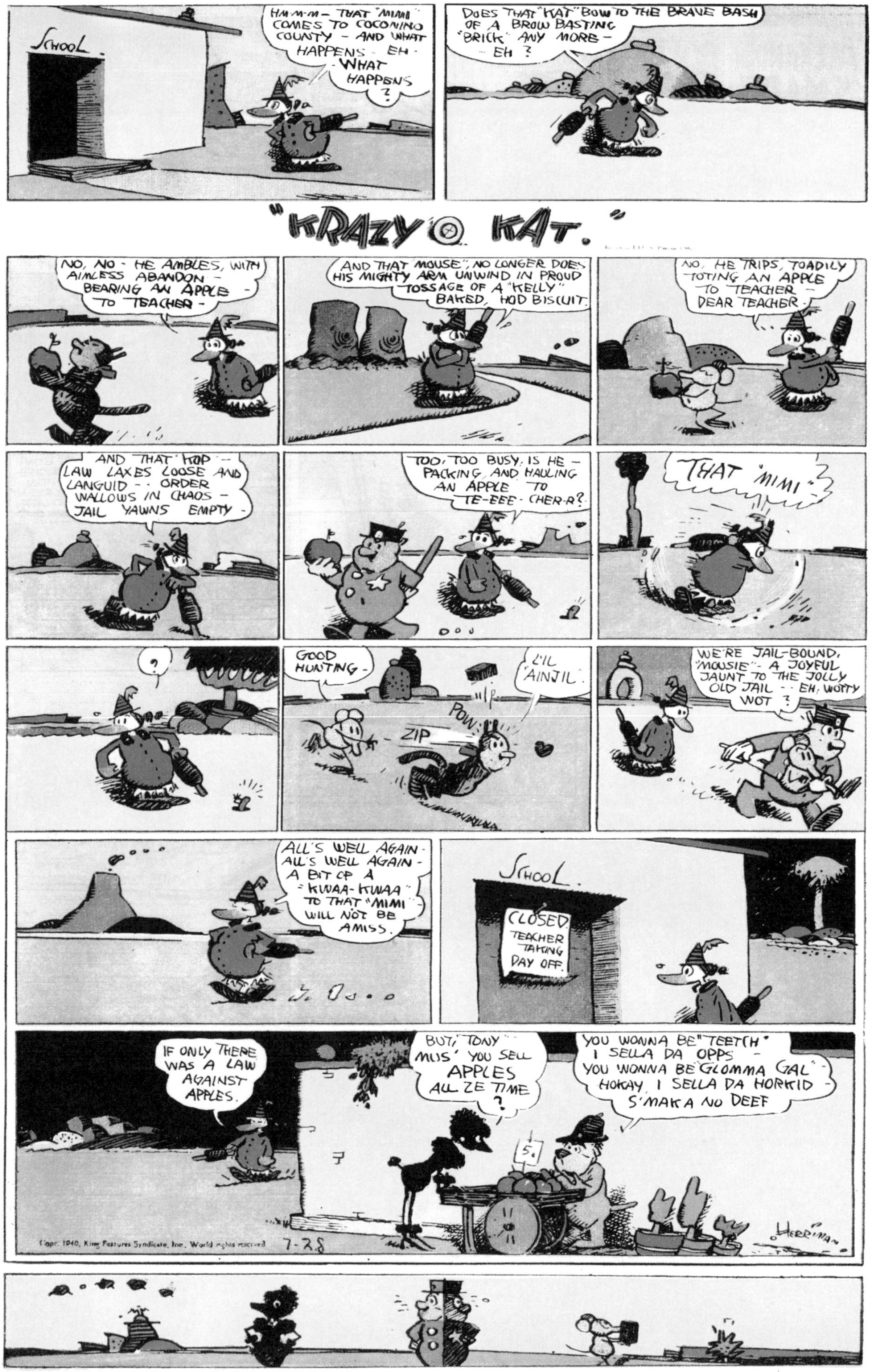
SCHOOL
HM-M-M - THAT "MIMI" COMES TO COCONINO COUNTY - AND WHAT HAPPENS - EH -
-WHAT HAPPENS ?
DOES THAT "KAT" BOW TO THE BRAVE BASH OF A BROW BASTING "BRICK" ANY MORE - - EH ?
"KRAZY KAT."
NO, NO - HE AMBLES, WITH AIMLESS ABANDON - BEARING AN APPLE - TO TEACHER -
AND THAT "MOUSE", NO LONGER DOES HIS MIGHTY ARM UNWIND IN PROUD TOSSAGE OF A "KELLY" BAKED, HOD BISCUIT.
NO, HE TRIPS, TOADILY TOTING AN APPLE TO TEACHER - DEAR TEACHER -
AND THAT "KOP" - LAW LAXES LOOSE AND LANGUID - - ORDER WALLOWS IN CHAOS - JAIL YAWNS EMPTY -
TOO, TOO BUSY, IS HE - PACKING, AND HAULING AN APPLE TO TE-EEE - CHER-R ?
THAT "MIMI"
?
GOOD HUNTING -
L'IL AINJIL
POW
ZIP
WE'RE JAIL-BOUND, "MOUSIE" - A JOYFUL JAUNT TO THE JOLLY OLD JAIL - - EH, WOTTY WOT ?
ALL'S WELL AGAIN - ALL'S WELL AGAIN - A BIT OF A "KWAA-KWAA" TO THAT "MIMI" WILL NOT BE AMISS.
SCHOOL
CLOSED TEACHER TAKING DAY OFF
IF ONLY THERE WAS A LAW AGAINST APPLES.
BUT, "TONY" - MUS' YOU SELL APPLES ALL ZE TIME ?
YOU WONNA BE "TEETCH" I SELLA DA OPPS - YOU WONNA BE GLOMMA GAL" - HOKAY, I SELLA DA HORKID - S'MAKA NO DEEF
5¢
Copr. 1940, King Features Syndicate, Inc. World rights reserved
7-28
HERRIMAN

July 28th, 1940.

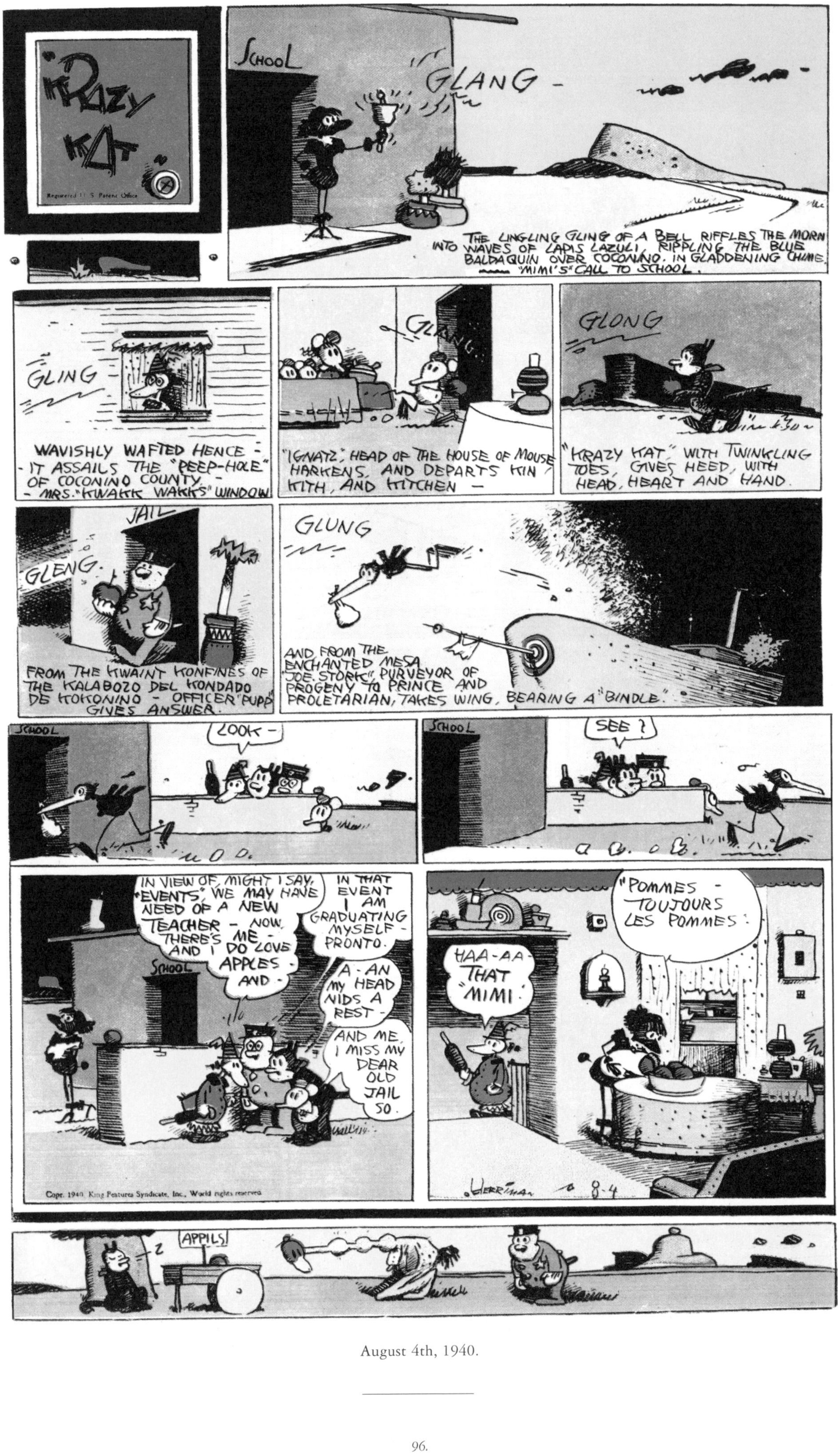
Krazy Kat
Registered U. S. Patent Office
SCHOOL
GLANG
THE LINGLING GLING OF A BELL RIFFLES THE MORN INTO WAVES OF LAPIS LAZULI, RIPPLING THE BLUE BALDAQUIN OVER COCONINO, IN GLADDENING CHIME "MIMI'S" CALL TO SCHOOL.
GLING
WAVISHLY WAFTED HENCE - IT ASSAILS THE "PEEP-HOLE" OF COCONINO COUNTY - MRS. "KWAKK WAKK'S" WINDOW
GLING
"IGNATZ," HEAD OF THE HOUSE OF MOUSE HARKENS, AND DEPARTS KIN, KITH, AND KITCHEN -
GLONG
"KRAZY KAT," WITH TWINKLING TOES, GIVES HEED, WITH HEAD, HEART AND HAND.
JAIL
GLENG.
FROM THE KWAINT KONFINES OF THE KALABOZO DEL KONDADO DE KOKONINO - OFFICER "PUPP" GIVES ANSWER.
GLUNG
AND FROM THE ENCHANTED MESA "JOE. STORK", PURVEYOR OF PROGENY TO PRINCE AND PROLETARIAN, TAKES WING, BEARING A "BINDLE".
SCHOOL
LOOK -
SCHOOL
SEE ?
IN VIEW OF, MIGHT I SAY, "EVENTS," WE MAY HAVE NEED OF A NEW TEACHER - NOW, THERE'S ME - AND I DO LOVE APPLES - AND -
IN THAT EVENT I AM GRADUATING MYSELF - PRONTO.
A - AN MY HEAD NIDS A REST -
AND ME, I MISS MY DEAR OLD JAIL SO.
SCHOOL
Copr. 1940, King Features Syndicate, Inc., World rights reserved
"POMMES - TOUJOURS LES POMMES."
HAA-AA "THAT "MIMI"
HERRIMAN 8-4
APPILS

August 4th, 1940.

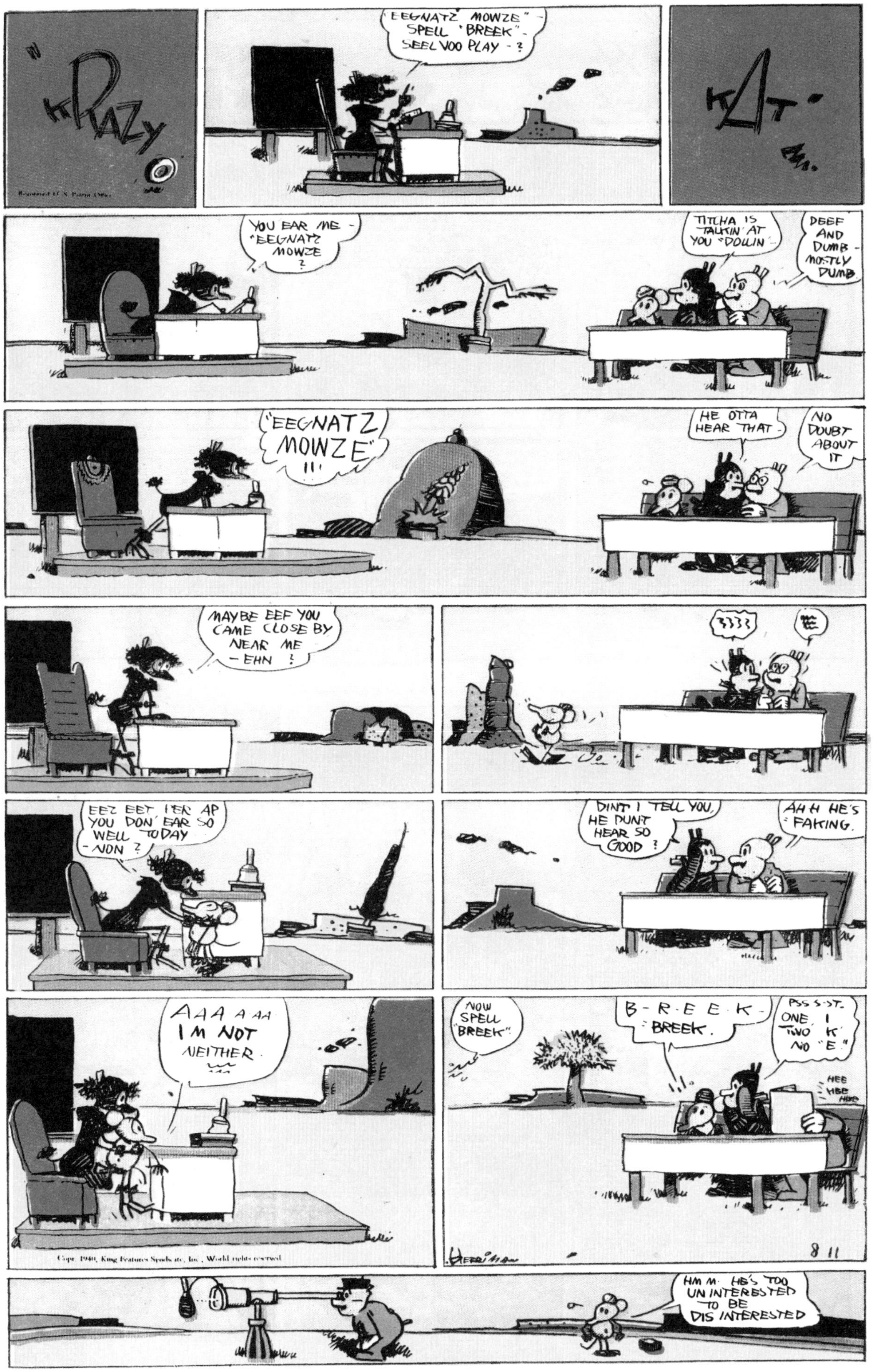

"KRAZY
Registered U. S. Patent Office
KAT"
"EEGNATZ MOWZE" - SPELL "BREEK" - SEEL VOO PLAY - ?
YOU EAR ME - "EEGNATZ MOWZE" ?
TITCHA IS TALKIN' AT YOU "DOWIN"
DEEF AND DUMB - MOSTLY DUMB
"EEGNATZ MOWZE" !!
HE OTTA HEAR THAT
NO DOUBT ABOUT IT
MAYBE EEF YOU CAME CLOSE BY NEAR ME - EHN ?
EEZ EET HER AP YOU DON' EAR SO WELL TODAY - NON ?
DINT I TELL YOU, HE DUNT HEAR SO GOOD ?
AH H HE'S FAKING.
AAA A AA I'M NOT NEITHER
NOW SPELL "BREEK".
B-R-E-E-K - BREEK.
PSS-S-ST. ONE "I" TWO "K" NO "E."
HEE HEE HEE
Copr. 1940, King Features Syndicate, Inc., World rights reserved.
HERRIMAN
8 11
HM M. HE'S TOO UN INTERESTED TO BE DIS INTERESTED

August 11th, 1940.

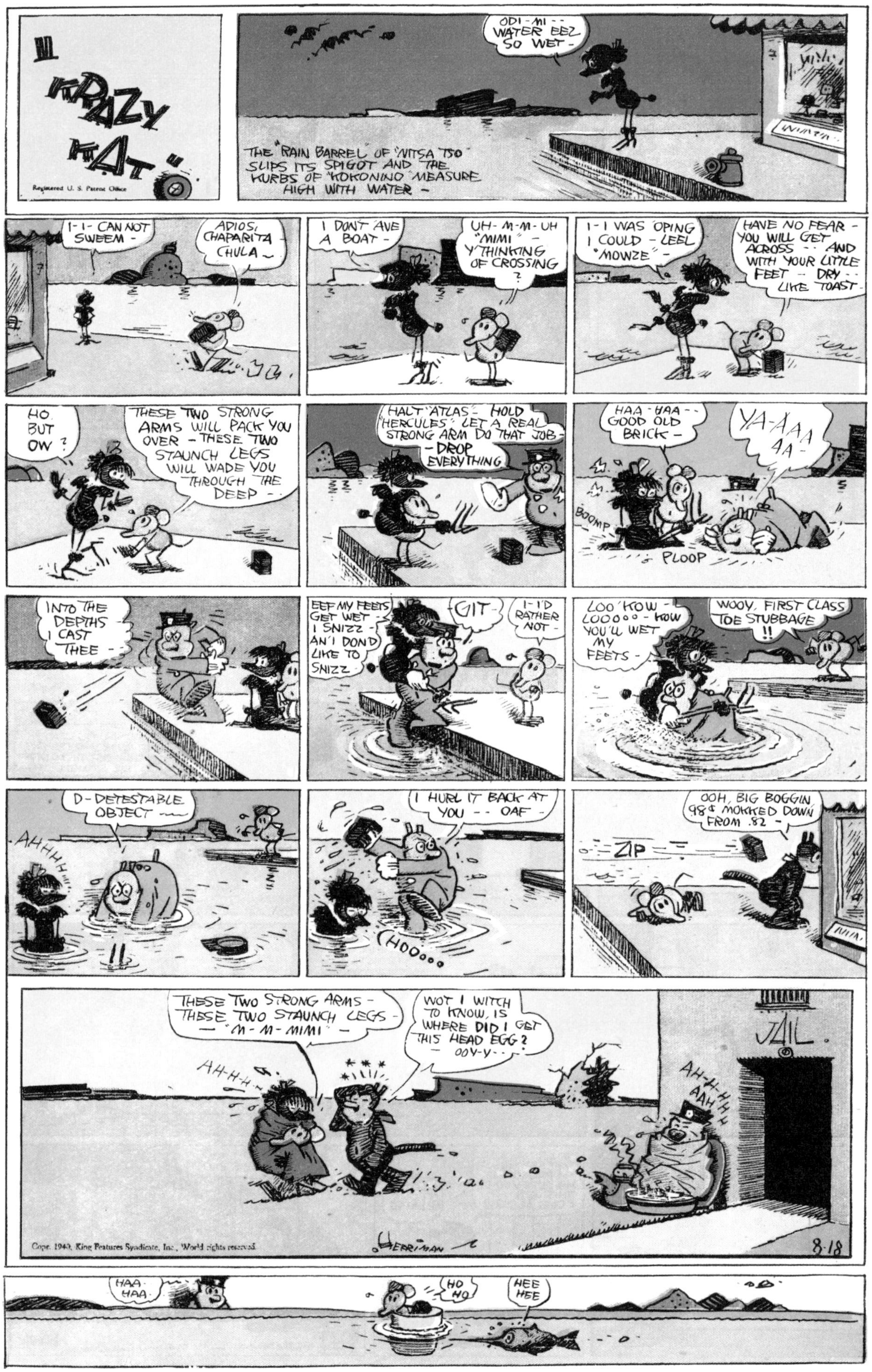
Krazy Kat
Registered U. S. Patent Office
ODI-MI -- WATER EEZ SO WET -
THE "RAIN BARREL" OF "NITSA TSO" SLIPS ITS SPIGOT AND THE KURBS OF "KOKONINO" MEASURE HIGH WITH WATER -
I-I- CAN NOT SWEEM -
ADIOS, CHAPARITA CHULA -
I DON'T AVE A BOAT -
UH-M-M-UH "MIMI" Y'THINKING OF CROSSING ?
I-I WAS OPING I COULD - LEEL "MOWZE" -
HAVE NO FEAR - YOU WILL GET ACROSS -- AND WITH YOUR LITTLE FEET -- DRY -- LIKE TOAST -
HO. BUT OW ?
THESE TWO STRONG ARMS WILL PACK YOU OVER - THESE TWO STAUNCH LEGS WILL WADE YOU THROUGH THE DEEP -
HALT "ATLAS" - HOLD "HERCULES" - LET A REAL STRONG ARM DO THAT JOB - DROP EVERYTHING
HAA-HAA -- GOOD OLD BRICK -
YA-AAA AA-
BOOMP
PLOOP
INTO THE DEPTHS I CAST THEE --
EEF MY FEETS GET WET - I SNIZZ - AN' I DOND LIKE TO SNIZZ -
GIT -
I-I'D RATHER NOT -
LOO'KOW - LOOOOO - KOW YOU'LL WET MY FEETS -
WOOY, FIRST CLASS TOE STUBBAGE !!
D-DETESTABLE OBJECT ---
AHHHH
I HURL IT BACK AT YOU -- OAF -
CHOOooo
ZIP
OOH, BIG BOGGIN, 98¢ MOKKED DOWN FROM .82 -
THESE TWO STRONG ARMS - THESE TWO STAUNCH LEGS - "M-M-MIMI" -
WOT I WITCH TO KNOW, IS WHERE DID I GET THIS HEAD EGG ? -- OOY-Y --
AH-H-H
JAIL
AH-H-H- AAH
Copr. 1940, King Features Syndicate, Inc., World rights reserved.
HERRIMAN
8-18
HAA-HAA
HO HO
HEE HEE

August 18th, 1940.

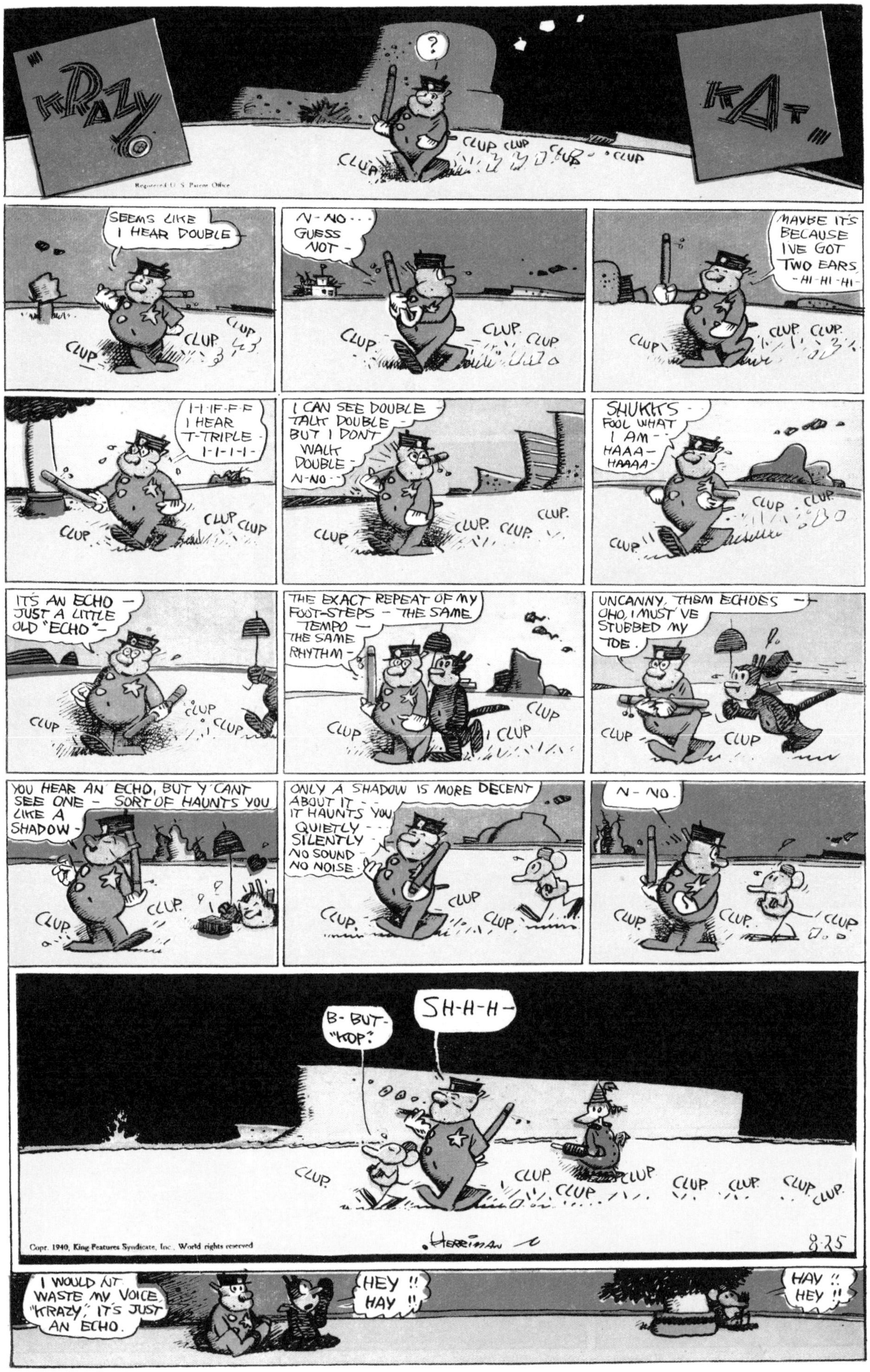

KRAZY
KAT
Registered U. S. Patent Office
?
CLUP CLUP CLUP CLUP CLUP
SEEMS LIKE I HEAR DOUBLE -
CLUP CLUP CLUP
N - NO - - - GUESS NOT -
CLUP CLUP CLUP
MAYBE IT'S BECAUSE I'VE GOT TWO EARS - HI - HI - HI -
CLUP CLUP CLUP
I-I-IF-F-F I HEAR T-TRIPLE - I-I-I-I -
CLUP CLUP CLUP
I CAN SEE DOUBLE - TALK DOUBLE - BUT I DON'T WALK DOUBLE - N-NO - -
CLUP CLUP CLUP CLUP
SHUKH'S - FOOL WHAT I AM - HAAA - HAAAA -
CLUP CLUP CLUP
IT'S AN ECHO - JUST A LITTLE OLD "ECHO" -
CLUP CLUP CLUP
THE EXACT REPEAT OF MY FOOT-STEPS - THE SAME TEMPO - THE SAME RHYTHM -
CLUP CLUP CLUP
UNCANNY, THEM ECHOES - UHO, I MUST'VE STUBBED MY TOE.
CLUP CLUP
YOU HEAR AN ECHO, BUT Y' CAN'T SEE ONE - SORT OF HAUNTS YOU LIKE A SHADOW -
CLUP CLUP
ONLY A SHADOW IS MORE DECENT ABOUT IT - - IT HAUNTS YOU QUIETLY - - SILENTLY - NO SOUND - NO NOISE -
CLUP CLUP CLUP
N - NO.
CLUP CLUP CLUP
B- BUT - "KOP."
SH-H-H-
CLUP CLUP CLUP CLUP CLUP CLUP CLUP CLUP
Copr. 1940, King Features Syndicate, Inc., World rights reserved
HERRIMAN
8-25
I WOULD N'T WASTE MY VOICE "KRAZY," IT'S JUST AN ECHO.
HEY !! HAY !!
HAY !! HEY !!

August 25th, 1940.

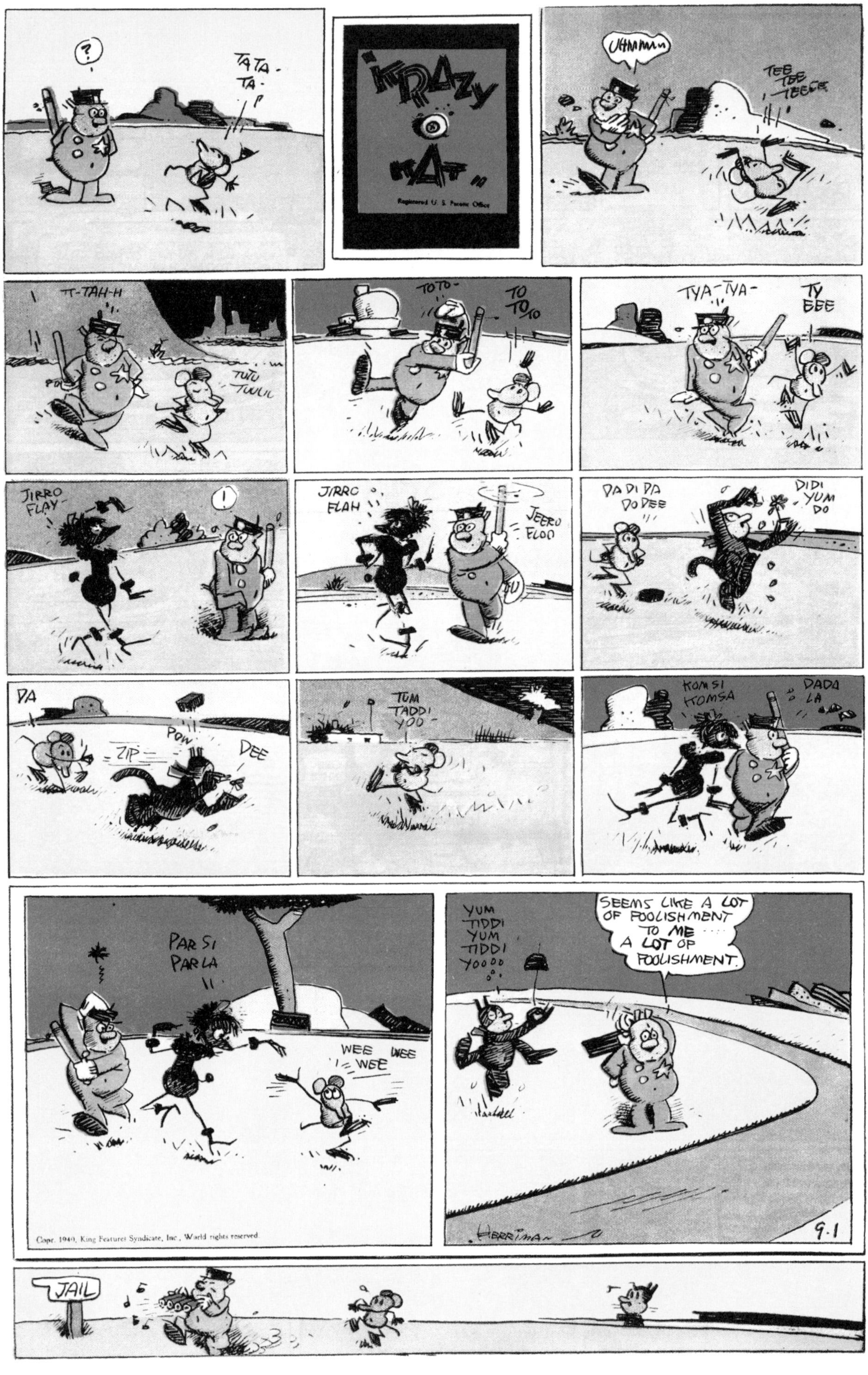
?
TA TA
TA
"KRAZY KAT"
Registered U. S. Patent Office
TEE TEE TEEEE
T-TAH-H
TUTU TUULL
TOTO
TO TO TO
TYA TYA
TY EEE
JIRRO FLAY
!
JIRRO FLAH
JEERO FLOO
DA DI DA DO DEE
DIDI YUM DO
DA
ZIP
POW
DEE
TUM TADDI YOO
KOM SI KOMSA
DADA LA
PAR SI PAR LA
WEE WEE WEE
Copr. 1940, King Features Syndicate, Inc., World rights reserved.
YUM TIDDI YUM TIDDI YOOOO
SEEMS LIKE A LOT OF FOOLISHMENT TO ME .... A LOT OF FOOLISHMENT.
HERRIMAN
9.1
JAIL

September 1st, 1940.

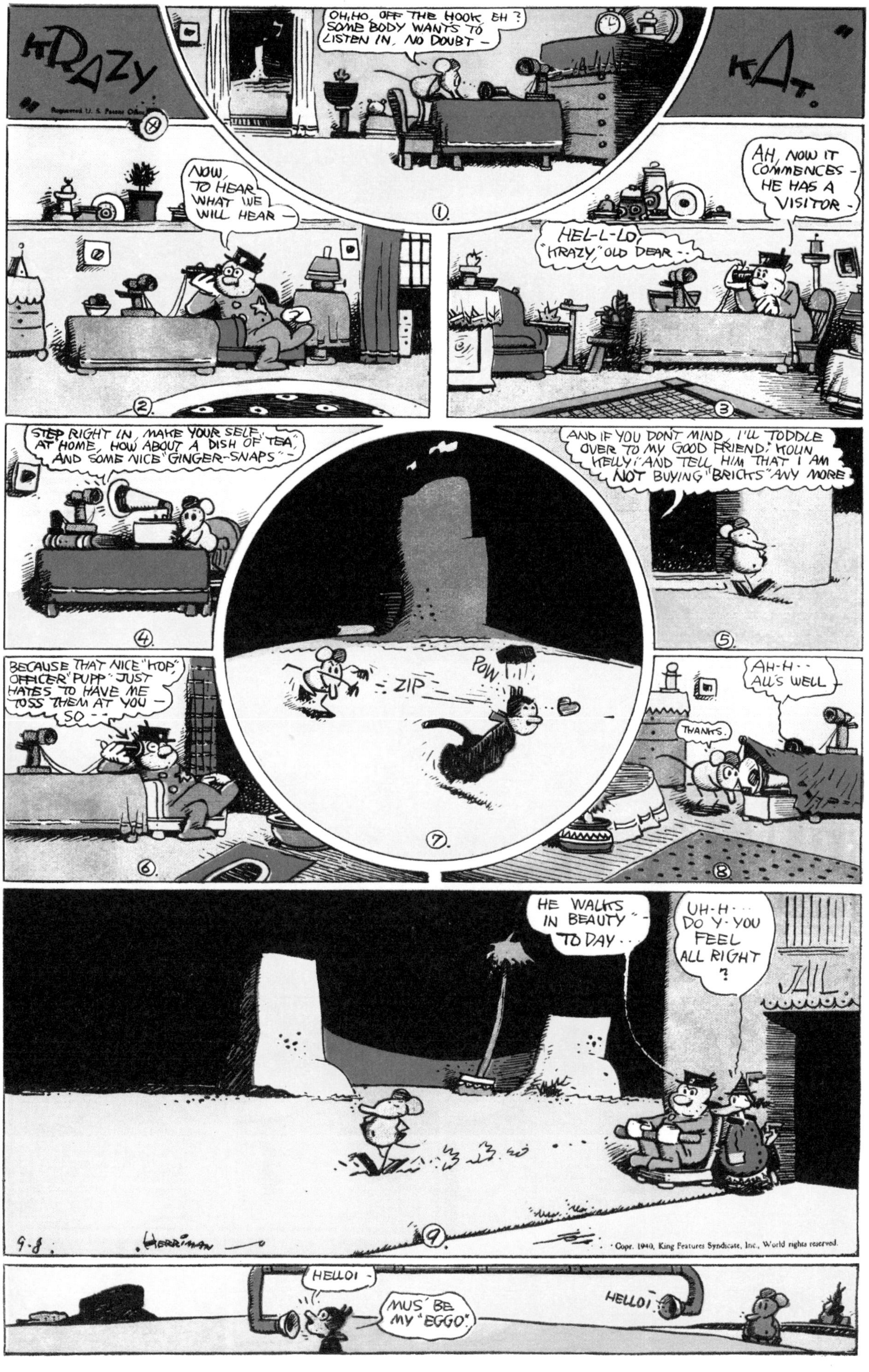
KRAZY KAT
Registered U. S. Patent Office
OH, HO, OFF THE HOOK EH? SOME BODY WANTS TO LISTEN IN, NO DOUBT -
NOW, TO HEAR WHAT WE WILL HEAR -
AH, NOW IT COMMENCES - HE HAS A VISITOR -
HEL-L-LO, "KRAZY," OLD DEAR - -
STEP RIGHT IN, MAKE YOUR SELF AT HOME, HOW ABOUT A DISH OF "TEA," AND SOME NICE "GINGER-SNAPS" -
AND IF YOU DON'T MIND, I'LL TODDLE OVER TO MY GOOD FRIEND, "KOUN KELLY," AND TELL HIM THAT I AM NOT BUYING "BRICKS" ANY MORE
BECAUSE THAT NICE "KOP," OFFICER "PUPP" JUST HATES TO HAVE ME TOSS THEM AT YOU - SO - -
ZIP
POW
AH-H - - ALL'S WELL
THANKS.
HE WALKS IN BEAUTY TO DAY - -
UH-H - - DO Y-YOU FEEL ALL RIGHT ?
JAIL
9-8
HERRIMAN
Copr. 1940, King Features Syndicate, Inc., World rights reserved.
HELLO!
MUS' BE MY "EGGO"
HELLO!

September 8th, 1940.

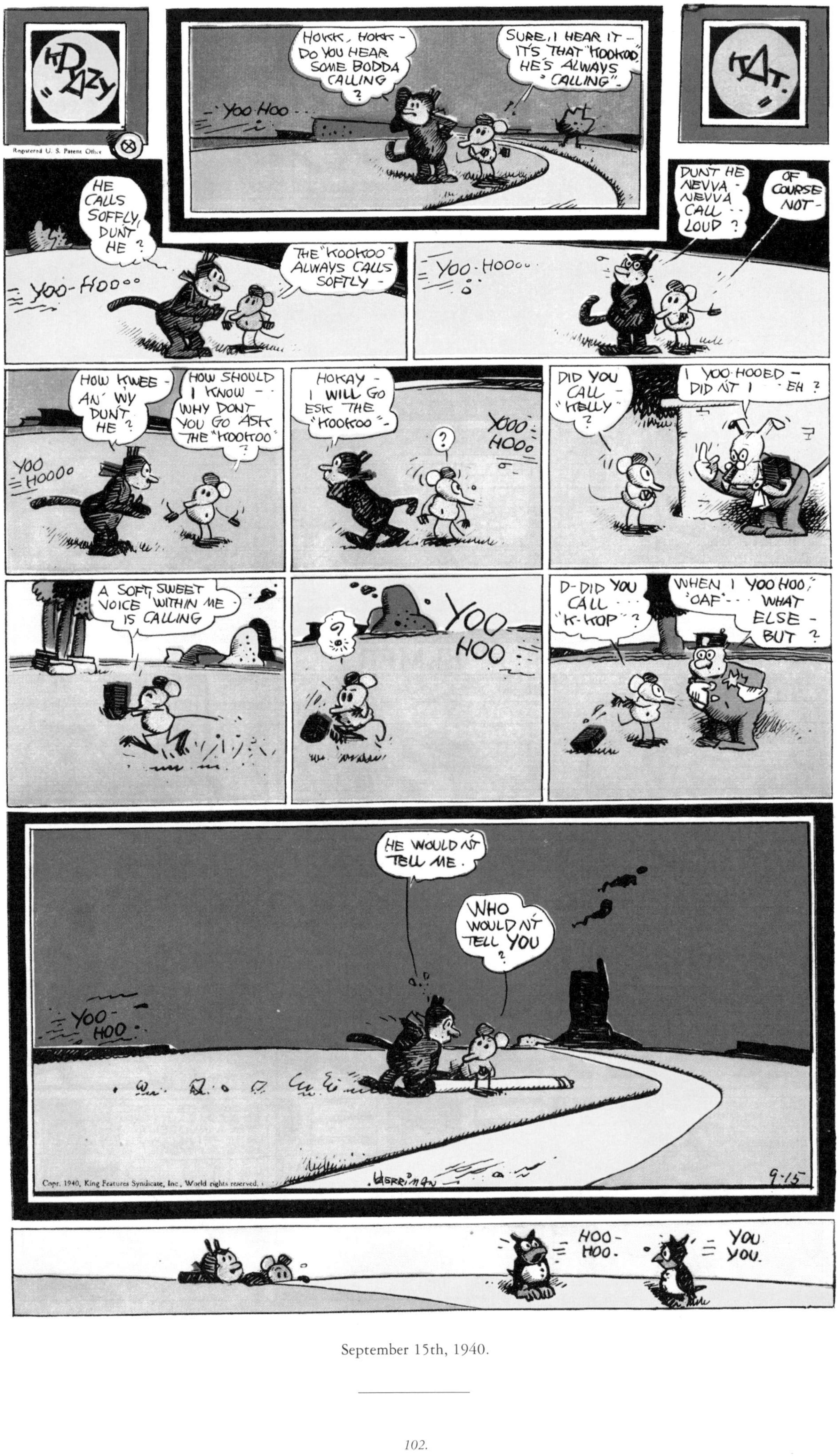
KRAZY
KAT.
Registered U. S. Patent Office
HOKK, HOKK - DO YOU HEAR SOME BODDA CALLING ?
SURE, I HEAR IT - IT'S THAT "KOOKOO" HE'S ALWAYS "CALLING".
YOO HOO
HE CALLS SOFFLY, DUNT HE ?
THE "KOOKOO" ALWAYS CALLS SOFTLY -
YOO-HOO
DUNT HE NEVVA NEVVA CALL LOUD ?
OF COURSE NOT -
YOO-HOO
HOW KWEE - AN' WY DUNT HE ?
HOW SHOULD I KNOW - WHY DONT YOU GO ASK THE "KOOKOO" ?
YOO HOOO
HOKAY - I WILL GO ESK THE "KOOKOO" -
YOOO HOO
DID YOU CALL "KELLY" ?
I YOO-HOOED - DID N'T I - EH ?
A SOFT, SWEET VOICE WITHIN ME IS CALLING
YOO HOO
D-DID YOU CALL "K-KOP" ?
WHEN I YOO HOO 'OAF' - WHAT ELSE - BUT ?
HE WOULD N'T TELL ME.
WHO WOULD N'T TELL YOU ?
YOO-HOO.
Copr. 1940, King Features Syndicate, Inc., World rights reserved.
HERRIMAN
9-15
HOO-HOO.
YOU YOU.

September 15th, 1940.

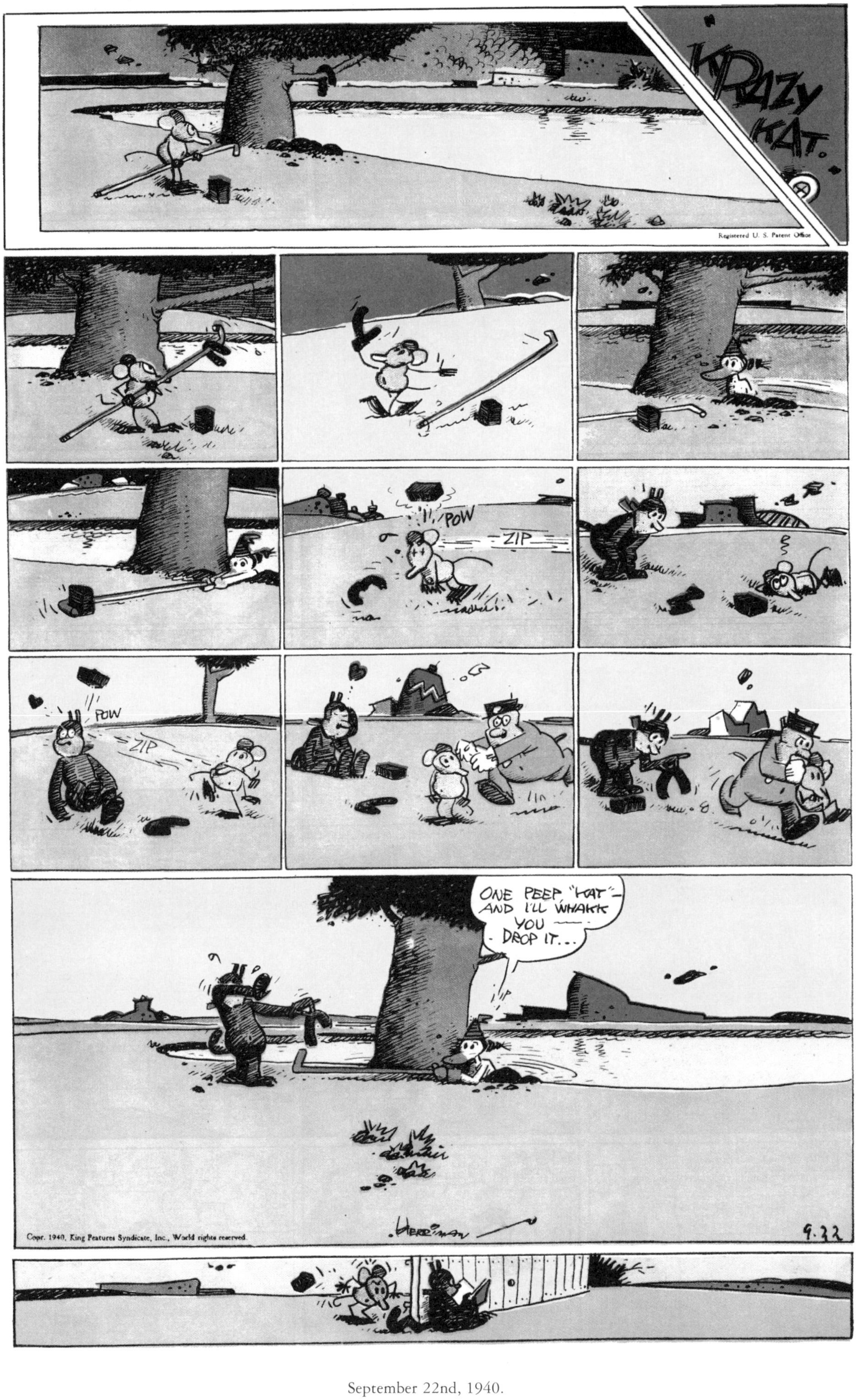
KRAZY KAT
Registered U. S. Patent Office
POW
ZIP
POW
ZIP
ONE PEEP "KAT" — AND I'LL WHAKK YOU — DROP IT...
Copr. 1940, King Features Syndicate, Inc., World rights reserved.
HERRIMAN
9.22

September 22nd, 1940.

IF WE HAD A NAVY - YES - BUT WE AINT - SO - WHAT GOOD IS IT ?
OFFICER "PUPP" PLANTS AN EYE UPON A POOL - AND PUZZLES THERE-AT - WONDER BESETS THE "LAW" - AMAZEMENT ASSAILS "ORDER."
"KRAZY KAT"
Registered U.S. Patent Office
A PEANUT FOR THAT BRICK - FAIR BARTER
"TRADER MOUSE" - ME.
POW
ZIP
MY BUTTER-FLY -
EH ?
ARE YOU FORGETTING THIS - ?
AH, NOW HAVE I USE FOR THAT POOL ? - 'T WILL SERVE TO DUCK A MOUSE AND A BRICK.
DID YOU HAVE TO SWIG IT DRY - YOU B-BIG - OAF ?
I COULD N'T HELP IT, "KOP" - THAT WAS A MIGHTY SALTY "GOOBER" -
OH, WELL - THERE'S ALWAYS THE JOLLY OLD JAIL.
ZIP
JAIL
Copr. 1940, King Features Syndicate, Inc., World rights reserved
HERRIMAN
9-29
JAIL.
?

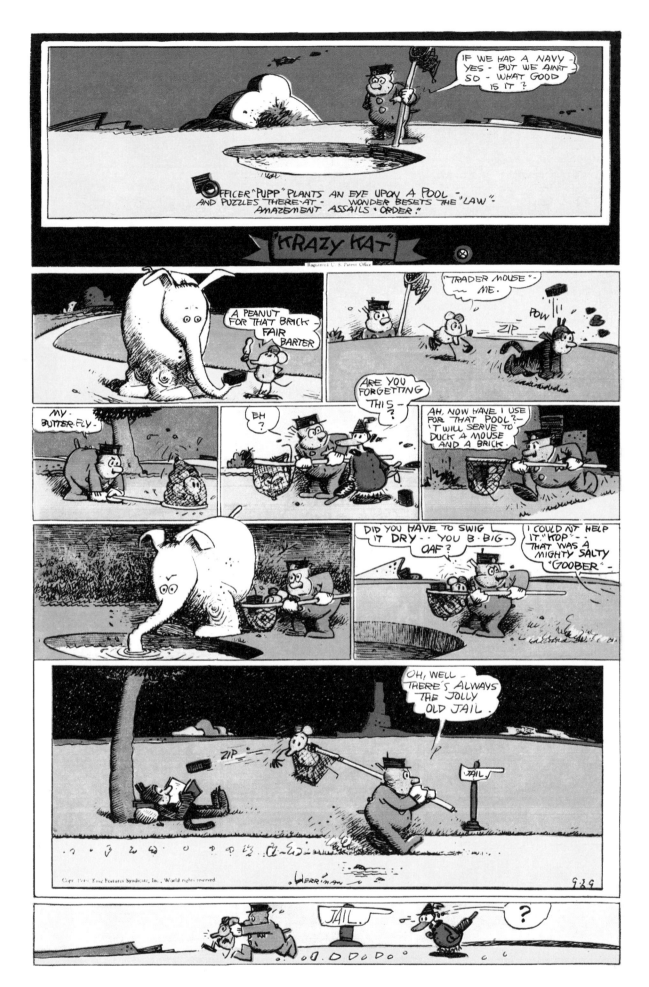

September 29th, 1940.

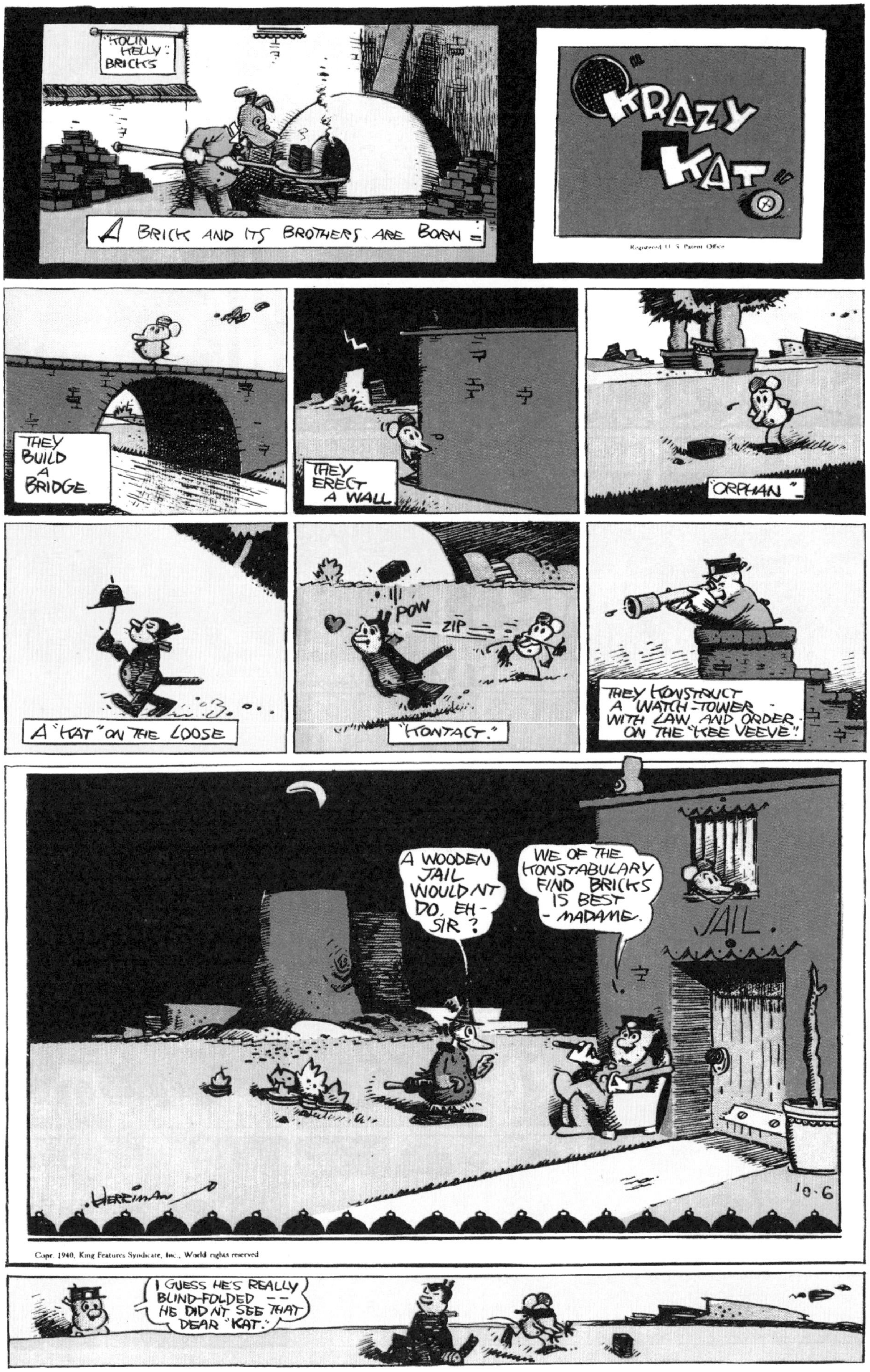
"KOLIN KELLY" BRICKS
A BRICK AND ITS BROTHERS ARE BORN =
"KRAZY KAT"
Registered U.S. Patent Office
THEY BUILD A BRIDGE
THEY ERECT A WALL
"ORPHAN"—
A "KAT" ON THE LOOSE
POW
ZIP
"KONTACT."
THEY KONSTRUCT A WATCH-TOWER WITH LAW AND ORDER ON THE "KEE VEEVE".
A WOODEN JAIL WOULD NT DO, EH SIR?
WE OF THE KONSTABULARY FIND BRICKS IS BEST - MADAME.
JAIL.
HERRIMAN
10-6
Copr. 1940, King Features Syndicate, Inc., World rights reserved
I GUESS HE'S REALLY BLIND-FOLDED -- HE DID NT SEE THAT DEAR "KAT."

October 6th, 1940.

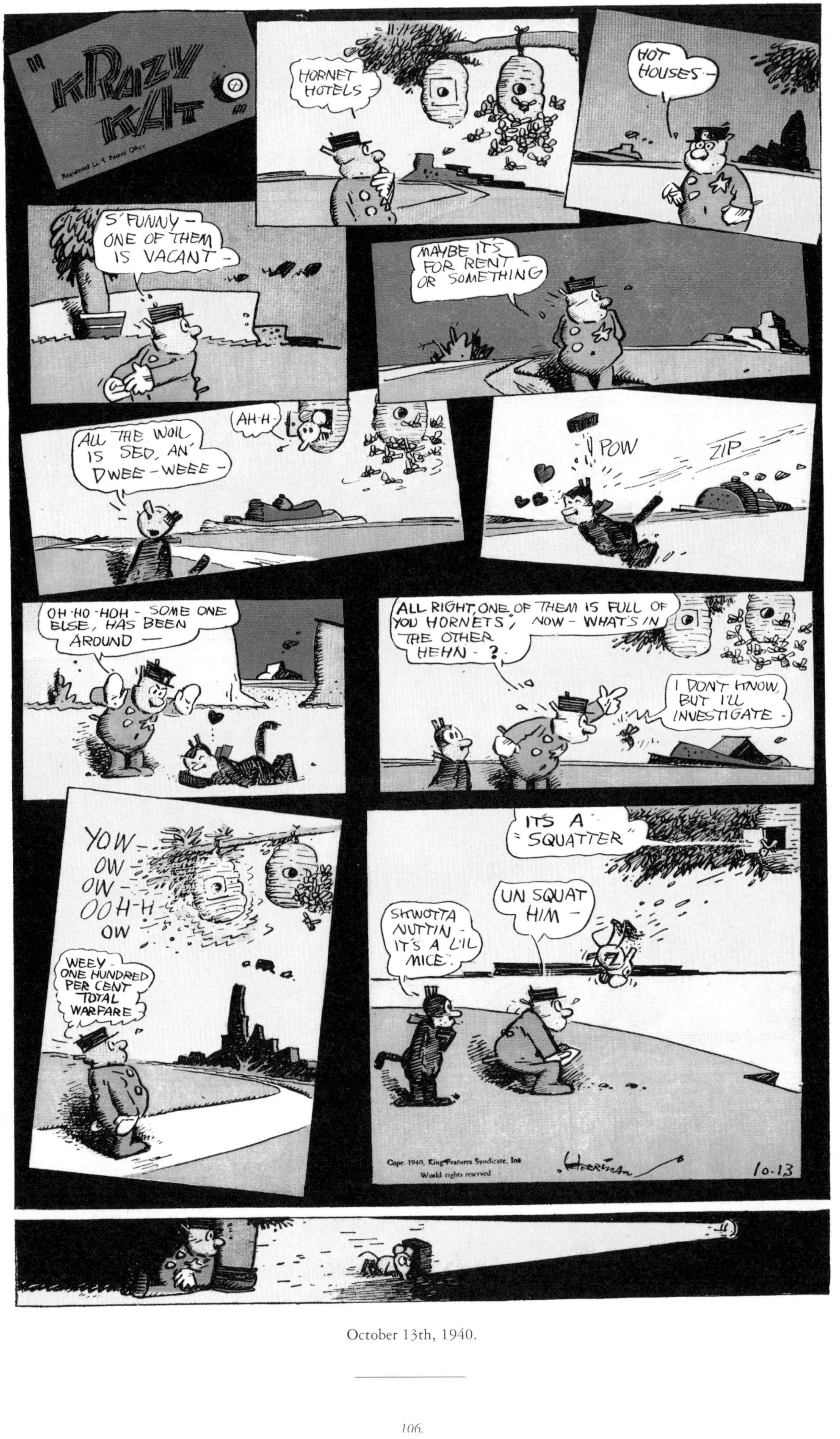
"Krazy Kat"
Registered U. S. Patent Office
HORNET HOTELS -
HOT HOUSES -
S'FUNNY - ONE OF THEM IS VACANT -
MAYBE IT'S FOR RENT OR SOMETHING
ALL THE WOIL IS SED, AN' DWEE - WEEE -
AH-H -
POW
ZIP
OH-HO-HOH - SOME ONE ELSE, HAS BEEN AROUND —
ALL RIGHT, ONE OF THEM IS FULL OF YOU HORNETS, NOW - WHAT'S IN THE OTHER HEHN - ?
I DON'T KNOW, BUT I'LL INVESTIGATE -
YOW - OW - OW - OOH-H - OW
WEEY - ONE HUNDRED PER CENT TOTAL WARFARE -
IT'S A SQUATTER
UN SQUAT HIM -
SHWOTTA NUTTIN - IT'S A L'IL MICE.
Copr. 1940, King Features Syndicate, Inc
World rights reserved
Herriman
10.13

October 13th, 1940.

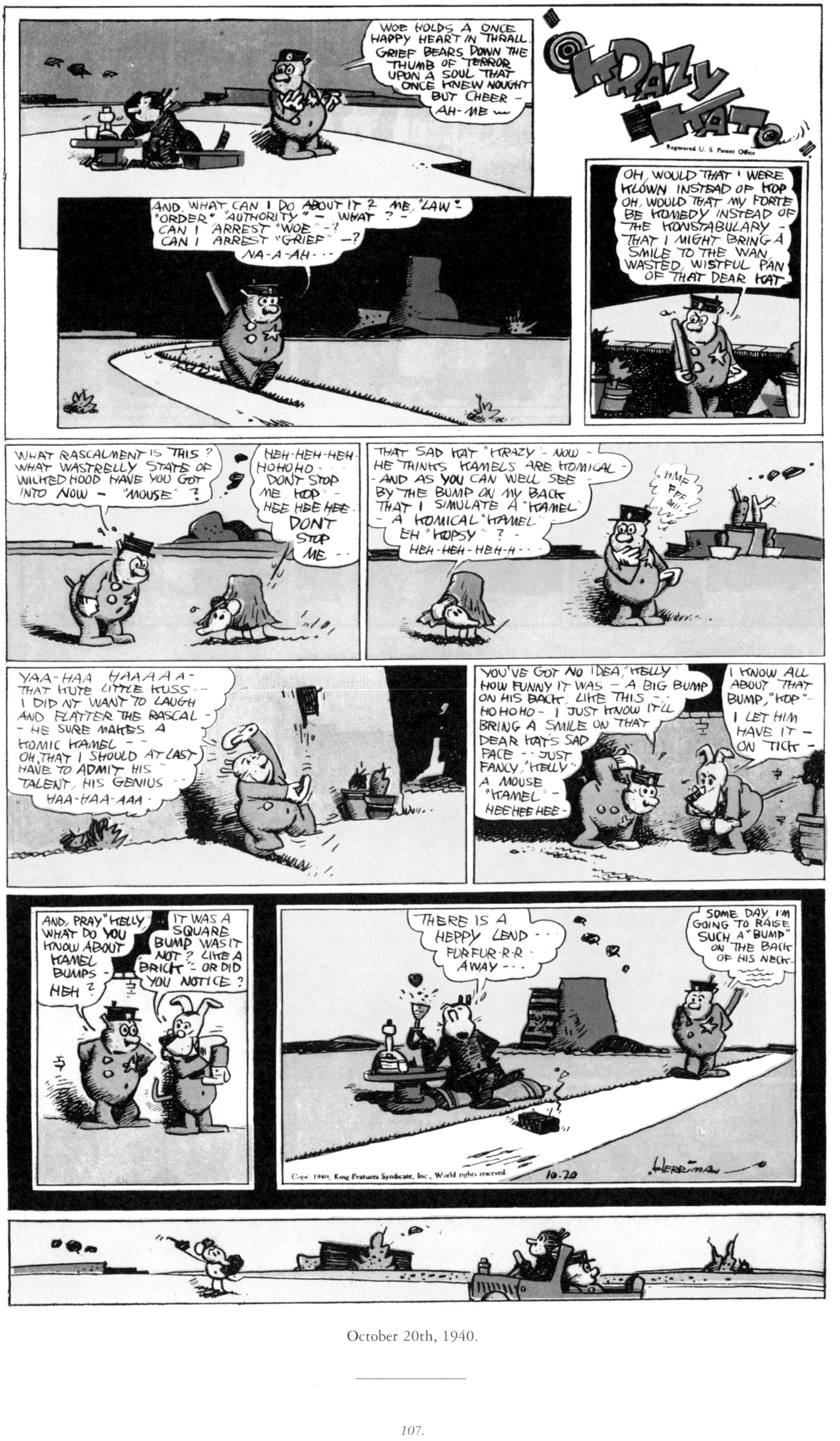
KRAZY KAT
Registered U.S. Patent Office
WOE HOLDS A ONCE HAPPY HEART IN THRALL. GRIEF BEARS DOWN THE THUMB OF TERROR UPON A SOUL THAT ONCE KNEW NOUGHT BUT CHEER - AH-ME ~
AND, WHAT CAN I DO ABOUT IT? ME, "LAW" "ORDER" "AUTHORITY" - WHAT? - CAN I ARREST "WOE" -? CAN I ARREST "GRIEF" -? NA-A-AH - -
OH, WOULD THAT I WERE KLOWN INSTEAD OF KOP OH, WOULD THAT MY FORTE BE KOMEDY INSTEAD OF THE KONSTABULARY - THAT I MIGHT BRING A SMILE TO THE WAN, WASTED, WISTFUL PAN OF THAT DEAR KAT
WHAT RASCALMENT IS THIS? WHAT WASTRELLY STATE OF WICKEDHOOD HAVE YOU GOT INTO NOW - "MOUSE"?
HEH-HEH-HEH HOHOHO - - DON'T STOP ME, KOP - HEE HEE HEE DON'T STOP ME - -
THAT SAD KAT "KRAZY" - NOW - HE THINKS KAMELS ARE KOMICAL - AND AS YOU CAN WELL SEE - BY THE BUMP ON MY BACK THAT I SIMULATE A "KAMEL" - A KOMICAL "KAMEL" - EH "KOPSY"? - HEH-HEH-HEH-H - -
YAA-HAA HAAAAA - THAT KUTE LITTLE KUSS - - I DID NT WANT TO LAUGH AND FLATTER THE RASCAL - - HE SURE MAKES A KOMIC KAMEL - - OH, THAT I SHOULD AT LAST HAVE TO ADMIT HIS TALENT, HIS GENIUS - - HAA-HAA-AAA -
YOU'VE GOT NO IDEA, "KELLY" HOW FUNNY IT WAS - A BIG BUMP ON HIS BACK, LIKE THIS - - HO HO HO - I JUST KNOW IT'LL BRING A SMILE ON THAT DEAR KAT'S SAD FACE - - JUST FANCY, "KELLY" A MOUSE "KAMEL" - HEE HEE HEE -
I KNOW ALL ABOUT THAT BUMP, "KOP" - I LET HIM HAVE IT - ON TICK -
AND, PRAY "KELLY" WHAT DO YOU KNOW ABOUT KAMEL BUMPS - HEH?
IT WAS A SQUARE BUMP WAS IT NOT? LIKE A BRICK - OR DID YOU NOTICE?
THERE IS A HEPPY LEND - - FURFUR-R-R AWAY - - .
SOME DAY, I'M GOING TO RAISE SUCH A "BUMP" ON THE BACK OF HIS NECK -
Copr. 1940, King Features Syndicate, Inc., World rights reserved.
10-20
HERRIMAN

October 20th, 1940.

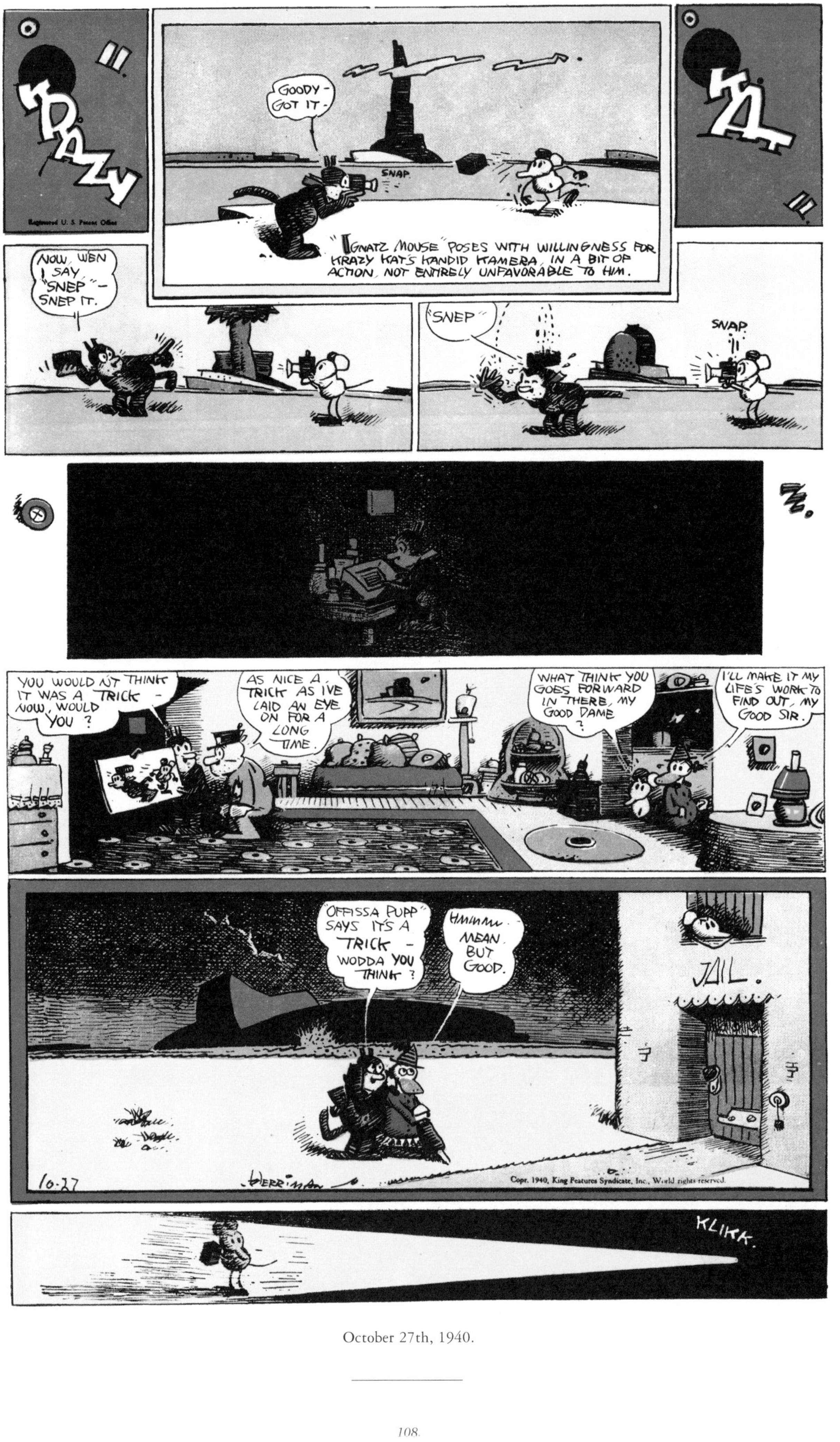
KRAZY
KAT
Registered U. S. Patent Office
GOODY - GOT IT -
SNAP.
"IGNATZ MOUSE" POSES WITH WILLINGNESS FOR KRAZY KAT'S KANDID KAMERA, IN A BIT OF ACTION, NOT ENTIRELY UNFAVORABLE TO HIM.
NOW, WEN I SAY "SNEP" - SNEP IT.
"SNEP"
SNAP.
YOU WOULD N'T THINK IT WAS A TRICK - NOW, WOULD YOU ?
AS NICE A TRICK AS I'VE LAID AN EYE ON FOR A LONG TIME.
WHAT THINK YOU GOES FORWARD IN THERE, MY GOOD DAME ?
I'LL MAKE IT MY LIFE'S WORK TO FIND OUT, MY GOOD SIR.
"OFFISSA PUPP" SAYS IT'S A TRICK - WODDA YOU THINK ?
HMMM - MEAN BUT GOOD.
JAIL.
10-27
HERRIMAN
Copr. 1940, King Features Syndicate, Inc., World rights reserved.
KLIKK.

October 27th, 1940.

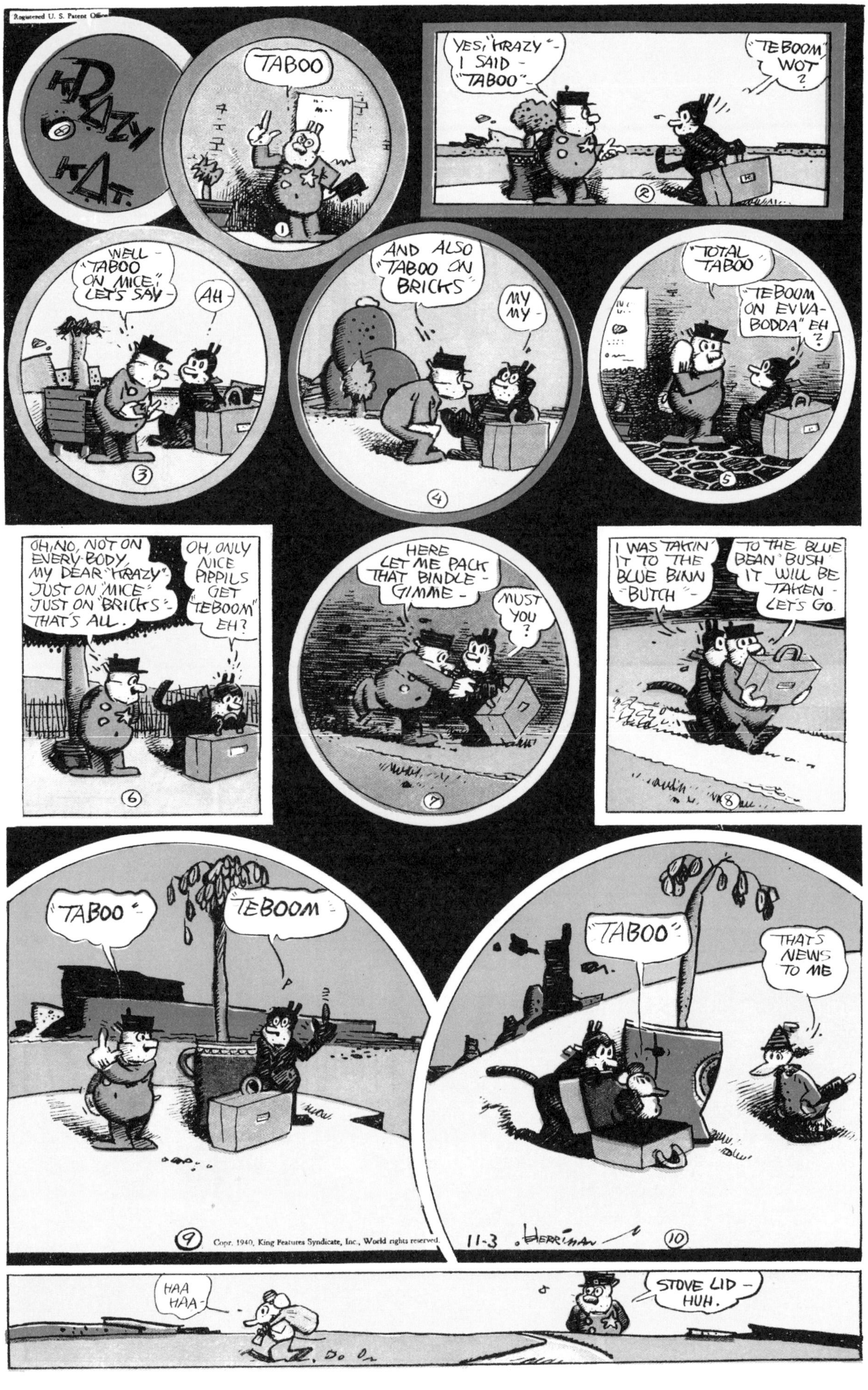

Registered U. S. Patent Office
KRAZY KAT
TABOO
YES, "KRAZY" - I SAID - "TABOO"
"TEBOOM" WOT ?
WELL - "TABOO ON MICE" LET'S SAY
AH
AND ALSO "TABOO ON BRICKS"
MY MY
"TOTAL TABOO"
"TEBOOM ON EVVA-BODDA" EH ?
OH, NO, NOT ON EVERY-BODY, MY DEAR "KRAZY" JUST ON "MICE" JUST ON "BRICKS" THAT'S ALL.
OH, ONLY NICE PIPPILS GET "TEBOOM" EH?
HERE LET ME PACK THAT BINDLE - GIMME -
MUST YOU ?
I WAS TAKIN' IT TO THE BLUE BINN "BUTCH"
TO THE BLUE BEAN BUSH IT WILL BE TAKEN LET'S GO.
TABOO
TEBOOM
TABOO
THAT'S NEWS TO ME
Copr. 1940, King Features Syndicate, Inc., World rights reserved.
11-3
HERRIMAN
HAA HAA -
STOVE LID - HUH.

November 3rd, 1940.

"KRAZY KAT"
Registered U. S. Patent Office
SYMBOL OF "SIN"
OH I'M NOT
MMM
THEN THAT "MOUSE" YOUR MASTER IS
AW- HE IS NOT
I-I-I'D BETTER SEE A DOCTOR
NOT IF HE SEES YOU FIRST.
I GAVE YOU MY WORD "KRAZY" - IT TALKED IT T-T-TALKED
WOT DID ?
THAT "BRICK"
DID THIS "BRIGG" - RILLY TALK "DOLLIN" ?
IT'S A HAUNT
NO
I ESKED IGNATZ "MICE" AN' HE SAID "NO"
LET'S GO ASK THE "BRICK".
Copr. 1940, King Features Syndicate, Inc., World rights reserved
HERRIMAN
11-10
KRAZY KWILT
IT'S ME, "DOLLIN"

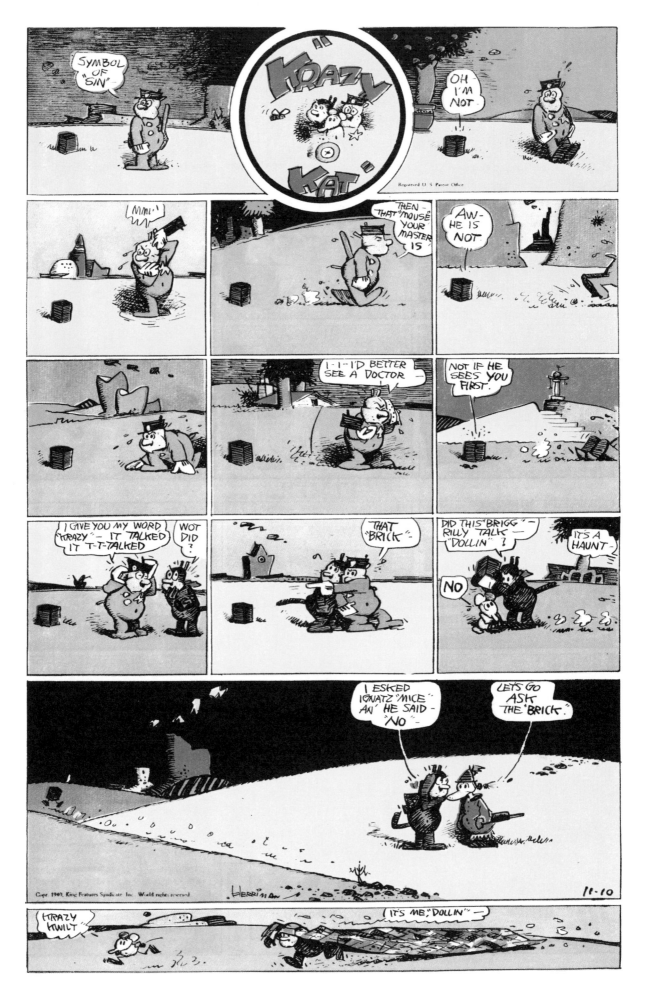

November 10th, 1940.

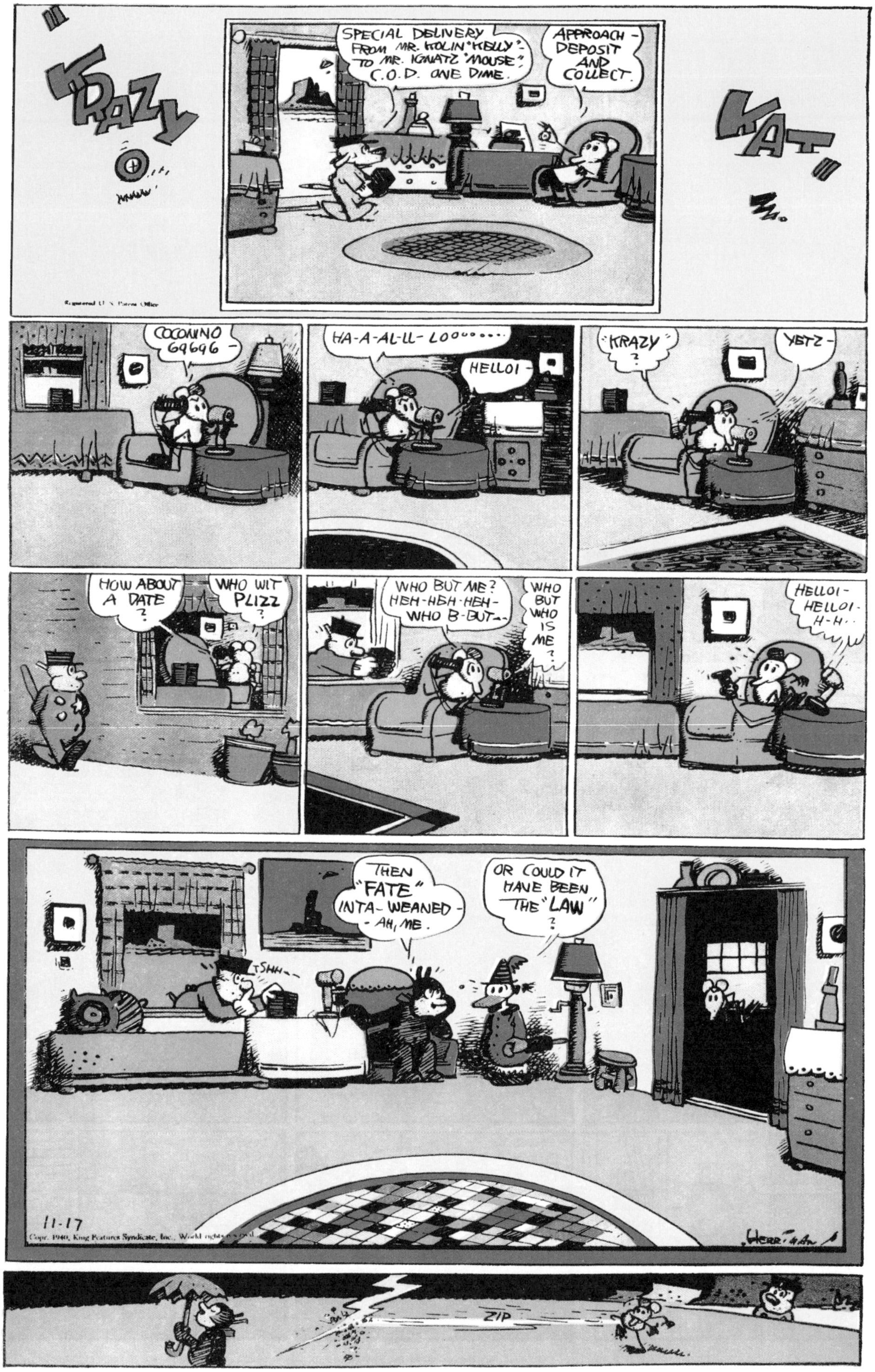
"KRAZY
KAT"
SPECIAL DELIVERY FROM MR. KOLIN "KELLY" TO MR. IGNATZ "MOUSE" C.O.D. ONE DIME.
APPROACH - DEPOSIT AND COLLECT.
COCONINO 69696 -
HA-A-AL-LL-LOO°°°°....
HELLO! -
"KRAZY" ?
YETZ -
HOW ABOUT A DATE ?
WHO WIT PLIZZ ?
WHO BUT ME? HEH-HEH-HEH- WHO B-BUT--
WHO BUT WHO IS ME ?
HELLO! - HELLO! - H-H..
THEN "FATE" INTA-WEANED - AH, ME.
OR COULD IT HAVE BEEN THE "LAW" ?
SHH--
11-17
HERRIMAN
ZIP

November 17th, 1940.

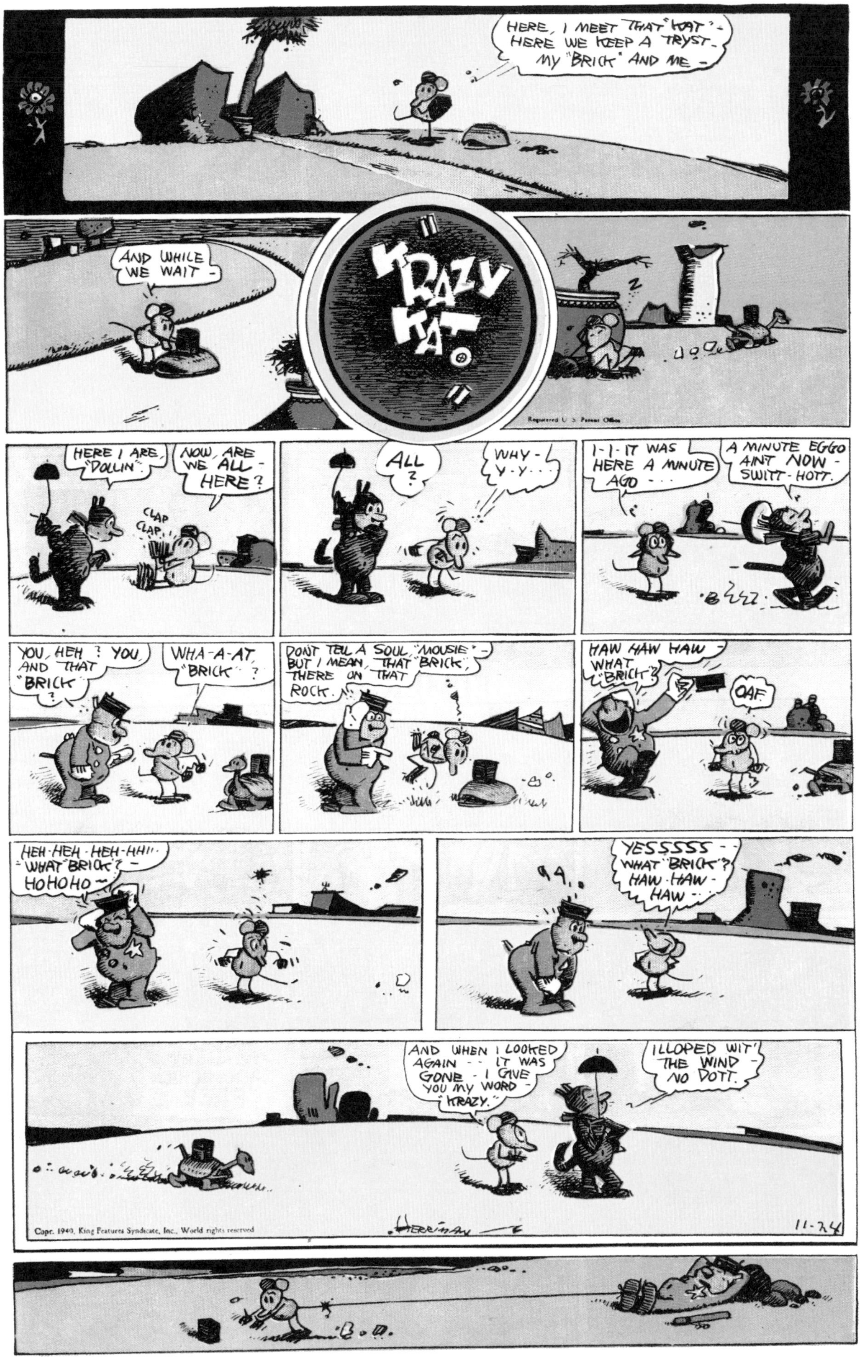
HERE, I MEET THAT "KAT" - HERE WE KEEP A TRYST - MY "BRICK" AND ME -
AND WHILE WE WAIT -
"KRAZY KAT"
Registered U. S. Patent Office
HERE I ARE, "DOLLIN".
NOW, ARE WE ALL HERE?
CLAP CLAP
ALL ?
WHY - Y - Y . . .
I - I - IT WAS HERE A MINUTE AGO - - -
A MINUTE EGGO AIN'T NOW - SWITT - HOTT.
BZZZ
YOU, HEH? YOU AND THAT "BRICK"?
WHA-A-AT "BRICK"?
DON'T TELL A SOUL, "MOUSIE" - BUT I MEAN, THAT "BRICK", THERE ON THAT ROCK.
HAW HAW HAW - WHAT "BRICK"?
OAF
HEH-HEH-HEH-HH!! - WHAT "BRICK"? - HOHOHO -
YESSSSS - - WHAT "BRICK"? HAW-HAW-HAW -
AND WHEN I LOOKED AGAIN - - IT WAS GONE - I GIVE YOU MY WORD - "KRAZY."
ILLOPED WIT' THE WIND - NO DOTT.
Copr. 1940, King Features Syndicate, Inc., World rights reserved
Herriman
11-24

November 24th, 1940.

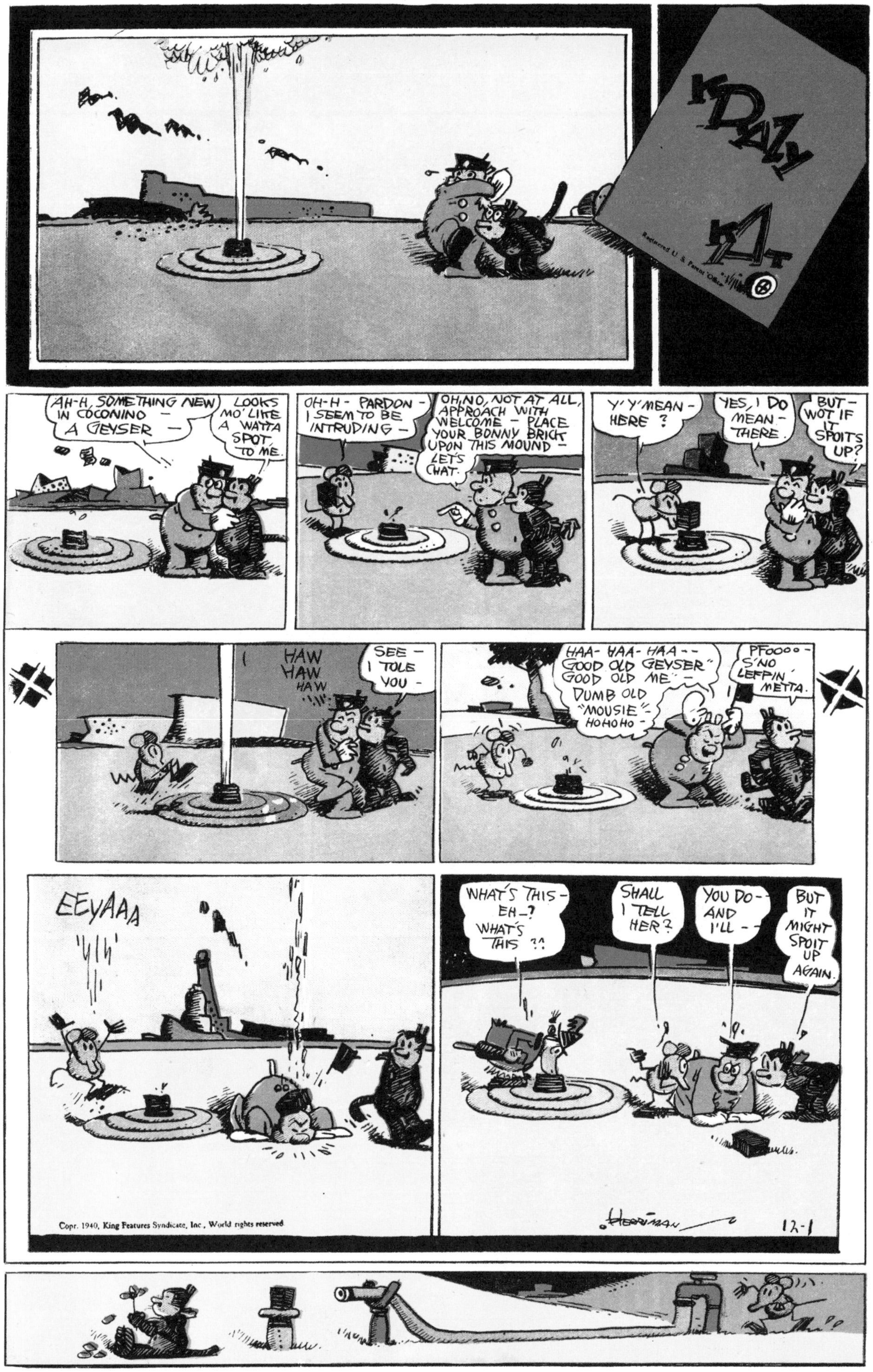
KRAZY KAT
Registered U. S. Patent Office
AH-H, SOMETHING NEW IN COCONINO — A GEYSER —
LOOKS MO' LIKE A WATTA SPOT, TO ME.
OH-H – PARDON – I SEEM TO BE INTRUDING –
OH, NO, NOT AT ALL, APPROACH WITH WELCOME – PLACE YOUR BONNY BRICK UPON THIS MOUND – LET'S CHAT.
Y'Y'MEAN – HERE ?
YES, I DO MEAN – THERE.
BUT – WOT IF IT SPOITS UP?
HAW HAW HAW
SEE – I TOLE YOU –
HAA-HAA-HAA -- GOOD OLD GEYSER" GOOD OLD ME – DUMB OLD "MOUSIE" – HOHOHO –
PFOOOO – S'NO LEFFIN' METTA.
EEYAAA
WHAT'S THIS – EH –? WHAT'S THIS ??
SHALL I TELL HER?
YOU DO – AND I'LL – –
BUT IT MIGHT SPOIT UP AGAIN.
Copr. 1940, King Features Syndicate, Inc., World rights reserved
Herriman
12-1

December 1st, 1940.

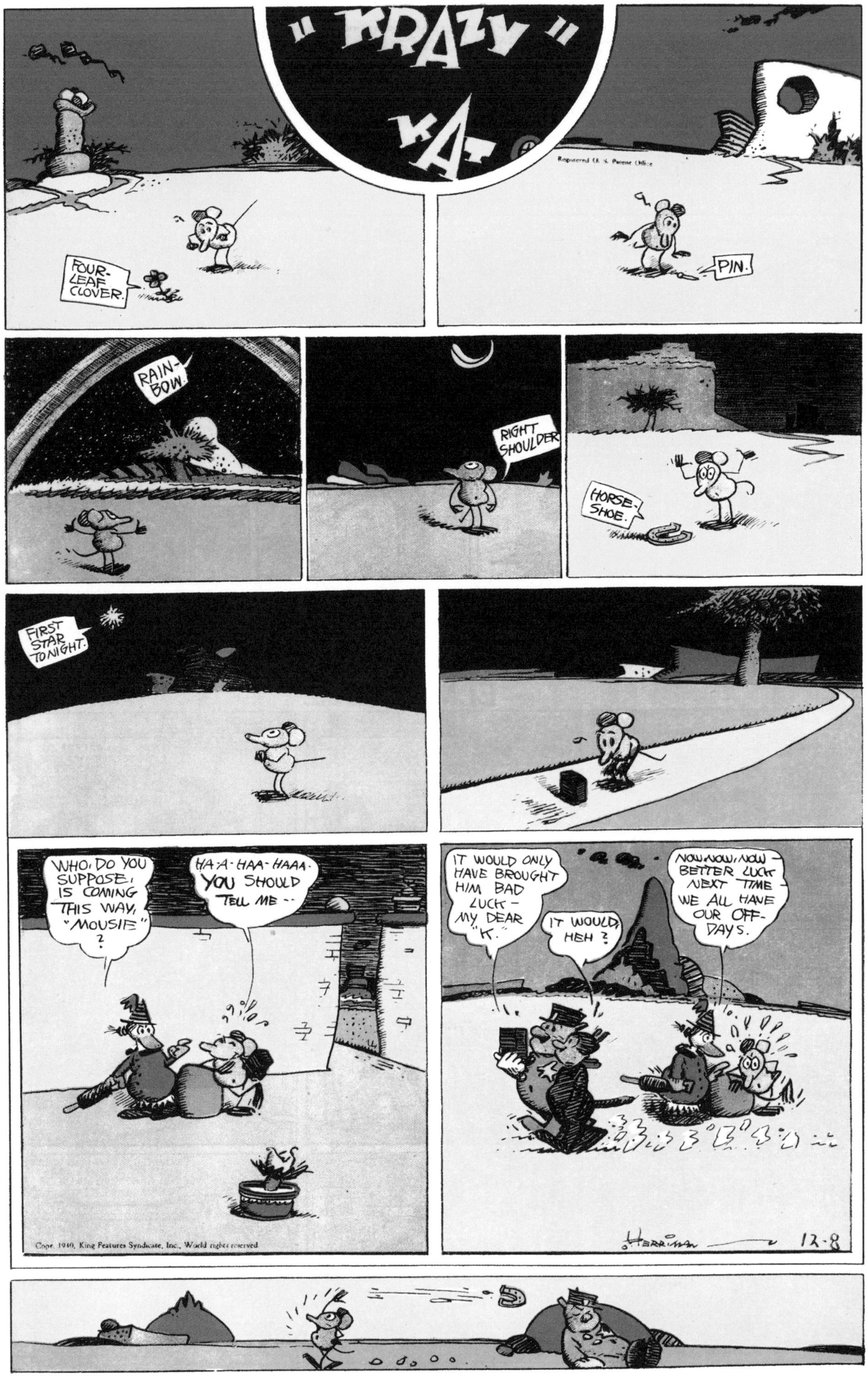
"KRAZY" KAT
Registered U.S. Patent Office
FOUR-LEAF CLOVER.
PIN.
RAIN-BOW.
RIGHT SHOULDER
HORSE-SHOE.
FIRST STAR TONIGHT.
WHO, DO YOU SUPPOSE, IS COMING THIS WAY, "MOUSIE" ?
HA-A-HAA-HAAA-YOU SHOULD TELL ME --
Copr. 1940, King Features Syndicate, Inc., World rights reserved
IT WOULD ONLY HAVE BROUGHT HIM BAD LUCK - MY DEAR "K."
IT WOULD, HEH ?
NOW, NOW, NOW - BETTER LUCK NEXT TIME - WE ALL HAVE OUR OFF-DAYS.
HERRIMAN 12-8

December 8th, 1940.

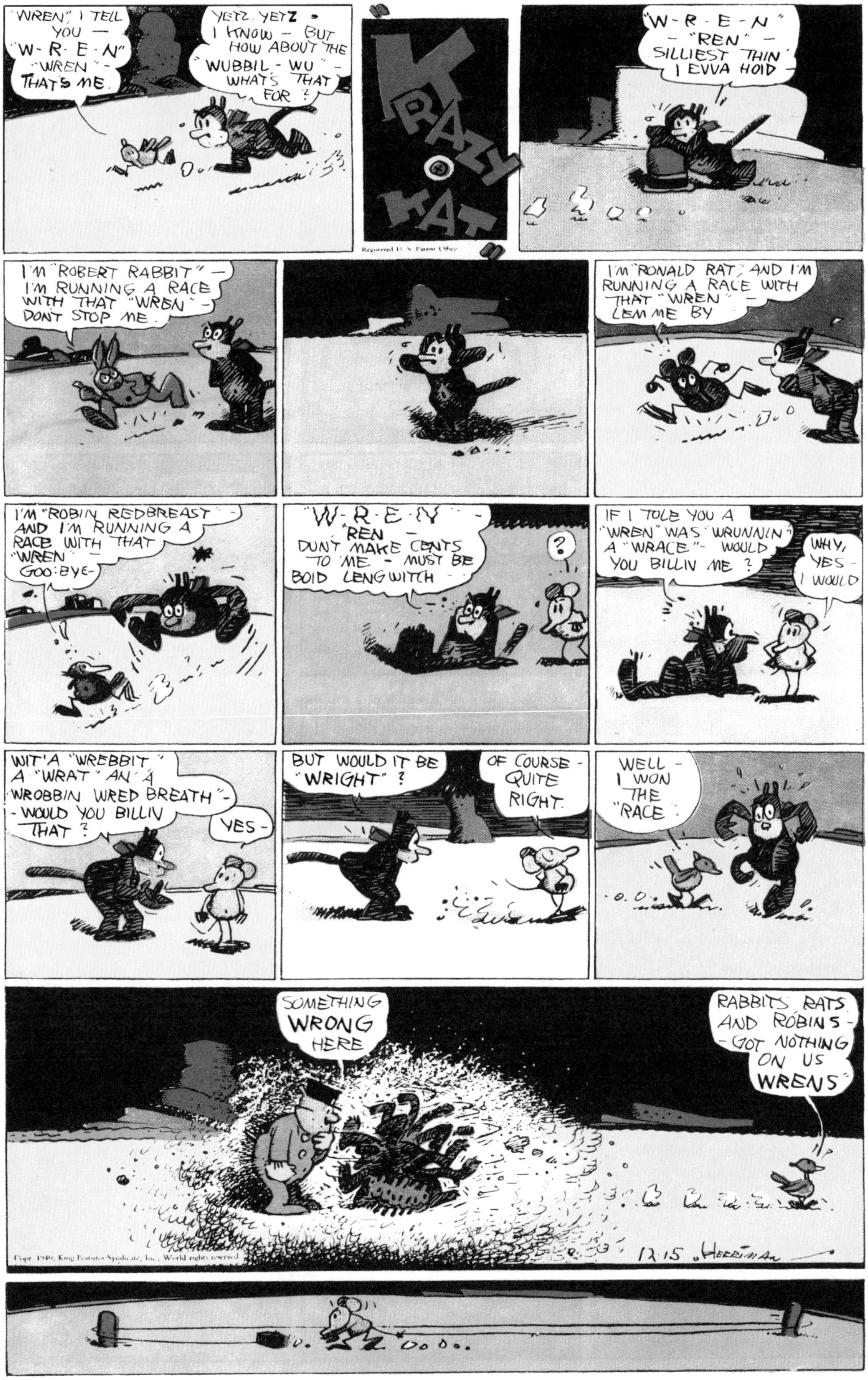

"WREN" I TELL YOU — "W-R-E-N" "WREN" - THAT'S ME.
YETZ, YETZ - I KNOW - BUT HOW ABOUT THE "WUBBIL-WU" - WHAT'S THAT FOR ?
KRAZY KAT
Registered U.S. Patent Office
"W-R-E-N" - "REN" - SILLIEST THIN' I EVVA HOID -
I'M "ROBERT RABBIT" - I'M RUNNING A RACE WITH THAT "WREN" - DON'T STOP ME.
I'M "RONALD RAT" AND I'M RUNNING A RACE WITH THAT "WREN" - LEMME BY
I'M "ROBIN REDBREAST" - AND I'M RUNNING A RACE WITH THAT "WREN" GOO'BYE-
"W-R-E-N" - "REN" - DUN'T MAKE CENTS TO ME - MUST BE BOID LENGWITCH -
?
IF I TOLE YOU A "WREN" WAS "WRUNNIN" A "WRACE" - WOULD YOU BILLIV ME ?
WHY, YES - I WOULD
WIT' A "WREBBIT" A "WRAT" AN' A "WROBBIN WRED BREATH" - - WOULD YOU BILLIV THAT ?
YES -
BUT WOULD IT BE "WRIGHT" ?
OF COURSE - QUITE RIGHT.
WELL - I WON THE "RACE".
SOMETHING WRONG HERE
RABBITS, RATS AND ROBINS - - GOT NOTHING ON US WRENS
Copr. 1940, King Features Syndicate, Inc., World rights reserved.
12.15 HERRIMAN

December 15th, 1940.

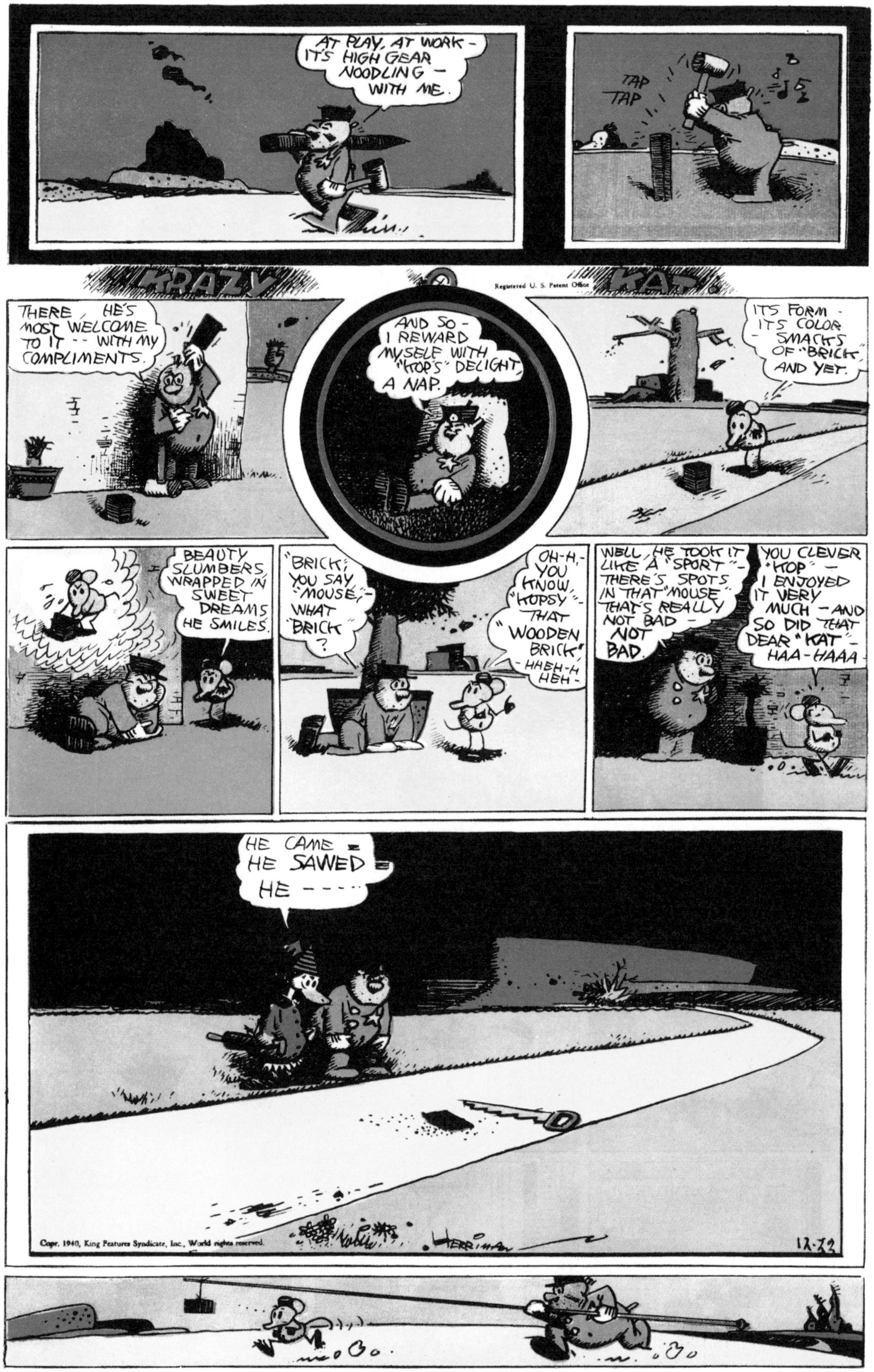

AT PLAY, AT WORK - IT'S HIGH GEAR NOODLING - WITH ME.
TAP TAP
KRAZY KAT
Registered U. S. Patent Office
THERE, HE'S MOST WELCOME TO IT -- WITH MY COMPLIMENTS.
AND SO - I REWARD MYSELF WITH "KOP'S" DELIGHT, A NAP.
ITS FORM - ITS COLOR - SMACKS OF "BRICK," AND YET.
BEAUTY SLUMBERS, WRAPPED IN SWEET DREAMS HE SMILES.
"BRICK," YOU SAY, "MOUSE," - WHAT "BRICK"?
OH-H, - YOU KNOW, "KOPSY" - THAT "WOODEN BRICK" - HHEH-H HEH -
WELL, HE TOOK IT LIKE A "SPORT" - THERE'S SPOTS IN THAT "MOUSE" THAT'S REALLY NOT BAD - NOT BAD.
YOU CLEVER "KOP" - I ENJOYED IT VERY MUCH - AND SO DID THAT DEAR "KAT" - HAA-HAAA
HE CAME - HE SAWED - HE - - - -
Copr. 1940, King Features Syndicate, Inc., World rights reserved.
HERRIMAN
12-22

December 22nd, 1940.

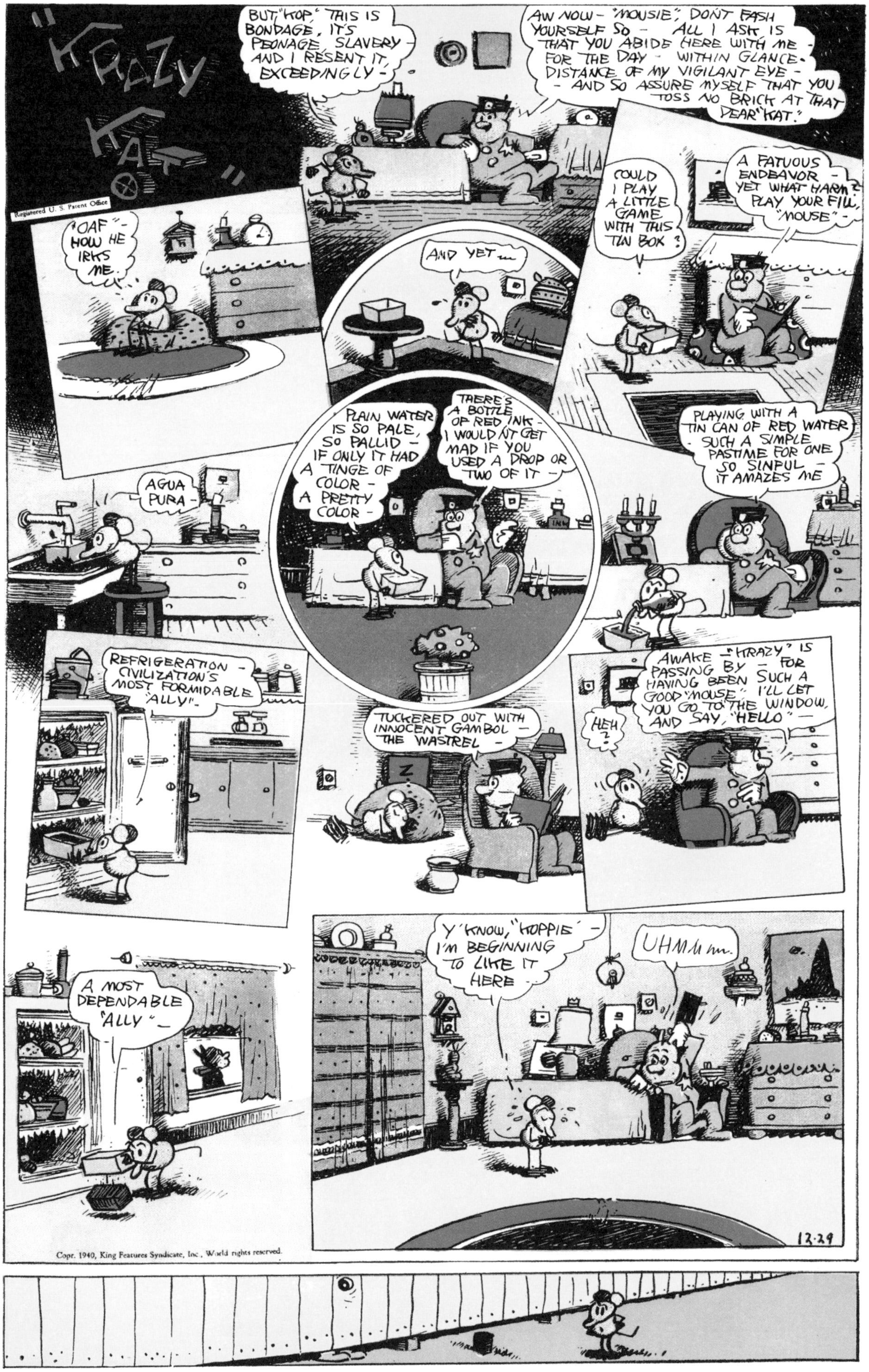
"Krazy Kat"
Registered U. S. Patent Office
BUT, "KOP," THIS IS BONDAGE, IT'S PEONAGE, SLAVERY - AND I RESENT IT, EXCEEDINGLY -
AW NOW - "MOUSIE," DON'T FASH YOURSELF SO - ALL I ASK IS THAT YOU ABIDE HERE WITH ME - FOR THE DAY - WITHIN GLANCE-DISTANCE OF MY VIGILANT EYE - - AND SO ASSURE MYSELF THAT YOU TOSS NO BRICK AT THAT DEAR "KAT."
"OAF" - HOW HE IRKS ME.
AND YET ...
COULD I PLAY A LITTLE GAME WITH THIS TIN BOX?
A FATUOUS ENDEAVOR - YET WHAT HARM? PLAY YOUR FILL, "MOUSE" -
AGUA PURA -
PLAIN WATER IS SO PALE, SO PALLID - IF ONLY IT HAD A TINGE OF COLOR - A PRETTY COLOR -
THERE'S A BOTTLE OF RED INK - I WOULD N'T GET MAD IF YOU USED A DROP OR TWO OF IT -
PLAYING WITH A TIN CAN OF RED WATER - SUCH A SIMPLE PASTIME FOR ONE SO SINFUL - IT AMAZES ME
REFRIGERATION - CIVILIZATION'S MOST FORMIDABLE "ALLY" -
TUCKERED OUT WITH INNOCENT GAMBOL - THE WASTREL -
AWAKE - "KRAZY" IS PASSING BY - FOR HAVING BEEN SUCH A GOOD "MOUSE," I'LL LET YOU GO TO THE WINDOW, AND SAY, "HELLO" -
HEH?
A MOST DEPENDABLE "ALLY" -
Y'KNOW, "KOPPIE" - I'M BEGINNING TO LIKE IT HERE -
UHMMmm.
12-29
Copr. 1940, King Features Syndicate, Inc., World rights reserved.

December 29th, 1940.

The IGNATZ MOUSE DEBAFFLER PAGE.

Our first order of debafflement this time calls for a return to the preceding K&I for 1937-38 and a look at the Kat pages for 6/6/37 and 6/13/37. The two-page gag sequence is obviously printed out of Herriman's intended order, despite the dates inscribed on the two pages by the strip syndicate, which led to out-of-order printing in the original newspaper printing. We doubt if any of our perceptive readers were puzzled by this easily noted screwup, or gave it more than a passing thought once the gag was enjoyed. (It should be noted, to clarify things, that the ink dates on all of our Kat pages were added by the syndicate, *not* Herriman, who dated his originals only in pencil.) But, after explaining things in our previous Debaffler section and telling all you good people that the two pages would now be published in correct order in K&I for the first time, *we* managed to follow the ink dates and print them as haywire as ever. So if anyone was seriously baffled by what they encountered in the last K&I, accept our shamefaced apologies herewith. (In the next printing, however…) Also, the DeBaffler note for 11/6/38 actually was meant to refer to the 11/13/38 strip.

1/1/39: But now, in order to get *au courant* with our bafflements, let's have a look at our very first Kat page this time, and ask everyone not to fail to note the engaging gyrations of the old party's mustachios, which seem to reflect the antic dance of the strip backgrounds in general.

1/29/39: Among early Kat strip students, this page was known as the Seesaw Episode, for some now inexplicable reason.

4/23/39: Apparently Coconino County can afford only one non-napping kop at a time.

10/29/39: Herewith Herriman commemorates the 1939 opening of the New York World's Fair, embleming the awesome event with the gaudy imagery of the Fair's once-famed mating of a trylon and a perisphere, here otherwise simply a shifting element in the strip's background.

11/5/39: Just why la belle Kwak-Wak wants to capture the flow of ink amuck baffles the DeBaffler.

11/17/40: "69696" — Apparently Garge thought he'd see if he could get away with this number — and he did.

Baffled by the oblong bricks of Kat art (usually unconnected to the strip continuity) which appear at the bottom of just about each and every Kat page? Their purpose was purely commercial, as it happens, and they were present so far as the syndicate was concerned simply to provide space for any advertiser that might want to use it for an oblong ad. All of the comic pages in the Hearst tabloid comics section of the 1930s and 1940s, from *Mandrake the Magician* to *Brick Bradford,* provided an identical space for advertisers which were widely used for the most popular strips, with advertisers being able to choose the strip locales they preferred. Happily for us the Kat pages were rarely chosen by any advertiser over the years, who reacted to the strip as did the mystified public at large. (Once exception being the Curtiss Candy Company, whose ads displace that bottom panel in three early-1940 strips here: 1/21, 2/4, and 2/18. Perhaps not coincidentally, that august company is still around, as are two of the three candy bars touted — Jolly Jack having long since gone to that great candy counter in the sky.) All thanks to William Randolph, who cheerfully eschewed revenue to keep his favorite strip in unsullied print.

And finally, the esteemed Jeet Heer (who also provided this volume's colorful introduction) has provided some aperçus and conjectures on several subjects, directly following. — B.B.

This is not tied to any one strip, but we should note that Herriman's daughter Bobbie (then known as Mrs. Barbara Pascal, wife of the screenwriter Ernest Pascal) died on November 14, 1939. She was only 30 years old. While this is admittedly purely subjective, I did get a melancholy feel to some of the strips in early 1940 (which must have been worked on at around the time Barbara died). In particular, I'm thinking of the Sunday page dated March 10th, 1940 where the three main characters disappear. It's almost a parable about love and death: the trio vanish one by one because they depend on each other. This is purely interpretation on my part but I think Herriman must have been thinking of Bobbie when he drew this strip.

The June 4th, 1939 strip is very curious — it reads like a birthday card. I did a check for everyone related to Herriman (his daughters, Louise Swinnerton) to see if any had a birthday around June 4th but came up blank.

In the strip of August 27th, 1939, Offissa Pupp says, "The world walks in beauty." This echoes an earlier phrase of his from September 11, 1938: "Today my world walks in beauty. Beneath me a good earth – a gracious glebe, lies in beauty…." As Patrick McDonnell, Karen O'Connell, and Georgia Riley de Havenon noted in *Krazy Kat: The Comic Art of George Herriman*, these phrases are inspired by a Navajo chant that runs as follows:

With beauty may I walk.
With beauty before me, may I walk.
With beauty behind me, may I walk.
With beauty above me, may I walk.
With beauty below me, may I walk.
With beauty all around me, may I walk.

And finally, In the October 15, 1939 strip, Officer Pupp refers to his confiscation of Ignatz's beans as a "noble experiment." That is the very phrase Herbert Hoover used to describe prohibition. This page might be read as an allegory about futile laws. — J.H.